THE
GOSPEL
AS
HISTORY

Institute for Ecumenical Research
Strasbourg, France

The Gospel Encounters History Series
Edited by Vilmos Vajta

In cooperation with Gunars Ansons, Günther Gassman, Marc Lienhard,
Harding Meyer, Warren A. Quanbeck, and Gérard Siegwalt

Already Published
THE GOSPEL AND UNITY
THE GOSPEL AND HUMAN DESTINY
THE GOSPEL AND THE AMBIGUITY OF THE CHURCH

The GOSPEL as HISTORY

Edited by Vilmos Vajta

Philadelphia
FORTRESS PRESS

Library of Congress Catalog Card Number 74–26348

ISBN 0–8006–0410–5

4526I74   Printed in the United States of America   1–410

Table of Contents

Preface

Do God's "holy" history with man and man's history with God have a universal significance? Is it a *single* history of God with his world— one which sanctifies our entirely secular history? These are the basic questions which this fourth and final volume of our Institute's series "The Gospel Encounters History" is trying to answer. As these questions are answered fundamentally in the affirmative, we feel it necessary to substantiate this understanding of God's history in its stark reality, even when dealing with the history of the oral and written gospel as taking place in the context of the history of the world.

The present volume systematically evaluates the results of theological research in which the question of historicity is presenting church and theology with new tasks and far-reaching decisions. *The Gospel As History* attempts to show two insights: first, the fact that history exerts considerable influence upon the linguistic structure of statements of faith and sets different emphases on their contents during different periods; second, the realization that this same history of mankind is continually being challenged and shaped by the gospel as the work and Word of God. God is in continuous dialogue with the world he created, and this dialogue is reflected in the ever-changing, ever-new forms of proclamation brought about by his Holy Spirit. It is in the very variety of his creative activity for the sake of the salvation of the world that God reveals himself as the eternally Unchangeable.

The issue of "scripture and tradition" receives new ecumenical emphasis in this context and forces us to re-examine our traditional positions. The exegetical, historical, and systematic contributions to this volume are intended to serve this purpose. Can the gospel handed down in proclamation, in dogmatic statements, and in the doxology of the congregation remain identical throughout the metamorphoses of history? This disturbing question is the one which our contributors intend to investigate.

We are pleased that a group of internationally known theologians has been able to cooperate in tackling a subject which is attracting so much attention in the field of ecumenical theology today. During a preparatory consultation between the authors and the editorial committee it became clear that the given theme demands to be examined from many different angles which must not be harmonized too hastily. The confrontation between the theologians is intended to give the reader an impression of the way in which God presents us with his truth in human dialogue. We wish to express our thanks to those who cooperated on this volume for having done so under these conditions.

Responsibility for the American edition of this fourth volume was carried specially by Dr. Gunars Ansons. Translations of essays originally written in German and French were provided by Miss Margaret A. Pater, Dr. Russell B. Norris, and Miss Barbara Hall. Mr. Herbert Grainger and Rev. William Dillon, S.A., assisted in the proofreading.

February 1974
Strasbourg, France

THE EDITORIAL COMMITTEE

I.

THE HISTORY OF GOD'S DEALING WITH HIS WORLD

Chapter 1

Works and Words of Jesus Christ

Introduction

The works and words of Jesus Christ in their indivisible unity constitute the history of Jesus Christ. In every bit of human history, not only in the history of Jesus Christ, words and works are closely related. For when we say "history" we mean an event of the past which is made up of free, human actions, "works," and to which we have access by means of a "word" which was connected with them at the beginning and transmitted to the following generations.

The nature of the relationship between works and words in historical transmission is a complicated question. First, the work of a person in the past is itself a unity of works and words, of action and speech. Only when an action is directed toward another person can it become an historical act. The fact that I washed my hands yesterday is certainly a past "event." But this event can never become an historical act because it was not directed toward another person. Every historical act has a linguistic meaning. It means something which concerns others. It is performed for, against, or with other people. In this sense, action is a form of the word, an "action-word." But by speaking we can also "en-act" an event, for example by commanding or by giving permission, so that our word is also an act (a work). Since our acts have a linguistic aspect and are thus also "words" in a certain sense, and correspondingly our words—because they concern others—are also to a certain extent "acts," every historical event is originally a unity of works and words. The original datum of history, the historical event, is an original and therefore indivisible unity of works and words.

Second, historical transmission, which enables later generations to gain access to the events of the past, is a combination of works and words. For the events of the past—even the very special events which took place within people of the past—are *past* in the strict sense of the word. They are no longer *here*. We can no longer call them into existence. We have no access to them as such, as so-called "facts." We cannot "experience" the events of the past as they were experienced by the people of that time. So one should not speak of "historical facts" because, strictly speaking, historical facts do not exist. The object of historical research and of the writing of history is therefore not the "historical fact," i.e., the past event itself, but historical transmission which is itself an account or discussion of the past event. The historical transmission which is the object of historical research is an account which has come down to us through a shorter or longer series of agents of transmission. The historical event which can become the object of historical research is never the "original" event of the past experienced by the contemporaries of the person who performed an historical act but the event as reported by the first witnesses and later agents of transmission.

The event of the past which is handed down (reported, testified to) is therefore always an indivisible unity of works and words, of the original work (which was itself a unity of works and words!) and of the word of the historical witnesses.

And the word which is related to the original event in the historical transmission is a word which interprets the work. The spoken word "expresses" the word hidden in the event. We call this the meaning of the work or action.

The interpretative function of the word which is indivisibly related to the work is the condition for any understanding of history. We only understand events from the past in so far as they speak to us. But they can only do this by virtue of the word hidden within them. The word of transmission expresses this hidden word so that the event can become comprehensible. True understanding of historical events comes about only when the word of the agents of transmission, including earlier historians, which speaks and explains them to us agrees with the word hidden in the original event. Consequently, historical truth is to be found in the identity of the concern expressed in the original event and in its transmission. It is possible and necessary to examine the reliability of the historical witnesses and to correct details of their witness, but it is not possible either to seek or to find the historical truth if the reliability of the historical witnesses is radically and consistently questioned from the very beginning. For such consistent scepticism about the "sources" would imply an *a priori* denial of the historical truth and thus of the possibility of historical research as a whole.

However, historical truth as the highest criterion for historical research must not be confused with the "correctness" which is the goal of the empirical natural sciences as an appropriate way of expressing all statements about the objects of "nature" on the basis of observing given (or experimentally induced) phenomena. For the historical truth can never be determined by observation but only understood in the understanding transmission of the historical witness which has come down to us.

History can therefore be treated as scientific research only because the object of historical understanding is of a linguistic nature.

Historical research is scientifically reliable in so far as it is able to grasp and transmit the word expressed in the sources and in their transmission as exactly as is humanly possible. Philological training is also necessary for this. But scientific historical research is more than philological erudition. The witness from the past must not only be faithfully translated but also examined to see if it is credible. Scientific historical research is fundamentally critical. But historical science is also more than the critical analysis of the "sources." The scholar does not arrive at the historical truth itself, either in philology or in a critical analysis of the sources. This happens only when he becomes involved in the business of hermeneutics. He has to try so to understand and to re-express the thing which was expressed in the past event and in its transmission that it is able also to speak to men of his day.

At the level of philology and historical criticism, historical research can display a certain "neutral" relevance which may give the impression that historical research should be subject to the same demand for objectivity as the natural sciences. But this is only apparently the case. Complete objectivity (in the sense of one's non-involvement in the thing testified to by the sources and the agents of transmission) would deprive historical research of its real scientific nature. An uninvolved, objective historical science would in fact have written off the knowledge of the historical truth before it started.

To the extent to which historical science is intended to serve historical understanding, it is of course closer to art than to empirical science. For art also expresses a truth which is not grasped by the observation of empirical data but by the interpretative understanding of a work. Writing history, which is really an art, is the final goal of historical research. Only through the writing of history, which itself becomes the recounting of history, can the historical truth from the past become a force to call forth a new history.

Consequently, it is meaningful to speak about God's history with the world only if God himself acts and speaks in time for, against or with men through human actions and human words. The history of God with his world is a divine-human history, the history of God's incarnation, which is condensed into the works and words of Jesus Christ. It is a genuinely human history which takes place in time and space and is transmitted and understood like any other human history. Its testimonies are subjected to the same philological, critical and hermeneutical methods. Nevertheless, it is a unique, "holy" history which cannot be compared with the rest of history. For in it God, the Creator, acts in a human way with man, his creature. But, precisely because God's history with men, i.e., the history of God's incarnation, is a holy history in the sense mentioned, it confronts the man to whom it comes in the testimony to the works and words of Jesus with the question: Is the God who is the active agent in the history of Jesus Christ perhaps also the real, active agent in "secular" history behind the many human doers of the works? Can this holy history perhaps become a sanctifying history? Is the sense of the holy history not perhaps to point to the whole history of mankind as a holy history, i.e., a history of God and his world? Is the holiness of God's history with his world to be found not so much in its difference from secular history but rather in the overcoming of the distinction between secular history and God's history with His world? Is the holy history holy precisely because it embraces the rest of history and fills it with its meaning? Is the holy history the only bit of human history which has a universal significance?[1]

I.
Jesus Christ as God's Work and Word

A. JESUS CHRIST AS GOD'S WORK FOR MAN

1. *The heart of God's history with his world*
Where history takes place, works are performed by men. In order for something to be able to be called an historical event, a work, as

was stated above, must "affect" the doer's fellow men. It must assume a linguistic form and for this reason it is always connected with a word. It is fundamentally impossible to set a limit to the significance of a historical event for others (i.e., people other than the doers of the work which constitutes the heart of the event). It not only has meaning for the contemporaries of the doer but also for later generations. As far as the tradition stretches from the event—both in space and in time—its significance also stretches. And its significance resides in the fact that the testimony to the event which once took place is a power which can call forth new works in a new history. This should not be understood as meaning only that the deeds of historical persons may serve as examples for the actions of people in later generations. The importance of past history as an example is really very limited. For, as everyone knows, "history does not repeat itself." For this reason the behavior of earlier generations cannot be copied, not even the moral virtues of historical "heroes." The real importance of history is contained in the experience which it conveys. From the tradition of history we come to know man (of which we are also a part) and his world (in which we ourselves also live) in a way which far transcends any theoretical knowledge of man (psychology) or of the world (philosophy). History provides us with a wider range of experience within which we can lead our historical lives.[2] The theoretical anthropological sciences only extend our knowledge, i.e., our general insight into man and his world. But they do not transmit a new experience of the life which we live as men in our world. Through history the world in which we live acquires, as it were, a new dimension of experience, the dimension of a common experience of the world.

It is the link between works and words in the historical event which in fact makes the relationship between earlier and later history within a historical whole possible at all. The word of the transmission preserves the meaning of the original event and introduces it to a new context of events. Thus history acquires the nature of the passage of time. History is a process; it constitutes a basically universal unity of experience and meaning which constantly transcends the limits of space and time. The course of history really has nothing to do with a chain of "cause" and "effect" in the sense of the "law of causality." Just as there are no "facts" in history, there are no "causes" and "effects" in the sense of natural science.[3] History constitutes an entity *sui generis* in which there are really no clear limits. History never goes around sharp corners. Indeed, the relationship between events is not present for empirical observation but is created by their transmission. In historical transmission there is a "before" and an "after" and a center. The events as such are not related in this way. Therefore, if there is a causal relationship between two or more events, it cannot shed any light on the meaningful relationship established by the transmission. Strictly speaking, causality is not an historical category at all. Where causality appears in history as an "explanation," history has usually been made into a natural phenomenon. Within a causal relationship there is no real "before," no real "after" and therefore no "center" either. In each bit of history which constitutes an entity in the tradition there is a "before," an "after" and a center.[4] The center is the place where the transmission of history which has already happened causes not only further but, in the full sense of the word, *new* history in a special, epoch-making way. If one point in the course of history is seen as a center in this way, it qualifies the history which precedes it as "pre-history" and that which follows as "post-history." If it were possible to speak of a universal course of history, it would also have to be possible to speak of a center of the whole history of mankind.

Now God's history with his world is in fact universal history itself in the sense that God is the Creator and Preserver of the world. When God acts for, against, or with men, when, in order to act in that way with men, he becomes man, his action embraces the whole world in every age. For God is eternal and omnipresent. There is no place and no time which can remain unaffected by his incarnation.

If the eternal and omnipresent God has started a history with his world, then this history, because it is a divine-*human* history, also has a course within which there is a center which gives it meaning.

In the history of God's incarnation the history of Jesus Christ constitutes the center. In him, i.e., in the Kingdom of God with men which became a reality in his life and works, in his death and in his resurrection, God's acts for his world reached their goal. The history of Jesus Christ is the place within the overall course of the history of God's incarnation which qualifies the preceding part as the pre-history and the subsequent part as the post-history of God's incarnation.

The pre-history of God's incarnation is the history of creation, i.e., the history of the election of Israel, in brief: the history reported by the Old Testament.[5] The post-history of God's incarnation is the history of the Church of Jesus Christ, the history of the redemption of the created world in and through the Church of Jesus Christ, that is, the history promised by the New Testament. The history of Jesus Christ in the narrower sense, the history of the man Jesus Christ testified to in the New Testament, can never be understood without that pre- and post-history if it is to be seen as the center of God's history with his world. It is of course possible to write a "life of Jesus"—how reliable remains an open question!—if his history is only understood as the personal history of a Jewish man who appeared as a prophet at the time of the first Roman emperors. This sort of "biography of Jesus" cannot take any account of the Old Testament. Not even the letter of the New Testament could be taken into consideration. The only possible sources would be the synoptics (and, with caution, perhaps the fourth Gospel as well). But if the history of Jesus Christ is considered to be the center of God's history with man, then of course the whole Bible and not only the New Testament or the Gospels must be called as a witness.[6]

But when we describe the history contained in the Old Testament as the pre-history and the history promised in the New Testament as the post-history of God's incarnation we should not understand "pre-history" only as a preparatory history and "post-history" only as a history of its effects. The pre-history is not the history which happened before and the post-history is not that which happened afterward; rather, pre-history is the history which happened first and post-history is that which happened last within the total course of the history of God's incarnation. Old Testament history, the history of Israel, and New Testament history, the history of the church, do not take place outside of the history of God's incarnation. If this were the case the history of Jesus Christ would not be the center of the history of God's incarnation. Both the history of Israel and the history of the church belong to the history of God's incarnation as the first and last phases of it. But they acquire their significance as the pre- and post-history of the history of God's incarnation from the center of that history, from the history of Jesus Christ. The history of the Old Testament acquires its meaning from the center to which it leads up.[7] The history of the New Testament receives its meaning from the center from which it springs. The history of Jesus Christ, as the center which unites that pre-history with that post-history, acquires its full meaning only when it is understood together with the pre- and post-history.

2. The Son of Man

In the center of his history with the world, God in Jesus Christ performs his saving act for man. As God's work, Jesus Christ is the Son of Man. This enigmatic description which Jesus applied to himself expresses the certainty that he came from God.[8] What the relationship is between Jesus' use of this title and the concept of the heavenly Son of Man as judge of the world in late Jewish apocalyptics is a much disputed question in New Testament research.[9] It is most probable that Jesus, in his reliance on the Heavenly Father to save him from the powers of death, somehow "identified" himself with the coming Son of Man-judge. The Son of Man-servant who has already come hopes, when his Son of Man-servanthood leads him to death, to be exalted as the Son of Man-judge after (in?) his death. Only if one interprets the identification of the poor and servant Son of Man, who has already come, with the coming heavenly Son of Man, as the expression of the hope of the Son of Man who has come, can one maintain that both the logia about the Son of Man who has come and those about the coming Son of Man express Jesus' understanding of his vocation.[10]

The Son of Man came to seek and save those who were lost.[11] When he has found them he leads them to God from whom they had strayed. Thus the Son of Man follows a definite path which leads from God to those who are lost and from them back to God. To follow this path in humble obedience is what Jesus calls his service.[12]

As the Son of Man who came to seek and save the lost, Jesus Christ is God's decisive work for man. He is the work of God because God sends and leads him. He does follow the path of his service as the Son of Man voluntarily, but because he follows it in obedience as the Son of the Heavenly Father he is the instrument by means of which the latter performs His work.

In the death and resurrection of Jesus Christ the way in which he is God's saving work for the world is made manifest. In dying and in being raised from the dead Jesus is no longer acting as a man among men. In his death and resurrection God alone is working in and with him. By allowing men in the death of Jesus to condemn and execute Jesus, the Son of Man, as a blasphemer, God prepares the way for his greatest work, the work of salvation itself, the resurrection by means of which He annuls for time and for eternity the judgment passed by man and thus accepts Jesus' service as Son of Man as a whole and declares it his own work. In and through Jesus the lost have been led back to God and by God himself. In Jesus' death and resurrection God made the whole service of the Son of Man his own work of salvation.

All the events of the pre-history of God's incarnation had this work of God as their goal. This work of God gave rise to all the post-history of God's incarnation.

But, as the pre-history of this action of God, the history of Israel makes the whole of extra-biblical history into the pre-history of God's incarnation. And, as the post-history of this action of God, the history of the church makes the whole future history of the world into the post-history of God's incarnation.

In its hope of the Kingdom of God Israel represents all men. Israel was chosen to represent all men through its waiting for the Kingdom of God.[13] And through its mission to the world the church imparts the fulfillment of Israel's hope to all men.[14] The church has been granted the favor of bringing to all men the salvation which it has received. This does not imply that the world apart from Israel wishes to be represented by Israel, or that the world apart from the church desires the salvation offered to it by the church. But it does mean that it is the will of God. It is God who causes Jesus Christ to be his work for the world and thus the center of the history of his incarnation. Thus—within the will of God—the crucified and risen Son of Man is not just any work of God but *the* work of God which constitutes the meaningful center of human history as a whole.

B. JESUS CHRIST AS GOD'S WORD TO MEN

1. *The revelation*

In the history of mankind, as we have seen, works and words are so interrelated that the word interprets the work, giving it its historical meaning by making the work a "linguistic event," enabling it to speak. The same applies to the history of Jesus Christ as the center of God's history with his world.

By making Jesus Christ, the Son of Man, to be his work, God also lets him, as his word, interpret this work. Thus it is impossible to speak of Jesus Christ as God's work without simultaneously speaking of him as the Word of God.

This is also what the New Testament does. In the prologue to the fourth Gospel Jesus is identified from the very beginning as the eternal Word of God's truth which became flesh (man) in him. Everything else which is said about him later in the fourth Gospel should be understood only as an elaboration of this fundamental insight. The principle of the fourth Gospel is that Jesus is the revelation of God.[15] The whole of his life, including his death and resurrection, is seen and understood as an indivisible whole which constitutes the revelation of the true God. He is life and light, the love and truth of God in human form, so that in him men have perfect fellowship with God.[16]

But it is not only the Gospel of John which recognizes Jesus Christ simply as the revelation of God. This recognition appears throughout the witness of the New Testament to Christ. In the fourth Gospel it is a clear line of thought and is developed in detail. But it is implicitly present in an undeveloped form as the basis of the synoptic Jesus tradition and of the Pauline kerygma of Christ. For everywhere in the New Testament the word and fate of Jesus are taken to be the final and decisive Word of God. This is expressed above all by the way in which Jesus is simply proclaimed as the fulfillment of the Old Testament, so that the Old Testament is related to him throughout. Nowhere in the New Testament is there the slightest indication that another person might come after Jesus as the revealer of the will of God. Therefore it is quite natural for all the so-called "messianic titles of sovereignty" also to be applied to him. He is *the* Christ. He is *the* Son of Man. He is *the* kyrios. He is *the* prophet who is to come. He is *the* Son of God. He is "the one who is to come." He is *the* shepherd. He is *the* light of the world.

When Jesus is described as *the* Word, *the* logos, he is not only being referred to as the one who, like the prophets before him, proclaims God's words; rather, he *is* God's Word even when he is speaking God's words. Because he is the Word of God, his words are one with his person, to which there is no analogy in the oracles of God proclaimed by the prophets. The Old Testament prophet may be able to explain his spoken words by symbolic actions. But nevertheless his oracles can be fundamentally separated from his person and his own life. The word of God which he has to proclaim "comes to him."[17] But Jesus is the Word of God in his own person. Therefore the words which he passes on as God's own words are basically indivisible from his person, from his life and death. The word of God which he pronounces receives its truth and power from the life which he leads. This cannot be said of the words of an Old Testament prophet. The words of Jesus are not a statement of a truth about God; rather, God is present with His power and truth in his words.

To put it another way: the words of God which are spoken by Jesus, the Word of God, are not only words of promise but words of fulfillment. In his person, in his life and death as the Word of God, the meaning of all the divine words he has spoken becomes clear, because the promise they contain is realized in a human life, in his life. All God's words of promise, his commands and his promises, are basically concerned with God's fellowship with man, i.e., God's incarnation. How the meaning intended here is to be understood, what the promised fellowship of man with God is like when it becomes a reality, is made manifest in the person of Jesus, in his filial obedience to the heavenly father. *Thus* he reveals God.

Jesus does not reveal God in a doctrine about God. Nor does he reveal God in supposedly divine virtues. As the revealer of God he is not a teacher of wisdom nor a demigod *(theios anthropos)*. As the Son of God he is the revealer of the Heavenly Father whose son he is. By means of his total submission to the Heavenly Father, in loving obedience and obedient love, his words about the nearness of the Kingdom of God and the mercy of the forgiving God who saves the lost acquire the fullness of their divine power and truth. No one else has proclaimed God's words *in this way*. The Word of God from his mouth can be compared only with the word by means of which God created heaven and earth from nothing; these words do what they say. They make the dead live.[18] No one before him knew God as Jesus revealed Him "full of grace and truth."[19]

2. *The dogma of Christ: true God*

As the Word of God Jesus Christ interprets himself as the work of God. Therefore he does not need to speak about himself as the Word of God. In the synoptic account we hear him speaking about the Kingdom of God and the Heavenly Father in such a way that it shows him to be the Word of God. His words about the Kingdom of God and the father in heaven are spoken by the obedient, servant Son of Man.

When he refers to himself he does not speak about his "nature" but about his way. This is the reason why he does not call himself Messiah, Son of David or Son of God, Lord or Savior, but applies to himself the term "man" (Son of Man) and perhaps also the expres-

sion "son" (without further definition).[20] This description of himself indicates only the way which he has to follow as God's servant.

It is significant for Jesus' so-called "self-understanding" that he
never speaks about his being the Son of God but only about his vocation as Son of Man and as Son (of God).

Therefore it is misleading to see the name "Son of Man" as a "title
of sovereignty." Messiah, Son of David, Son of God, Lord, etc. are
"messianic titles of sovereignty." But the way in which Jesus uses the
description "Son of Man" (man) for himself does not make it one
of the messianic titles of sovereignty. It describes the way which God
has to follow if he wishes to seek and find the lost, the way which the
servant of God follows in his name.

Nor is it the function of the Johannine "I am" statements to express Jesus' "self-understanding." They also describe the path of the
Son's calling: bread, light, the shepherd, the resurrection, the way,
the truth, the life, etc. These descriptions are intended as a call to
follow Jesus on his path. Behind them there are Old Testament images which, when applied to Jesus, secretly point the way which will
lead through death to heavenly glory and which invite the disciples
to follow this way as well. Even John 10:30 and 14:9 are not declarations of himself as the Messiah but statements about God, the
Heavenly Father, who makes Himself manifest through what He does
with the Son. This can be seen particularly clearly in John 5:19-30.

The historical question as to whether Jesus himself speaks in a
more "synoptic" or a more "Johannine" way can hardly be answered.
What is more important is the other question: is there an agreement
in content between the synoptics and the Gospel of John in their
presentation of Jesus' understanding of his calling? To this question
we must say "yes."

The way in which the Gospels present Jesus Christ as the Son who
does not teach that he is the Son of God but who *is* God's Son when
he proclaims the Kingdom of God and does the will of God as the
servant Son of Man, is the way the church's dogma about Christ con-
fesses him. That Jesus Christ, the Son of Man and the revealer of
God, is God's work and God's word in an indivisible unity, is expressed by the dogma in the phrase, "he is true God." He is not a
divine man but God who became man. If Jesus Christ were not the
very work and Word of God, God would not have started a history
with man. Only on the condition that the dogma about Christ states
the truth can one speak about a history of God with man.

II.
The Works and Words of Jesus

A. THE MIRACLES OF JESUS

1. *The Son of Man as a High Priest*

The Son of Man came as God's work for men to lead men to God. But he can only do this if men go with him voluntarily, "follow" him. Therefore God's history with man includes a history of man with God. Otherwise the history which God started with man would not be a genuinely human history, because man would only be a human thing which was treated purely mechanically. In this sense one must speak of man's "cooperation" with God (in Christ!). But this in no way entails a "synergistic" understanding. The work which God performs for man, the work of salvation, is exclusively God's work. Man does not cooperate with God in that work! This situation is made clear in the Christological dogma by the statement that the divine and human natures must not be confused. Jesus Christ is God and man in one person, not a god-man or a man-god. Man cooperates with God in that God's history with him, i.e., God's work of salvation for him, calls forth his own history with God, a history which is not a divine but a human history. As the human history which is *called* forth by God's history with man, the history of man with God is the history of the answer to God's call. Man's co-operation with God is man's response to God's call. This history is also an indivisible unity of works and words. It too has a center. And Jesus Christ is that center also.

Therefore here too there is a pre-history and a post-history. The pre-history is the history of man's search for God, the "history of religion."[21] The post-history is the history of man's finding God, the "history of faith." And the center is Jesus Christ as the representative of all men before God, the head of a new humanity reconciled to God.

The history of religion and the history of faith as the pre- and post-history of the real history of man with God in Jesus Christ draw their meaning only from the center, from the history of the Son of Man who stands before God in place of all men in order to open up their own way to God.

As the Son of Man-servant sent by God and subjected to suffering and death, Jesus Christ is considered to be God's work. As the one who followed this path voluntarily and sacrificed himself to God,

Jesus Christ is considered to be the representative of the man who allows himself to be found and led back to God, the high priest of all men.

It is well known that the Letter to the Hebrews has set out a theology of Jesus, the high priest, which is closely related to the Johannine theology.[22] In the fourth Gospel, Jesus is also presented as the priest who "sanctifies" himself for his own in order to lead them back to God, although the terms "priest" or "high priest" do not occur in this context. And in the synoptic tradition Jesus is also presented as the one who follows voluntarily and gives his life for "many," especially in the passages about Jesus' last meal with his disciples.

The Son of Man did not come to be served but to serve, and to give up his life as a ransom for many; the Son of Man is going the way appointed for him in the scriptures.[23] And as he goes this way he gives the disciples the bread and the wine with the words about the sacrificed body and the blood shed for many; there the Son of Man is the high priest of man whether he is given the name or not.

In and through his taking the place of the many, men can pass through death with him to the father. Those whom he represents are not separate from the reality of his return to the father in heaven; rather, they are taken with him on his way. That is why this meal is constantly repeated "in memory of him."

But it is not only his disciples who are taken with him. Since Jesus' vicarious action is the center of man's history with God, it also embraces the pre-history (the history of religion) and the post-history (the history of faith). As the high priest of men Jesus Christ follows the way of the servant Son of Man through death to eternal life as the voluntary representative of all the lost.[24] They are taken up into his free service in so real a way that they are also able and permitted to go with him voluntarily, and not only the believers who have found him but also the seekers of the various religions to whom the Good News has not been proclaimed. Jesus Christ, man's high priest, is "the eldest among a *large family* of brothers"; he has brought "many sons to glory."[25]

2. *The Miracles of Jesus—Works of the High Priest*

The works of the high priest, Jesus Christ, are miracles. All of Jesus' works, not only those called "the miracles," are miracles in so far as they bring lost people into the saving reality of God. The mir-

acles are wonders performed by God, not because they are "supernatural events" but because they are performed as a consequence of
an unbroken relationship with God, i.e., a "natural," childlike relationship of man to God, his creator, which is not destroyed by sin.[26]
Because they are in this sense "unusual" (strange) human acts they
constitute the "signs" of the Kingdom of God which has already
dawned and in which God lives with men in an unbroken relationship of the creator to his creature. The miracles are human acts performed by the servant Son of Man by means of which he vicariously
realizes for all men man's "natural" life with God.[27]

For this reason, Jesus' miracles are human acts which make it possible and, if they are accepted in faith, true that lost men are permitted to live with God in his Kingdom through no merit of their
own. The miracles of healing remove all the obstacles which sickness
and death have placed in the way of an unbroken relationship of
man to God. The raising of the dead and the healing of the sick
essentially belong together.[28]

In addition to the healings, however, the fellowship of meals
which Jesus has with the lost must also be described as a miracle. It
is through the fellowship of eating that total solidarity is established
between the Son of Man-high priest and all those whom he serves.
They sit at table with him in God's Kingdom. The fellowship of
meals and the raising of the dead belong together as miracles of the
Kingdom of God. This was quickly sensed by Jesus' opponents.
Therefore they fight particularly against the healings he performs on
the Sabbath, i.e., as works which are performed for God in a special
sense, and his meals with tax collectors and sinners.[29]

Finally, the suffering (and death) of Jesus, if it is seen as his voluntary act of obedience, is a miracle. Indeed, it is the last miracle
which embraces all the preceding ones. For by dying of his own free
will he removes everything which is still able to separate the lost sinner from God. His voluntary death is the last and final sacrifice
which opens up the way for all lost men to God once and for all. His
voluntary death is the completion of the priestly service which was
the essence of all his human activity.[30] All of Jesus' miracles bind to
him the people whom he represents as a priest before God. They
impart to other people the living fellowship with Jesus, the Son of
Man-high priest.

As signs of the dawning Kingdom of God, all of Jesus' miracles
have an eternal significance for all people, not only for those who

experienced the individual miracles personally. The healings have an eternal significance not only for the sick who experienced them but for all sick persons, including those who are never healed. The raisings of the dead do not only have eternal meaning for the daughter of Jairus and her parents or for Lazarus and his sisters but for all those who are going to die. This explains why there are many parallels to Jesus' miracles both in Israel and in the non-biblical history of religions. Together with such parallels the miracles of Jesus are the signs of the dawning of the Kingdom of God and tokens of the coming end of the world. Each healing of the sick points to a future in which there will be no more sickness. Each raising of the dead points to eternity in which death will have been overcome forever. Each Lord's Supper points to the life to come in which full fellowship between God and man will be a reality.

The miracles of Jesus are made real at all times as signs of the perfect rule of God among men by the report in the Gospels. By means of preaching in the church they remain signs of hope for all those who live in this world without hope, for the despairing, the oppressed, the discouraged, in short: for all the lost people whom the Son of Man came to seek and to save.

Thus a genuine "theology of hope" is always a theology of the miracles performed by the high priest, Jesus Christ, for all men.

Two things should be noted here. First, it is of decisive importance that the miracles of Jesus really took place. If they were freely invented, legendary ideas they could not give hope to anyone. The Gospel tradition testifies unanimously that Jesus worked miracles. This fact does not exclude the possibility that we may have critical doubts about individual miracles and have to admit that here and there the account of a miracle contains "legendary additions." But if it were decided that Jesus had worked no miracles at all then the belief in him as the high priest of all men would be destroyed. Second, it is of decisive importance that the future of all men depends on works which Jesus has already performed and not on works which they themselves have to perform, perhaps with his assistance. The renewal of the world, which is the essence of the church's hope for the world, will take place at the second coming of Jesus Christ beyond the history of mankind. A renewal of the world within the confines of the world and of history can certainly be the subject of passionate expectation. But it can never become the essence of the hope of the Church. Hope which looks forward to the coming of Jesus Christ is not a utopia and it expects nothing from revolutions.[31]

The history of faith, as the post-history of the history of man with God in Jesus Christ, is the history from which men draw the courage to bear the present which God has given them and in which they find the persistence to wait for the future promised them by God because of the miracles performed for them by Jesus Christ. His miracles enable them to be co-priests with him who have free access to God in him. Together with him they bring the whole world to God as a thank-offering. Therefore, they, like the contemporary revolutionary utopians, cannot scorn the present time which God has given them. But they can still less join the reactionary inhabitants of the world in unreservedly affirming the world as it is in its self-satisfied hostility to God. The miracles of Jesus Christ have unhinged the old world for them once and for all. And the new world of which the revolutionary utopians dream also belongs to this old world. "Here we have no permanent home, but we are seekers after the city which is to come."[32]

B. THE PREACHING OF JESUS CHRIST: WORDS OF THE KING IN THE KINGDOM OF GOD

1. *The royal teacher*

Just as the Word which Jesus Christ is (the revelation of God) explains the work which he is (the Son of Man), so the word which Jesus Christ pronounces explains the works which he does. The unity of his word and his works constitutes the center of man's history with God.

The word which Jesus Christ pronounces is the Gospel of the Kingdom of God. In his preaching Jesus Christ is and remains the herald of God's Kingdom. His words about the Kingdom of God, like those of the Baptist, are first an announcement of the Kingdom, a "kerygma." But what is specific to the words of Jesus about the Kingdom of God is not the kerygma as such. The announcement of the nearness of the Kingdom of God is something Jesus has in common with his forerunner. He simply presupposes the kerygma and can therefore proclaim even the nearness of the Kingdom in a kerygmatic way.[33] But his own message, which is by no means a mere repetition of the Baptist's preaching, is essentially doctrine, didache, not kerygma. Unlike the Baptist, Jesus appears as a teacher (rabbi). And his followers were disciples in the literal sense, i.e., pupils. Jesus *teaches* in the synagogues and on the sea shore. He *teaches* with authority and not like the Scribes. The use of parables, which he developed in a most original way and which constitutes the heart of his preaching, is a secret *teaching* about the Kingdom of God.[34]

It is characteristic of the image which the Gospels give us of Jesus that what he says is either doctrine or prayer. He teaches in the midst of the people. Even his so-called "disputations" are a form of doctrine. In the solitude before God he prays.[35]

Just as his miracles manifest the presence of the Kingdom of God, so his doctrine elucidates its nature. Thus Jesus' teaching explains his works. But this should not be understood to mean that everything he says is exclusively an interpretation of the different miracles, although there is food for thought in the fact that both the synoptics and John (in particular) often situate words or discourses of Jesus in direct relation to a miracle which has just been performed.

But the miracles are not isolated events. As such they could only be seen as amazing bits of magic. And it was only his enemies who considered him to be a magician, precisely because they did not want to believe his Gospel.[36] Jesus' teaching about the Kingdom of God makes clear to the faith of his disciples the way in which his amazing works are precisely not magic but God's miracles. For his teaching about the Kingdom of God is a promise from God of a new life for men as children of God, free from all sin and evil. Only where this teaching is followed through faith in the word of Jesus is it possible also to believe in the works of Jesus as God's miracles, as a real anticipation of the perfect Kingdom of God.[37] In this sense it is true that Jesus' words explain his works.

As the teacher who explains the coming Kingdom of God, Jesus performs a royal service. Through his teaching, which is thoroughly human teaching, God himself exercises His kingly rule over men. As the teacher of the Kingdom of God he is its king. As the king in the Kingdom of God he is its teacher. It is characteristic of the Lordship of God which is present in Jesus that God exercises his kingly power over the people on this earth through the teaching of Jesus. Therefore as king of the Kingdom of God Jesus is a teacher; his kingly power is that he witnesses to the truth.[38]

As the teacher of the Kingdom of God Jesus royally represents God to the men of this world. His teaching is therefore, in the strictest sense of the word, human speech. This applies both to its form and to its content. The form of Jesus' teaching is human in so far as it uses the everyday language of men. Jesus does not declaim a philosophy. He does not impart a mysterious gnostic knowledge. His parables are little examples from everyday life or stories from familiar workaday situations. But the content of Jesus' teaching about the Kingdom of God is human too because Jesus explains it as God's Lordship over men as they really are and live. The Kingdom of God certainly belongs to the future. In its perfect form it is the subject of eschatological hope. But Jesus demonstrates through his teaching in what way the coming Kingdom of God intervenes here and now as a present power in man's life. Wherever this really happens the Kingdom of God is not only a thing of the future, but is already present precisely as an eschatological reality. The presence of the coming Kingdom of God in man's everyday existence is the theme of Jesus' teaching about the Kingdom of God.[39] Therefore it is precisely his teaching about God's kingly rule which deals with man's existence. In this sense an "existential interpretation" of this teaching is the only appropriate one.

But this certainly does not mean that a general "doctrine about man" can be derived from the teaching of Jesus. Jesus' teaching shows what it means that God is present among men again—like before the Fall! In his teaching Jesus represents God! But he does not set out general truths about human existence. He does not teach ethics. He does not present a political program. He does not supplement our knowledge about human psychology or sociology. This insight is the unrelinquishable truth of the Lutheran doctrine of God's two realms.[40] If one tries to make Jesus' teaching "useful" for one's own philosophy or policy, to build it into one's own program in some way, one is then denying Jesus' royal authority which he exercises through his teaching. One cannot "use" or "exploit" the teaching of Jesus. One may not "make it relevant." As the king in the Kingdom of God, he does not fit into our ranks. He does not wish to be the king of a corpus christianum. He does not intend to justify revolution, not even a just, social revolution. His teaching cannot be transformed into a teaching which is ours. He rules in the Kingdom of God with his truth alone. But he does allow a kingdom of the world to exist in separation from the Kingdom of God. "Then pay Caesar what is due to Caesar, and pay to God what is due to God."[41]

However, he does not leave this kingdom of the world to exist in peace! Through his teaching he brings the Kingdom of God into the furthest corner. Thus not even the emperor in Rome and his representatives in Jerusalem could live in peace as long as he was there. If, on the other hand, he had transformed his teaching into a political program such as the Zealots had, it would have been a simple thing for the emperor to get rid of him, just as it is a simple matter for any dictatorship today to cope with a church which is involved in politics.[42] One can tackle politics by political means. But how can one tackle a power which is apolitical in the strict sense but which for this very reason can have major political consequences?

2. *The dogma about Christ: true man*

Being the center of man's history with God, Jesus Christ is true man, as the dogma about him testifies. His miracles are human works. They promise man's new, redeemed life in the Kingdom of God. They are works of the Son of Man who is himself the work of God and as such true God. In this sense they are all works of God. But precisely because they are works of the Son of Man, who is himself true God, they are human works, since in all of his miracles he performs the high-priestly service of leading men to God. In all of his miracles he takes the place of men in such a way that he brings them back to God along his path of suffering and death. The way which he follows with his miracles as the high priest of all men is the way of man to God and to eternal life. Therefore the people whom he represents before God will also have a share in his miracles. Because he himself is the work of God, true God, Jesus' miracles are also "divine" works. But they are not "divine" in the sense of "not human" or "superhuman." As the works of God who became man, the miracles of Jesus are so profoundly human that it is an easy matter to laugh at them or to deny them. Therefore Jesus' miracles are part of his humiliation. They by no means reveal his divine majesty. This is the reason why the New Testament stories of the miracles bear no more than the slightest resemblance to the miraculous legends of other religions. Of course the crowds often praise Jesus' miracles (or God because of them!). But also because he is a miracle-worker Jesus is accused by the authorities. He performs miracles on the Sabbath and is thus a transgressor of the divine law. Because he drives out demons they accuse him of being in league with the devil. His association at table with the lost earns him the nickname "glut-

ton and drinker, a friend of tax-gatherers and sinners."[43] Thus all
the miracles which he works are an integral part of his indigent human life.

That the miracles of Jesus are profoundly human in their very
"divinity" is brought out particularly clearly by the fact that they
are often performed with prayer.[44] They are not the "powerful
deeds" of a demigod but works of God, which the Son of Man exe-
cutes in obedience as a servant. The fact that Jesus is shown to be at
prayer so often in the synoptic tradition demonstrates most clearly
that in all his works he is truly man: the obedient Son of Man.

But the words of Jesus are human words as well. In his teaching
about the Kingdom of God he certainly does represent God among
men. In this sense, all his teaching is the word of God. God himself
expresses his truth through his teaching. But Jesus' teaching is not
the word of God in the sense of being a non-human or superhuman
word. On the contrary, as we have already seen, the words in Jesus'
teaching are profoundly human. He speaks in his teaching as a man
to his fellowmen. And it is in this way, e.g., in the straightforward
language of his parables, that he expresses God's truth and wisdom.

Jesus' teaching, because it is human speech, is also an integral part
of his human abasement. His teaching is rejected by his opponents.
They accuse him of blasphemy.[45] On several occasions they try to set
a trap for him.[46] Even his disciples misunderstand his teaching.[47] He
does not want to convince people with proofs. He resolutely refuses
to substantiate his teaching with a sign from heaven.[48]

But the profound humanity of the works and words of Jesus
should by no means be seen as a "shortcoming." Only as genuinely
human works and words can they constitute the center of man's history with God.

The statement in the Christological dogma about the true humanity of Jesus Christ therefore expresses the indispensable condition for
a history of man with God.

However, the Christological dogma does not only state that Jesus
Christ is true God and true man but also that his two "natures" (divinity and humanity) are united in one single person without being
confused or separated.

This means that in one person, Jesus Christ, God's history with
the world and man's history with God are so closely related that the
one "history" can never take place without the other. God cannot
start a history with man and take it to its conclusion without keeping

the door open for a corresponding human history, a "history of re-sponse." And men can have no other history with God than the "his-tory of response" which is included in God's history with them. But in the correspondence between these two histories—a history in which God is the agent and a history in which man is the agent—God still remains God and man man. The two histories are held to-gether in the works and words of Jesus Christ. Nevertheless, a care-ful distinction must be made between the work and the word which he is, on the one hand, and the works which he does and the words which he speaks, on the other. For on the one hand Jesus Christ is the center of a history brought about by God and on the other he is the center of a history which men experience. In the first case the pre-history is the history of God's deeds for the people of Israel and the post-history is the history of God's deeds in the church. In the second case the pre-history is the history of man's expectation, the history of religion, and the post-history is the history of finding, of fulfillment, the history of faith. There is certainly a correspondence between the history of Israel and the history of religion; they con-verge because they move in the same direction. But they are not iden-tical. And in the same way there is a correspondence between the his-tory of the church and the history of faith because they both have the same origin, Jesus Christ. But they are not identical. For in the one history, in the pre-history of Israel and in the post-history of the church, God comes to man. In the other history, in the pre-history of religion and in the post-history of faith, man comes to God. But the distinction between the two histories ("natures") can never separate them. For they have the same center in one person, Jesus Christ, who is both God and man.

Therefore the truth of the dogma about Christ is the prerequisite for any meaningful reference to a history of God with his world.

III.

The Works and Words of Jesus Christ in the
History of the Church and in the History of Faith

A. THE HISTORY OF THE CHURCH

1. *Baptism*

The history of the church is the post-history of God's history with man in the sense that it originates from the center of that history in Jesus Christ. This means, on the one hand, that in it God's history with the world continues. It also takes place today among us. On the other hand it means that, in its relationship to the history of Jesus Christ in the narrower sense, the history of the church has no new or independent content. The content of the history of the church as post-history is God's work and word in Jesus Christ. The work of God which Jesus Christ constitutes, the Son of Man who leads men to God, is present among us in baptism in this post-history.

Just as Jesus, the Son of Man, as God's saving work for men, came to the lost to seek and save them, so Jesus, the Lord, comes to all the lost in baptism to seek them and to admit them to the Kingdom of God.

Baptism is administered in the name of Jesus or, rather, into the name of Jesus. Like the name of God the name of Jesus Christ is not merely a way of referring to a particular person. The name of Jesus Christ is the name of Lord which was given to him at the resurrection, the name of God. Therefore the whole wealth of Jesus' life is concentrated in his name. But it is the man, Jesus, the son of Mary who was crucified under Pontius Pilate, who was given the name of God at the resurrection. The Lord (kyrios) is called Jesus. This is why from the very beginning the human name of Jesus and the divine name "Lord" have been united in the church's creed. The name Jesus Lord (or Jesus Christ) is the name of the one who is both God and man, God's only begotten son, born of the virgin Mary. His name always embraces the whole content of the historical life of Jesus of Nazareth. Wherever his name is known, called upon, proclaimed or worshipped, the whole wealth of Jesus' human life is present from his birth in Bethlehem to his crucifixion on Golgotha. But he is not only made present by means of remembering the past; he is present and alive just as he was during his life on earth. The "historical Jesus" speaks and acts wherever his name is known and called upon as the name of the Lord. For the fact that *Jesus* is kyrios means that his unique life as a man is not over like the life of all other mortals which can then be "made present" only by memories, but that it is and remains present everywhere and at all times in his name, the name Jesus kyrios, in its divine and human fullness. Only because his name is the name of the Lord can people from all nations and of all times be baptized into his name.

Just as the "historical Jesus," the Son of Man, during his lifetime gave to the lost with whom he associated the same right as he himself had, namely that of living in the Kingdom of God as children of the heavenly father, simply by being with them, so the same Jesus after his resurrection and exaltation gives to the lost with whom he associates through baptism in his name the same right to live before God simply by the gift of the Holy Spirit, which he has linked with his name. Thus baptism is the sacrament of justification by faith. The right of the Son of Man, who is present either physically during his lifetime or in exaltation in the Holy Spirit, to live as a child of God before him can be received by a man as his own right only through faith. As the righteousness of the Son of Man, the righteousness of faith given in baptism is the righteousness of "another," i.e., no man can acquire ("earn") this right by his own behavior (by "works of the law"). He can only receive it if another, the Son of Man who has this right for eternity, shares it with him, brings him into his fellowship. This happens in baptism.

In baptism in his name, Jesus Christ is the work of God for the world today, as he was during his earthly life as the Son of Man sent by God to the lost. The history of the church is the genuine post-history of the history of the Son of Man, Jesus Christ, because God performs in the church today through baptism the same work for men as he performed in Jesus' day in him and through him for the salvation of mankind.

It is the same work. Baptism into the name of Jesus gives the baptized the rights of the historical Son of Man. By baptism he is brought into the same church as that which the historical Jesus gathered around himself. God's work, which this Jesus constituted in his service as the Son of Man, he now constitutes through baptism for the lost who are alive now. The name of Jesus, linked with the Holy Spirit, creates a living fellowship of men today, not with a purely heavenly being, not with a "Christ of the kerygma or of faith" who has no "continuity" with the historical Jesus, but with the historical Jesus. For, if there is a "Christ of the kerygma or of faith," he is quite certainly identical with the "historical Jesus" or he is a mere invention. The Christ (of the kerygma, of faith) always bears the historical name *Jesus*. The name into which people are baptized is: *Jesus (Christ) kyrios*.[49]

The curious idea that "justification by faith" is a dated doctrine of the Reformation in the sixteenth century, which therefore has nothing to say to "the man of today" and should consequently be replaced by other, up-to-date theological terms, would probably never have appeared if it had not been forgotten that justification—

irrespective of the theoretical reflections of theologians on justification—is the work of God for the world which is the foundation for everything else and without which the world is and remains lost. Man can only receive *the* work of God in faith, by accepting the promise which God has linked with baptism. That there may possibly be men "of today"—they presumably also existed yesterday and the day before yesterday—to whom God's work in baptism "says nothing" can only be stated, if it is true, as a sheer fact. But it can in no case bring theologians—Lutheran theologians in particular—to deny that which God does in baptism.

On the contrary, it should be the task of Lutheran theologians to criticize the way in which justification by faith alone has been presented in orthodox Lutheran theology, in pietism and in the Enlightenment. One ought to examine whether or not the doctrine of justification, which "is unable to say anything to the men of today," is perhaps a psychologized and anthropocentric perversion of the biblical and Reformation witness to God's work in baptism. It should be examined whether perhaps, instead of starting with the real lost condition of man without God, the starting point was some "feeling of guilt" which upset a mental harmony. And, above all, it should be considered whether the theology of those centuries has gradually made "faith" into a "religiosity" which was and is an unbearable yoke of law for the "weary and heavy laden." It is quite possible that the justification theories of the centuries following the Reformation may say nothing "to the men of today." But then the time would have come not to replace justification by faith alone with another, more up-to-date doctrine but, on the contrary, to witness to justification by faith alone in the right way, i.e., to point to God's work for the world through Jesus Christ in baptism. It is not a matter of "feelings," of "soothing the conscience"[50] or of answering distressing questions ("problems") which we ask ourselves. It is a fundamental matter of our existence: whether we shall remain in death without the living God or whether we shall allow ourselves to be "rescued from the domain of darkness and brought away into the kingdom of his dear Son" in baptism through God's work. The world will certainly not be helped by a better theology, not even by the abandonment of a supposedly outdated theology, but only by the work of God. The church is to continue the work of God, i.e., baptism. It is to baptize people and to teach the baptized to observe everything that the Lord, in whose name they were baptized, has commanded. Then justification takes place as the work of God received by faith. And where this happens, where men are justified through God's work in baptism, the testimony to justification, the praise of God for his work of salvation, "says something" to those who have been justified.

Where baptism is administered as God's work for the world, real church history takes place. There people are born again as children of God. There people begin to live in this world in the perfect freedom of the children of God; as free children of God they live *in* this world. Their life history becomes part of "secular" history, the history of their nation, their class, the world. Seen "from below" the history of the church is not a special history. If one considers only the men who play a part in the history of the church (as historical scholars do), i.e., if one forgets that the history of the church is a part of *God's* history with his world, then the history of the church is in fact only a small part of the history of mankind and perhaps not even a particularly important or interesting bit of history.

In secular history the baptism of a child is not a world-shaking event but an old habit which the parents have not yet given up and which cannot be of any importance except within the close family circle where it is the occasion for a special meal. But if one looks at the history of the church "from above," as the post-history of the history of the Son of Man, Jesus Christ, and thus as an integral part of the history of God's incarnation, then the baptism of a child, as the work of God in Jesus Christ for a new human being who still has his life in this world ahead of him, is the greatest event in a person's life, and the act which the church performs when it brings people to baptism is the most important historical act that can be performed at all. If baptism is the continuance of God's saving work, constituted by Jesus Christ, for new people each time, then each act of baptism which takes place in the church is a sign that in the very banal human "history of the church" God continues his history with men. And then there can be no doubt that the church, its ministers and its congregations, have no task in this world bigger and more important than administering holy baptism. Wherever baptism is administered real church history takes place. It is there that people are born of water and the Spirit to the perfect freedom of the children of God. Because there are such free people alive in the world, the world has a future. Its history is not a history of decay but a history of fulfillment, a holy history, God's history with the world.[51]

2. The Church of Jesus Christ

The *Word* of God, which Jesus Christ is, which interprets the *work* of God which he is, the revelation of God in him, takes the form of the Church of Jesus Christ in the post-history of God's incarnation, the history of the church.

The Church of Jesus Christ is the people of God, "the Israel of God,"[52] reborn through the baptism of its members. Since they have received their right to exist before God by baptism into the name of the Lord Jesus, in him they are now God's children, God's people. But in him they are now also obedient children of God, as he is. "When Israel was a boy, I loved him; I called my son out of Egypt."[53] This election of Israel has been fulfilled in Jesus, the servant Son of Man. Everyone who has been baptized into his name, and has thus received in him the right to divine sonship, is a member of this Israel of God.[54]

The Church of Jesus Christ as the people of God, in the election and justification imparted to it in Jesus Christ, is indeed "Jesus Christ existing as the church." This expression, introduced by Dietrich Bonhoeffer, explains the Pauline term "body of Christ."[55] The church can be described as the body of Christ, as *corpus Christi mysticum,* because it is Jesus Christ existing as the church. If Jesus Christ, the Son of Man, the Lord, gives to his church his own right to live as a child before God, then he stands in its place before God as the high priest of all men, then he exists as the church. The church of those baptized into the name of Jesus Christ by no means loses its identity by justification through faith. It is not absorbed into him in some mystical way. As the people of God it retains its own existence in Jesus Christ. But in its own existence as the church, as God's people, it is justified only in him. Only in him does it have access to God. This means that he exists before God as the church. With him, around him and in him he has the brothers whose priest he is: "Here am I, and the children whom God has given me."[56] He can say to his church—and at the baptism of each of its members he has said—"I exist before God as the church which you are." But the church cannot say, "I am the body of Christ. Therefore I exist before God as Christ." If the church were to say this, it would have exchanged justification by faith, which it has constantly to receive anew in Christ's promise, for a justification by works which it discovered within itself.

Jesus Christ is the word of God to the world. In the post-history of the history of God's incarnation he is the Word which reveals God to the world, the word of revelation, by existing as the church. Therefore the Church of Jesus Christ cannot ignore the call to exist as the word of God to the world. "You are light for all the world. A town that stands on a hill cannot be hidden."[57]

Just as Jesus, the Son of Man, revealed the fatherliness of God by his own filial trust and his filial obedience to the heavenly father, so Jesus Christ existing as the church reveals God, his Heavenly Father, by the trust and obedience of all of its members. The church in its deeds and in its suffering is the divine word of revelation to the world, as was the Son of Man.

The deeds of the church, which are the deeds of its members, reveal God in so far as they are performed in the perfect freedom of the children of God. What is revealed by the deeds of the children of God is the fatherly goodness of God. "And you, like the lamp, must shed light among your fellows, so that, when they see the good you do, they may give praise to your Father in heaven."[58]

Good deeds are good, not because they show that the doer is "good" but because they are of benefit to those for whom they are done. *They* cannot see the goodness of the doer and it is no concern of theirs. They see that these works are a help to them. And therefore they thank not the doer, whom they probably do not always know, but God, the father in heaven. By means of what has happened to them they have seen something of the fatherliness of God which they had not experienced before in this way. And for this they thank their heavenly father.

Thus the action of the church which reveals God to the world is not some Christian morality. We can ignore the question whether or not there is such a thing because, if it does exist, it cannot possibly reveal the fatherliness of God to man. Good works are certainly performed by Christians. But, since the goodness consists of the help which others receive, good deeds—like visiting the sick or giving bread to the hungry—can and must be performed by non-Christians as well. The fact that it is a good work does not make it "Christian." Good works are services to one's neighbor, not the fulfillment of a law of virtues. For this very reason it is of no importance whether the person serving is known or not to the one whom he serves. For the latter is not supposed to see the former's moral goodness and recognize it as such but the good work itself. And he should not thank the doer but the father in heaven for the goodness which he has received.

This means that the church cannot reveal God by means of Christian laws which it may support but only by means of service which cannot make a striking impression as *its* service, i.e., as a "Christian" act or as a "church" activity. True service, which consists of good works for the people in the world, is a worldly service, a service performed by Christians in the world and for the world, a service which must always and without exception be performed together with non-Christians and in such a way that it is irrelevant and, for the sake of the world, must be irrelevant what or how much is done by Christians and what or how much by non-Christians. According to the words of Jesus "non-Christians" who do good are not against "Christians" but for them. They are coworkers with Christ who are in fact already following the path that leads to baptism.[59] The church's service to the world must retain the genuine worldliness demanded of it. This is the only way for it to be part of the word of God which the church is.

If the church, instead of rendering worldly service to its neighbor, tries to impose a "Christian" order on the world (the theocratic error), it ceases in this erroneous legalism to be God's word to the world. By a theocratic attitude, in all its forms, the church reveals not the fatherly goodness of God but merely the church's desire for "influence."

The suffering of the church is an essential part of the word of God to the world. That which is not made manifest by service to the world is revealed by suffering. Because the church suffers for the sake of Christ, one can see that it has no righteousness of its own. It only has Christ. He is its "Christian-ness," its only righteousness before God. For this very reason the church has to be able to give up everything else in order to keep him. A church which is under the cross cannot wish for a theocracy. Through suffering it learns that it is not granted any Christian morality, any Christian politics, any Christian order or any influence over others in the name of Christ. There is only one thing in it which is Christian. And that is not a thing or an object but the living Christ himself. All that otherwise remains for it is worldly service. Suffering ensures that this is the case and that this is seen to be so. Without suffering, the word which the Church is can be misunderstood along theocratic lines to imply that Christians could be an example to "non-Christians" by their "Christianness"; that one should see *them* and thank *them* instead of seeing their works and thanking God. But where the church also suffers, God himself fends off this error.

The link between serving and suffering in the relationship of the church to the world corresponds to prayer in its relationship to God. The prayer of the church cannot be seen as such by the world. To a certain extent it belongs to the *disciplina arcana* of the church.[60] But in prayer the church discovers that its service and its suffering come from the same fatherly goodness. Through prayer it learns to accept both worldly service and suffering for the sake of Christ in gratitude as a gift from God. If the church receives this gift in secret it does not need to appear in public in a theocratic way as a Christian power. In the world outside, the church is satisfied with the works of service and with suffering, if this is demanded of it, both of which the world can see only in worldliness.

B. THE HISTORY OF FAITH

1. *Holy Communion*

As the history of the church is the post-history of God's history with man which springs from its center in Jesus Christ, so the history of faith is the post-history of the history of man with God which springs from its center in the high-priestly miracles and kingly teaching of Jesus Christ.

The miracles performed by Jesus Christ during the time of his earthly life—the miracles of healing, the table fellowship and his voluntary, sacrificial death—are continued in the church through Holy Communion after his resurrection and exaltation. We have already seen that the history of faith, as the post-history of the history of man with God in Jesus Christ, is the history in which men find the courage to bear the present time given by God, and receive the perseverance to wait for God's future from the miracles performed for them by Jesus Christ. By means of his miracles they are incorporated into his priestly service and become his fellow priests who have access to God in him.

The importance of the Eucharist is that in it the living fellowship between the sinners justified by baptism and the Son of Man-high priest, Jesus Christ, is made real. Holy Communion is the high-priestly work of Jesus Christ in the church, the contemporary miracle which sums up within it all the historical miracles of Jesus. In

the church's "doing in memory of him" Jesus Christ's voluntary
sacrificial death is present. The eucharistic anamnesis is the church's
sacrifice of thanksgiving which the high priest, Jesus Christ, unites
with his own sacrifice of thanksgiving, his voluntary death, and offers
to the Heavenly Father in his name. In Communion the fellowship
of the meal takes place between all the baptized, who receive the
body and blood of Jesus Christ in faith in the form of bread and
wine, and Jesus Christ and all his saints in all places and at all times.
In the fellowship of this meal all those who have become one with
Jesus Christ and with his saints have also become one with God in
heaven. Because the sacrifice of thanksgiving and the Communion
bind man to the God who is universal, self-giving love, all those who
take part in this meal in faith are sent out from the table of the Lord
directly into the suffering, godless world to be physically sacrificed
there in loving service.

With these three aspects—anamnesis (the eucharistic sacrifice),
Communion and loving service (the self-sacrifice)—the Eucharist
participates in the eschatological significance of the historical miracles of Jesus. In anamnesis, Communion and loving service the congregation at Communion anticipates the worship of heaven, the eternal fellowship of mankind which has been redeemed and the glorifi-
cation of the whole creation.[61] In all three relationships the whole
emphasis is placed on the "incarnational" unity of Spirit and body
in the sacrament. Although the preaching of the church as a linguistic manifestation has a physical side, the spirituality and corporeality
of man's salvation in Jesus Christ is only fully manifest in the Eucharist. Wherever the Eucharist is neglected in the life of the church,
there is usually little regard for the corporeality of salvation. Only
when proclamation and Holy Communion are indivisible parts of
one cultic act in the worship of the church has the church taken the
miracle of the incarnation really seriously. By means of the unity of
body and Spirit in the eucharistic gift, the church is bound simultaneously to the invisible God and to the visible world which He has
created. The visible fellowship of Communion in the church's Sunday worship prevents it from so "spiritualizing" its fellowship with
God, with man and with the world of living creatures that the corporeality of its existence and thus also of its eternal salvation is forgotten.

This dual relationship with the invisible God and the visible
world, established by Holy Communion, is the work of Jesus Christ

in the church. It is a miracle of his which brings about this dual relationship of man in Holy Communion. The historical effects of the
dual relationship of man with God and the world cannot be
"planned" by the members of the church. Rather the church under-
goes this relationship as a work wrought for it by its Lord. But this
by no means implies that the church is passive or indifferent in its
attitude to the contemporary history of which its members are a part.
How could this be possible if it is linked to the world? But it means
that it cannot arrange its active participation in the history of the
nation and the world, in which its members spend their earthly life,
along theocratic lines and must act responsibly in the freedom of the
children of God in a "worldly" way together with other children of
the world. Once again we must note the truth of the Lutheran doctrine of God's two realms.

If the church allows its life in the world to be determined by the
miracle of Jesus Christ in the Church, by the sacrament of the
Eucharist, its history as an integral part of the history of mankind
will also be and remain a history of man with God in the world. It
is a history of faith and, as such, can never be directly demonstrated.
But because it is a history of faith it constitutes a great power in the
history of the world.[62]

2. Preaching

In their unity the works and words of Jesus Christ constitute the
history of Jesus Christ. This is true when his history is seen as the
center of God's history with the world, but also when it is seen as
the center of man's history with God. Thus in the history of faith
the words of Jesus are also linked with his works because they interpret the latter.

Jesus Christ's miracle in the church, Holy Communion, is thus
accompanied by the words (the teaching) of Jesus Christ in the
Church, preaching. The preaching of the Church is the way in
which the teaching of Jesus goes out into the world and forward
through time after his resurrection and exaltation. The preaching of
the church is not the independent word of contemporary preachers.
Therefore they are exempt from any concern about the "relevance"
of their word and its "effect." "We must be regarded as Christ's sub-
ordinates and as stewards of the secrets of God. Well then, stewards
are expected to show themselves trustworthy."[63] This apostolic word

is the supreme law for the preacher in the church. His preaching is and should be nothing less than the teaching of Jesus Christ, but also nothing more. For this reason preaching must be based on the text of the Bible. Any attempt to preach in worship on non-biblical texts—on a text from Dag Hammarskjöld, for example[64]—can only be permitted on condition that it is made clear to everyone that this is not the preaching of the church but only an "address," which can certainly also be given in the church, which is, however, only the "word" of the preacher and not the word of Jesus Christ.

But to say that preaching must be strictly based on the text of the Bible certainly does not mean that the preacher may only repeat biblical quotations. The text of the Bible witnesses to the Gospel, the joyful news, which must be proclaimed as such to the listeners of today. The fact that the church today must extract the teaching of Jesus Christ from the biblical texts in its preaching includes the task of hermeneutics. Jesus' teaching about the Kingdom of God is of universal application. Therefore it must and can be interpreted aright for the people of every place and time. Without interpretation the teaching of Jesus can never be rightly preached. A mere repetition of biblical words and phrases would be a misinterpretation of the Gospel. What matters is that, by means of the right interpretation of Jesus' teaching in preaching, the Kingdom of God which he proclaimed should be enabled to intervene here and now in the lives of men in accordance with its universal significance. In so far as Jesus' teaching about the Kingdom of God lays emphasis on man and his world, the interpretation of Jesus' teaching which is necessary here can certainly be called an "existential interpretation." But man's existence in his world should not be misinterpreted in an "existentialist" way. The conception of existence which is limited to the individual and absolutizes the free decision or choice of the living agent does not correspond to the reality of man living as God's creation.

A view of existence inspired by Marxism, which does not disregard society and things, and a view of man influenced by psychoanalysis would at least be formally nearer to Jesus' teaching about the Kingdom of God than the existential interpretation of a Rudolf Bultmann derived from Kierkegaard and the theological neo-Kantianism of Wilhelm Herrmann. If it is at all necessary to speak about a "concept of existence" offered to man through the preaching of the

Gospel, it must be remembered that man "understands" his existence as a creature of God reborn in Jesus Christ to eternal life only
in the sense that he knows his Creator and the World in which the
Creator has set him, i.e., he believes in and obeys God and accepts
the world as God's gift, and not because he sets himself up as an
autonomous being. An understanding of existence in the view of the
Christian faith is not a "self-understanding"; it is not acquired by
man's "acquiring" his "self" in contradistinction to a heteronomous
will of God or to causal natural laws. On the contrary, in faith man
understands "himself" *in* (not in contrast to) God, *in* God's creation, *in* Jesus Christ, *in* the church. And this "being in," which is the
form of the believer's existence, is made possible only when man
turns intentionally to God, the world, Christ and the church, and
not by any kind of existential analysis of a direct intention to be
himself.

If this is forgotten faith is reduced to a "worldless," socially and
politically sterile "inner life," which is a clear contrast to Jesus'
teaching about the Kingdom of God and is therefore of no value as
a "preliminary understanding" for the interpretation of the Gospel.

The existential interpretation in the church's preaching, which
relates the teaching of Jesus to the concrete life of contemporary man
in his world, must not combine his teaching with a view of the world
or of life from any other source, which is a great temptation in an
age of totalitarian thinking like our own. On the contrary, it must
set the reality of the Kingdom of God, which is both liberating and
limiting, over against all the demands and expectations of the kingdoms of this world, so that the people who are living in the world
with the expectation of the Kingdom of God are simultaneously set
free for sacrificial love and bound by faithfulness to the love which
serves. The social and political "effect" of the church's preaching
does not reside in "ideas" which it could propagate—for preaching
does not propagate "ideas" or "programs" and is never "relevant" in
this sense—but in its attitude to the world ("the freedom of the captives"[65]) which is the expression of faith in its truth.

The teaching of Jesus in the church's preaching is inseparably
linked with the miracle of Jesus in the church's Holy Communion
to constitute a history of faith. Only where they are found together
in the life of the Church and of its members does the history of faith
take place.

Conclusion

In the introduction, the question was asked as to whether holy history, God's history with man and man's history with God, is of universal significance. Is it a history of salvation which sanctifies the history of the world? Does its holiness turn the whole of secular history into a history of God with his world? These questions must receive an unconditional, affirmative answer—that was the conclusion of the preceding reflections on the works and words of Jesus Christ. When one compares secular history, the history of the world, with holy history—the history of Jesus Christ, the history of the church, the history of faith—one can see that the "history of the world" is and remains a separate history in so far as it is the product of self-love (*amor sui*). Holy history, on the other hand, is governed by the love of God and of one's neighbor (*amor dei et proximi*) and is therefore simply universal history.[66]

It is the faith and the hope of the Christian church that holy history will finally sanctify the whole history of the world. Sometime the Kingdom of God will encompass and perfect all the kingdoms of the world.

But, because the love of God which became history in Jesus Christ can only vanquish self-love through sacrifice, through voluntary death for the enemies of God, the path to the perfection of the history of the world leads through a history of the church and of faith which is marked by the sign of the cross, i.e., the sign of the sacrifice of love. Only a church under the cross, not a Church triumphant with "influence," can and will be "the church for the world."[67] It is the church for the world above all because it prays for the world as it is, for the world which from time to time will again persecute the church. It believes all things, hopes all things and suffers all things for the world which does not know God. It exists for the world to which all the children of God on this side of death belong with body and soul as well. Thus, under the cross of Jesus Christ, until he comes again in glory, the "works and words of Jesus Christ" take place as God's works for and God's words to the world which he created and which belongs to him for ever.

—*Translated by* MARGARET A. PATER

NOTES

All biblical quotations have been taken from the New English Bible.

1. From the overwhelming wealth of works on the nature and meaning of history, the following list of individual philosophical and theological writings comprises some which have been of help to the author: H-G. Gadamer, *Wahrheit und Methode*, 2nd edition, Tübingen, 1960. H. I. Marrou, "Comment comprendre le métier d'historien, L'histoire et ses méthodes," *Encyclopédie de la Pléiade XI*, Paris, 1961, pp. 1467-1539. R. Wittram, *Das Interesse an der Geschichte*, Göttingen, 1958. Idem, *Zukunft in der Geschichte*, Göttingen, 1966. H. Butterfield, *Man on His Past*, Cambridge, 1955. G. J. Renier, *History. Its Purpose and Method*, London, 1950. E. H. Carr, *What Is History?*, London, 1961. W. Dray, *Laws and Explanation in History*, Oxford, 1957. A. Richardson, *History Sacred and Profane*, London, 1964. R. Niebuhr, *Faith and History*, New York, 1949. H. Berkhof, *Der Sinn der Geschichte*, Göttingen, 1962. O. Cullmann, *Salvation in History*, London, 1967. W. Pannenberg, *Basic Questions in Theology*, London, 1970, Vol. I, pp. 1-181. Idem, *et al., Revelation as History*, New York and London, 1968. J. M. Robinson and J. B. Cobb, Jr., ed., *The New Hermeneutic. New Frontiers in Theology*, New York, Evanston, and London, 1964, Vol. II. J. Moltmann, *Theology of Hope*, London, 1967. Idem, *Perspektiven der Theologie*, Munich, 1968. Idem, *Mensch*, Stuttgart, 1971.

2. Gadamer, *op. cit.*, pp. 329-449. Wittram, *op. cit.*, pp. 110-122.

3. Renier, *op. cit.*, pp. 179-188 and 221-243.

4. Carr, *op. cit.*, pp. 87-156.

5. In the Bible, creation is an historical and not a cosmological term. The creation of the world and the election and guidance of Israel belong to a history, to creation.

6. This was established by Martin Kähler as early as 1892 in his little book which was of such great importance for the evolution of the "Formgeschichte" (history of form) school, *The So-called Historical Jesus and the Historic Biblical Christ*, Philadelphia, 1966. One may criticize some of the details of Kähler's work. The main point of his criticism of the "biography of Jesus" remains irrefutable. ". . . and one will not be able to depict the historical Christ without establishing his identity by means of the Old Testament, without bringing to bear the Old Testament background and also the Old Testament coloring to the life which he leads before and in his Father. Thus every section of our Bible contributes toward giving us a complete picture of Jesus the Christ. This concerns above all the church's work with the Word of God; the mature Christian, however, can also become aware of it in his study of the Bible and implement it silently for himself by growing into this testimony step by step. And this is what we mean when we speak of the *biblical* Christ." (Translation by R.P.) *Op. cit.*, 1953, pp. 67-68.

7. This insight is becoming increasingly prevalent in Old Testament scholarship, especially in Germany; cf. C. Westermann, ed., *Essays on Old Testament Hermeneutics*, Richmond, Va., 1963. G. von Rad, *Old Testament Theology*, Edinburgh and London, 1962-65, Vol. II, pp. 319-409. A. G. Hebert, *The Throne of David*, London, 1941. Idem, *The Authority of the Old Testament*, London, 1947. Idem, *When Israel Came Out of Egypt*, London, 1961. F. Mildenberger, *Gottes Tat im Wort*, Gütersloh, 1964. G. E. Wright, *God Who Acts*, London, 1952.

8. Mark 2:10; 2:28; Matthew 11:19; 18:11; Luke 17:22; 19:10.
9. Rudolf Bultmann and the German New Testament research which follows him consider, under the lasting influence of W. Wrede, *The Messianic Secret*, Cambridge and London, 1971, that Jesus did not describe himself as the Son of Man but that this description of himself was put into his mouth after the resurrection by the church which identified him with the heavenly Son of Man of apocalyptic thinking. The only genuine Son of Man *logia* are those which speak of the coming Son of Man-judge of the world with whom Jesus did not identify himself. Thus R. Bultmann, *Theology of the New Testament*, London, 1965, Vol. I, pp. 26-32. H. E. Tödt, *The Son of Man in the Synoptic Tradition*, London, 1965, is an attempt to provide the basis for this theory by studying the history of the tradition. Non-German New Testament research is generally of the opposite opinion—that Jesus did in fact describe himself as the Son of Man (man). The most detailed criticism of the view of the Bultmann school has been undertaken by E. Schweizer, *Lordship and Discipleship*, London, 1960; cf. idem, *Neotestamentica*, Zürich and Stuttgart, 1963, pp. 56-92. The hypothesis of Bultmann and his followers is in any case improbable because there can be no explanation of the fact that the description "Son of Man" ("man") occurs eighty-three times in the New Testament as Jesus' description of himself and only once in the mouth of someone else (Acts 7:56) if Jesus did not call himself the Son of Man. Moreover it appears nonsensical that the Church, if there were no inducement to do so, should have put an interpretation of the expression "Son of Man" which was foreign to it and indeed meaningless into the mouth of Jesus, namely the concept of a humbled Son of Man who had already come. For according to this theory the Church originally knew only the apocalyptic meaning of the "title" Son of Man, partly because of Jesus' references to another coming Son of Man and partly because of its own identification of this other with the risen (non-earthly) Jesus. In fact the whole theory is a methodological invention which lacks any historical probability.
10. R. Prenter, *Connaître Christ*, Neuchâtel, 1966, pp. 75-149.
11. Matthew 18:11; Luke 19:10.
12. Mark 10:45.
13. Genesis 12:3.
14. Matthew 28:19-20; Romans 10:18.
15. John 1:18.
16. 1 John 1:3.
17. Jeremiah 1:4; 2:1; Ezekiel 1:3, etc.
18. John 1:1-3; 5:21.
19. John 1:14.
20. O. Cullmann, *The Christology of the New Testament*, London, 1963, pp. 152-164 and 306-314.
21. The expression "history of religion" is meant here in its broadest sense. The history of philosophy is to a large extent part of the history of religion in this sense. If the history of religion, understood in this way, is seen as the pre-history of the history of man with God, which has as its centre the high priestly service of Jesus Christ, then the way in which the second Vatican Council adopted a positive evaluation of the non-Christian religions must be considered to be theologically legitimate. The challenge contained in this approach should not be neglected by Protestant theology. Cf. *Lumen Gentium* 16; *Nostra Aetate*; *Ad Gentes 3*. P. Tillich, *Christianity and the Encounter of World Religions*, New York and London, 1963.

22. O. Cullmann, *op. cit.*, pp. 83-107.
23. Mark 14:21. "In the scriptures" may refer, for example, to Ezekiel 12:1 ff.
24. *Ad Gentes 3*.
25. Romans 8:29; Hebrews 2:10.
26. The miracles of Jesus are "signs," i.e., advance signs of the coming Kingdom of God, Matthew 11:4-6; 12:28; but they are not "signs of proof," intended to demonstrate the authority of Jesus. Jesus refuses to provide a "sign from heaven" by way of proof, Matthew 12:39.
27. Matthew 9:35-36; 8:16-17; 12:15-21.
28. Matthew 11:5.
29. Matthew 11:19; Luke 19:7; Mark 3:1-6.
30. Mark 10:45. The concept of Jesus' miracle developed here is based on the relationship described in the preceding remarks between the service of the Son of Man, on the one hand, understood along the lines of Isaiah 53, and the miracles or Jesus' redemptive death, on the other.
31. "After the church's having presented the heavenly Christ in a one-sided way for so long in word, sacrament and hierarchy, they (that is: committed Christians) are now seeking a fellowship with the crucified Son of Man who, in the hungry, naked, prisoners and those without rights is waiting for the actions of the righteous." (J. Moltmann, *Gott in der Revolution. Diskussion zur "Theologie der Revolution"*, Munich, 1969, p. 70.) If this fellowship with the suffering Son of Man is seen first as an alternative to the presence of the heavenly Christ in word and sacrament (and hierarchy?) and second as a solution to the crisis of identity in Christianity brought about by the revolutionary situation, then it has nothing to do with "Christianity" as understood by the Bible. In the same lecture Moltmann asks the question, "Will Christianity decay along with the predominance of Europe and with the pre-industrial era? Or does Christianity itself contain an immanent revolutionary potential which can be discovered, consciously recognized and translated into practical social action?" (*Ibid.*, p. 69). The answer to this question, which Moltmann was expecting from the student conference in Turku, is already implied in what he himself says in the following sentences: "Without self-criticism in Christianity there can be no real presence of Christians in the places where revolutionary decisions are taken in the world. Therefore it is necessary for resolute groups to bring the revolution of freedom into the existing churches. The Christian faith is concerned with God in Christ. But the crisis of its identity is caused by its no longer being certain why it exists. It is well aware where it comes from but it no longer knows exactly where it is going. Therefore the future makes it so helpless. But one does not only acquire one's identity from a theoretical reminder of one's origin; in practice identification with and commitment to the tasks of the present for a greater future are a part of it. When Christians come to rediscover why they exist, they will also rediscover who they really are" (*ibid.*). If it is correct to assume that the personified Christian faith, to which both "knowledge," "origin" and "direction" as well as "not knowing" and "helplessness" are attributed, is identical with the "Christians" mentioned in the last sentence quoted, one must say "no" to the whole approach. If "Christians" see themselves as a Christian, believing church and wish to seek and perhaps find their identity in this understanding of themselves, they must hear and believe the promises of God. When they have thus found their identity as "Christians" or as the Christian church, they must and will "commit themselves" to acting in the world, naturally also in the political field and, in

certain situations, probably also "in the places where revolutionary decisions are taken." But if they try to discover their identity in their own commitment and not in faith in God's promises, they will most certainly lose this identity completely and irrevocably. They would then be giving up their identity with the Christian faith and seeking a new identity in the "revolution."

32. Hebrews 13:14.
33. Mark 1:15.
34. Mark 1:21; 6:2; 13:10; Matthew 4:23; 9:35; 13:54; Luke 4:15-30; John 6:59; 18:20; Mark 4:1; Luke 5:3; 13:22; Mark 12:35; Luke 23:5; the parables as doctrine: Mark 4:2-34.
35. Luke 5:16; 6:12; 9:18; Mark 1:35, etc.
36. Matthew 12:24.
37. Where Jesus does not find faith he performs no miracles: Matthew 13:53.
38. John 18:37; Mark 1:27.
39. In the "Sermon on the Mount" Matthew has put together an "address" by combining bits of teaching to present Jesus' teaching from this angle: Matthew 5-7.
40. Cf. R. Prenter, "L'interprétation de la doctrine des deux règnes," in *Revue d'Histoire et de Philosophie Religieuses*, 1963, 3, pp. 239-249.
41. Matthew 22:21.
42. Here it is not possible to go into the revolutionary interpretation of the person of Jesus which has become "modern" again. For a discussion of this misinterpretation of the Gospel tradition reference may be made to the following works: O. Cullmann, *Jesus und die Revolutionären seiner Zeit*, Tübingen, 1970. M. Hengel, *War Jesus Revolutionär?* Stuttgart, 1970. B. Gerhardsson, *2000 ar senare*, Stockholm, 1972, pp. 43-49.
43. Mark 2:12; 3:2; 3:22; Matthew 11:19.
44. Mark 6:41; 7:34; 8:12; John 11:41.
45. Mark 2:7.
46. Matthew 22:15; cf. Mark 8:11; 10:2.
47. Matthew 16:6-12; 22-23; Mark 10:35-45.
48. Matthew 12:39.
49. Greater detail of the reasons for the view of baptism into the name of Jesus Christ as expounded here can be found in: R. Prenter, *Connaître Christ*, Neuchâtel, 1966, pp. 42-52.
50. *Confessio Augustana XX*, 12-22. It cannot be denied that Melanchthon here anticipates the shift in the conception of the doctrine of justification which we find in late orthodoxy and in pietism. If one places too much emphasis on these pastoral considerations in the interpretation of the Reformation doctrine of justification, one does not do justice to the nature of the Pauline and Lutheran doctrine of justification by faith alone. This doctrine is concerned with man's right before God, not with the "pacifying" of his own heart. That the man who is justified before God can live "peacefully" and happily does not mean that God declares him justified for this reason. For in times of temptation—and precisely in temptation when one's "peace" is lost—he may and should rely on the fact that God, who declared him justified in baptism, cannot lie. Because the conscience is not at peace, faith which is under attack clings to the right which it has been promised.
51. For a criticism of the doctrine of justification in connection with the Assembly of the Lutheran World Federation at Helsinki in 1963, see especially G. Gloege, *Gnade für die Welt. Kritik und Krise des Luthertums*, Göttingen, 1964; also: P. Tillich, *Systematic Theology III*, Chicago, 1963, pp. 221-228.

52. Galatians 6:16.
53. Hosea 11:1.
54. Cf. *Lumen Gentium* 9-10.
55. D. Bonhoeffer, *Sanctorum Communio*, London, 1963. R. Prenter, "Jesus Christus als Gemeinde existierend. Ein Beitrag zum Verständnis Dietrich Bonhoeffers," in *Lutherische Monatshefte* Jhg. 4, 1965, p. 262-267.
56. Hebrews 2:13.
57. Matthew 5:14.
58. Matthew 5:16.
59. Mark 9:40.
60. D. Bonhoeffer, *Letters and Papers from Prison*, London, 1953. Cf. R. Prenter, *Dietrich Bonhoeffer und Karl Barths Offenbarungspositivismus. Die mündige Welt*, Munich, 1960, Vol. 3, pp. 11-41. H. Müller, *Von der Kirche zur Welt*, Leipzig, 1961, pp. 393-400. A. Dumas, *Une théologie de la réalité: Dietrich Bonhoeffer*, Geneva, 1968, pp. 215-233. G. Meuss, *Arkandisziplin und Weltlichkeit bei Dietrich Bonhoeffer. Die Mündige Welt*, Munich, 1961, Vol. 3, pp. 68-115.
61. In connection with the ideas developed in this paper cf. R. Prenter, *Connaître Christ*, pp. 52-74. Idem, A Lutheran Doctrine of Eucharistic Sacrifice. *Studia Theologica Scandinavica*, 1965, Vol. 19, pp. 189-199. Idem, La fondation christologique du ministère. OIKONOMIA, Oscar Cullmann zum 65. Ceburtstag gewidmet, Hamburg and Bergstedt 1967, pp. 239-247. Cf. *Lumen Gentium* 10-11; *De Sacra Liturgia* 7-11.
62. The unplanned "effect" of the life of the children of God on the history of the world is expressed in the concept of the gift of grace, the charisma. The forces of the faith which bring about history are charismatic. Therefore they cannot be contained within any sort of theocracy. However they are effective in secular history.
63. 1 Corinthians 4:1-2.
64. This really was tried in Scandinavia in an "experimental service!"
65. "Die Freiheit der Gebundenen" (the freedom of the captives) was the original title of the Festschrift für Karl Barth (Theologische Aufsätze) 1936. The freedom of the captives is the charismatic life.
66. According to Augustine (*De Civitate Dei*), the struggle of the love of God against the love of self is the essence of history.
67. Uppsala 68 Speaks, Geneva, 1968, Section II: Renewal in Mission, especially part II, Opportunities for Mission, p. 30, "The Church in Mission is the Church for Others." Cf. *Gaudium et Spes*, pp. 40-45.

Chapter 2

God's World and the Individual

A. THE CHANGES IN THE OUTWARD SETTING

The Gospel basically has always been preached for the individual, even in the days when it was accepted in practice by whole nations under the guidance of their kings. The word of the Gospel in fact always requires the "yes" of faith, and faith can only be born in the heart of the *indivdual.*

In the course of history the Gospel has never been preached without the preacher's working with the presupposition, in some form or another, that the world in which the individual listener found himself was *God's world,* God's creation. This presupposition can also be found at many points in the expressions used by the Gospel, e.g., in the expressions "forgiveness of sins" or "redemption." The individual has got lost in a world in which he could really have lived as a child of God if he had not destroyed his true life by his very aberration. "Forgiveness of sins" and "redemption" are meaningful words only if one assumes that they put something in order and thus make something "whole" again.

This means that certain quite irreligious phenomena in the world are interpreted as the work of God—birth, rain, sunshine, bread, water, and so on. All of these phenomena are described in the Bible, both in the Old and the New Testaments, as God's creations. But the fact that they are mentioned in the Bible does not mean that man's access to them is through the Bible. On the contrary, they are already present in the world; they are present in the world *of all men*—the Bible only refers to them. And this is precisely where the difference lies between God's world and the Gospel. The Gospel comes *from* the Bible; it *comes to us* from the Bible. If it is not heard in the words of the Bible it cannot be heard in the world.

The distinction made between the "universal" and the "specific" by K. E. Løgstrup is necessary, in my view.[1] The universal is present and affects man's life in general everywhere in the world. But the specific must be brought about within a historical process by a word which is preached. And in this historical process the Gospel today relates more directly than ever before to the *individual*.

As a general rule, and especially in the present century, attention is rather directed to interpreting the Gospel and not to interpreting the world as God's world, that is not to belief in God as the Creator. This strong concentration on the Gospel, i.e., on the second article of the Creed, however, was never as one-sided in any earlier generation in church history as it is today. There has always been special emphasis placed on the affirmation of those statements in the Creed which the unbelieving world around the church has denied. There have been times, particularly at the beginning, during the Gnostic period, when the belief in God as the Creator was expressly rejected by heretics. At that time the doctrine of creation was especially emphasized by the church.

There are plenty of signs to indicate that now, in the twentieth century, we are living with a new form of gnosticism. The vigor with which the first article of the Creed is brushed to one side seems to echo the first century. One thing is quite clear: if our generation had to draw up a Creed, it would never put belief in the Creator at the beginning of it. But there, in the first part of the whole, the reference to the Creator still stands today in the church's Sunday confession of faith—and it stands there for very good reasons. It refers to the world as God's world.

Now that we have provisionally described the reason for contrasting "God's world," on the one hand, with the "individual," on the other, it is possible to have a better understanding of the subject-matter of this first section: "The Changes in the Outward Setting." It is easier to see what this is about if one outlines briefly four periods of church history. In each of these periods the *world* has been understood differently and yet in such a way that in all four periods it has been presented as *God's* world. Of course, the position of the *individual* and the task of preaching the Gospel have also been understood differently in each period.

The four periods are: (1) the period of the minority churches before the fourth century, (2) the period of cooperation with the Roman Empire and the related period of medieval unity in Europe, (3) the period of the dissolution of this unity and the related period of national states and national churches (confessionalism), and (4) the new period of minority churches developing today and the related internationalization of the church (an "exodus" from a secular identity with the Western national states).

In general it can be said that the following is of special importance for our overall subject, "The Gospel as History": the orginal diversity in the interpretation of what the "Gospel" is, which was lost in the cooperation of the church with the state—first with the Roman Empire and then with modern national states—is coming into existence again in the modern situation.

From the very beginning there were *four* Gospels and in the Early Church before the fourth century there was a much greater tolerance of diversity than was allowed in the Roman Empire or later in the confessional national states. In this sense the situation today offers a new opportunity of re-establishing something which existed at the very beginning.[2]

One the other hand, the attention devoted to the other task, that of "interpreting the world," is slighter today than ever before. At the time of the early minority churches there was a gnosticism with a clear and logical structure which compelled the church to turn its attention to its responsibility for interpreting the world: one could see what the consequence would be of losing the faith in the Creator. And in the two periods of cooperation with the state which followed, Christians always occupied responsible positions in the world, which made it necessary to reflect on God's Lordship over the world—which is not brought about by preaching the Gospel to the individual.

But today those who preach the Gospel do not occupy positions of direct political responsibility. They do talk "about the world" (about the world rather than about heaven!) and can say more or less anything that occurs to them—and they do say it, but the fact that they themselves may become gnostics in the process is a danger which they hardly notice.

The subject with which we are concerned, "God's world and the individual," must therefore have two main emphases. The Gospel has a history and it must change in order to retain its continuity—that is the one side. But the Gospel can remain the Gospel only if it is not seen in isolation—that is the other. Wherever it is proclaimed in the world, it is always preached in God's world, against the background of creation and the law. And the Christian interpretation of the world as God's world also has a history. Precisely because man's life in creation is part of the universal, because it simply *is there*, it can be interpreted *as creation* by using the greatest possible variety of terminologies and patterns of thought.

Thus transformation, change which still retains continuity, will be a main point for discussion in both cases.

1. The minority situation before the fourth century

In these first three hundred years there was not yet any close co-operation with a government, neither in the original Jewish setting nor in the Roman Empire. The congregations were often house churches or small groups and owned no public meeting places. The church's concept of itself was of a wandering, missionary church; it was constantly moving toward the end of the world. Its life was in a sense a life for those outside of its fellowship, those who were not members but to whom it felt itself to have been sent.

If one is looking in this early period for a parallel to the later relationship between church and state, the best parallel is that of "the old Israel." Israel was a nation chosen by God; Israel had the Law and "the promises" (Romans 9:4) and yet it said "no" and thus remained outside the door. On a number of occasions an attempt was made to find a way of living with Israel and its norms (e.g., Acts 15). This attempt was necessary because, as a partner, Israel exercised an influence on the everyday life of the members of the Christian congregation. And each of these attempts had the same result as all the later modifications of the church's coexistence with the state: Christians acted without their action being based directly on the *Gospel*.

The eating of meat in certain cases, circumcision, keeping the Sabbath, etc., belonged to this collection of actions which could have been performed or not in complete freedom on the basis of the Gospel. But then they became governed by a predetermined code because the other factor, the synagogue, was nearby and was a significant partner which also influenced "the weaker brothers."[3] Every rule of this sort has temporal limitations and necessarily so. When the rule is laid down its abolition is already in the air, as it were. The rules which were laid down in Acts 15 were never abolished by the congregation itself. It goes without saying that a new situation (without the synagogue as a partner) will abolish them.

But the Gospel can never be superseded in any situation. Of its own accord it has full authority to create new church orders, e.g., it fixes Sunday worship for the first weekday after the Sabbath (John

20:26; Revelation 1:10), and in situations of conflict it can destroy old and sacred church orders (e.g., Galatians 2:10-14). Because the Gospel has this sovereignty and because it is the only one sent out to reach people throughout the world, it takes on all sorts of different languages, terminologies and ways of thinking. This is why there are *four Gospels*.

This diversity is a result of the diversity of the audiences, of the differences in ways of thinking, which have already marked the listeners, the *addressees* of the Gospel. If at some later time a holy book about liberating events were to have been written, it is unthinkable that such a holy book would have contained the same succession of events in four different editions. The desire for unity and conformity even in terminology and expression was later taken for granted and promoted by the state. This applies both to the emperor in the Roman empire and to the kings and princes of the national state during the period of confessionalism.

But at the beginning this was *not* the case. The young church at the time of the martyrs was conscious of its own inner unity and could tolerate diversity for precisely this reason.

2. Cooperation with the Roman Empire

The general political trend in the fourth century was different from that of the sixteenth century, indeed it went in the opposite direction. As the Roman empire developed, small national states with their own languages disappeared and a unity was created with a common language, Latin. After the Reformation the unity of Europe disappeared and relatively small national states emerged with services of worship in their own languages. Both developments were defended to a certain extent on biblical grounds.

The emperor himself, Constantine the Great, interpreted his victory as a consequence of divine intervention. Eusebius in his *History of the Church* lends support to this view.[4] The eschatological future with its peace between the nations was being prevented, according to Eusebius, by the hostility of the national states to one another; but now this future is a reality: peace reigns and a uniform language has begun to prevail among the people. To a certain extent Jewish conceptions of the predominance of the future of the Hebrews are being used here to support a quite different empire.[5]

It is quite obvious that this political unity put an end to pluralism in the church which it was previously possible to tolerate without divisions. There were different Christologies from the very beginning. Antioch, Asia Minor, Alexandria, etc. stood for different emphases which were held in tension but were not capable of dividing the states at the time of the martyrs. Where the state wanted to suppress or persecute something, the hostile leaders of the state turned against the *one thing* that all of these Christologies had *in common*, the faith in Christ itself, the center of the diversity. But now, after the beginning of the fourth century, tensions in the church represent threats to the state.

For the state demands unity. The same demand for unity, which had led to the persecution of the Christian Church for disturbing the unity before the fourth century, now resulted in the rigid unity of this church, i.e., in division. The emperor and the state authorities summoned councils, took part in the drafting of confessional statements and thus also shared the responsibility for condemning heretics. These are platitudes from church history with which we are all familiar. But there are two considerations of importance here, one relating to the past and one to the future.

When we look back we can see that a relative diversity, which was not felt to be a weakness in the minority period and at the time of the persecutions, became suspicious at this point and therefore rapidly came to an end. The lack of agreement between Asia Minor and Rome about the date of the Easter festival is a good example. There was real conflict and tension but Irenaeus considered that a church could survive without division although two different Easter festivals were celebrated within it at different times.[6] Later on, groups within the church were divided from one another as a result of conflicts which were no greater; they only became intolerable because the church had become responsible for civil legislation and therefore *could* not tolerate differences.

If we look to the future we shall see that this Constantinian unity constituted a preparatory stage of the confessional divisions of the seventeenth century. Then, too, there is a total union of church and empire, but in such a way that each national state is linked with a church of a particular confession which a citizen, who wishes to enjoy civil rights, has to accept (the right to work, to marry, etc.). And precisely this combination of a confession with civil rights is coming to an end in the twentieth century; it is disappearing in all parts of the West, more quickly in some countries and more slowly in others.

3. *The collapse of medieval unity and the growth of the national states*

We have just indicated the typical characteristics of this period. What must be added is first and foremost the *combination* of factors which brought about the new situation. The concentration on the Gospel alone and the neglect of the first article of the Creed caused a curious division of the factors involved. From a "religious" point of view something happened in Wittenberg, and the events there "fitted in well" with other outward events of the same period which are considered to be purely political factors. As historians, we put the religious and political factors together in order to interpret what happened. In this way we divide up a life which was only *one* life for those living at the time.

In fact the following are all interrelated: the discovery of the Gospel, the development of national states which governed their own concerns independently and free from Papal control, the invention of printing and the holding of public worship in the languages of the various nations. The factors at the end of the list are just as "religious" as the exegetical discovery at Wittenberg.

According to the conviction which the exegete in Wittenberg, Martin Luther, derived from the Bible, the medieval, "mixed" state, in which the church exercised fundamentally secular power, is in fact a state which contradicts the Gospel. The development of the northern European national states is in agreement with the Will of God—from the point of view of the Christian faith; it happens "according to the Word of God."[7] The same applies to the other events —printing and the use of the national language. These events enable the Gospel to *live!* Indeed, how could it exist without them, i.e., penetrate into the hearts of men?

It is here that the belief in the *Creator*, which also comes at the beginning of the Creed, becomes important. The various factors are interpreted together and should not be divided up by us at a later time into secular and religious factors. If we divide them we force our own sectarian religion *upon* the sources—*in* the sources there is no such sectarian religion! Objectively speaking, everything is secular, including the exegetical work in Wittenberg.

The fact that this unity of church and nation constitutes a *risk*, a risk for the purity of the Gospel, is another matter. Every combination of something from the Gospel with something human which is separate from the Gospel constitutes a risk for the purity of the Gos-

pel. This was the case at the very beginning of the church's history
when the first rules were introduced concerning the church and
Judaism, before there was any question of the state being a partner.
Any rule of this sort is subject to the principle: as soon as the rule
is introduced, its abolition is in the air; in this realm everything has
temporal limitations, everything passes away.

The danger of judaizing Christianity became evident very early;
the danger of captivity to the empire and to the gradually incomprehensible Latin services became visible (and intolerable) later on;
and soon after the Reformation there arose the equally obvious and
equally intolerable danger of confessionalism in the national
churches. The thing that *prevails*, that does not pass away and that
must continually make itself new clothes in order to be able to preserve its identity and continuity, is the Gospel.

After 1648 and the Peace of Westphalia, during the period of national states and confessional churches, this danger became particularly evident. At that point the confessional boundaries were laid
down more or less geographically; even the Roman Catholic church
became a denomination from the point of view of the state. Thus
the unity of the church with the worldly realm became almost total
for the *individual*. A Swede was a Lutheran, an Englishman was an
Anglican (at least for short periods during the seventeenth century),
a Frenchman was a Catholic, etc. This unity did not last long *in the
form of total identity*—conceptions of tolerance soon came into being
—but as a phenomenon of partial unity it still exists in many countries today (e.g., in marriage and education laws).

But, and this is important, this unity is breaking down more and
more as the days go by. It is quite obvious in which direction this
process will go in the future.

4. The new minority situation and secularisation

What is meant by the new situation? There are features which
occur in a number of places and which must be seen in conjunction
in order to identity the whole. *First*, in its legislation society is becoming more and more separated from the church. Compulsory
teaching in schools, that is the knowledge which every citizen is
"compelled" to acquire, a teaching which used to be determined
confessionally, is no longer in the hands of the largest church in the
country. Biblical passages (and their influence) are vanishing from
the wording of laws governing marriage and divorce. The same

thing is happening in other fields of penal and civil law. *Second,* the local church reacts negatively to a nationalistic limitation of the Christian ethos to actions and activities which are of benefit only to one's own country. *Third,* there is a growing positive concern for those in need in countries other than one's own.[8]

These only appear to be three trends. In fact, they all constitute *one* movement. Just as the scattered church was drawn after the fourth century from many places and many languages into the structural unity of the Roman Empire by a single gathering movement which brought about conformity and uniformity, and just as the church departed from this artificial (Latin and papal) unity and entered a phase of symbiosis with the new national states and their laws after the sixteenth century, so the church now is abandoning these national states and seeking a new foothold in international responsibility for nations and countries which do not yet enjoy a life of human dignity.

Naturally this change in the outward situation of the church is secondary in this case as well. The world has changed and therefore the church is changing too.

The national states would have come about even without the Reformation; modern internationalization is an established fact. If numerous large industries today have larger budgets than the majority of national states and if these industries are already actively planning, building and exploiting workers at an international level, the traditional sovereignty of the individual states in decisive areas is merely an illusion. And when Swedish working groups are flown to Malta to have their meetings there because the Swedish hotel prices are too high, then in a sense Malta has become the place of work for northern Europeans (the flight time is no greater than the time which a car driver requires to travel from his suburban apartment to the center of Stockholm, i.e., to his place of work) .

But this change in the world is not a change which is "foreign" to the church because it is a change in *God's* world, that is in the very world in which God is at work today as the Creator. The leper in Africa, who used to be so far away from us that our help could not reach him quickly enough, is so close to us today—because of what God has done—that we can see him on television and reach him in an airplane, both almost directly, in a day or a night. This is new— just as new as were printing and the other external changes of the sixteenth century.

But this newness is not only a question of new (international) links with situations of need which were far away from us in the past. It also involves a break with older expressions of solidarity with our own country. Ever since the beginning of the confessionalist era of the national states the churches had been shut in their own countries; there recent legislation is now pushing them aside.

When everything is added up, the contemporary changes in the outward setting constitute a uniform movement in a remarkable way which represents a return to the original situation before the fourth century and also a forward movement. What will happen in the future has never existed before. The martyr church of the second century still had the future unity of the Roman Empire in front of it, a situation which will not arise again. And behind it this same martyr church probably had the synagogues of the old Israel, which were to be found here and there in the large towns, but no parish churches with towers and cemeteries in which the name of Jesus Christ has been cut into walls and stones for centuries. The future minority church in Europe (and to some extent in America), however, will have this in front of it every day.

And yet, along with Africans and Asians who do not have this past, its eyes are turned to the future. Here the most important factor will be the discovery of positive plurality. The forward movement toward new international responsibility is a return to the diversity of expression in the preaching of the Gospel. Just as the early Christian Gospel took on a number of different forms in order to be able to reach different audiences, so the Gospel today must take many forms, become multiform. This is the only way for it to say the same thing everywhere, that is for it to be uniform.

But this presupposes diversity within the old churches, within the former national churches. Once they were marked by uniformity, a uniformity which was one element of the unity of the state. Now that they have been severed from this external unity, now that they are no longer legally required to maintain uniformity, they can calmly rely on their inner unity and tolerate what the early church also tolerated—after all it had four Gospels, and Paul as well, and the Letter to the Hebrews as well! All of these New Testament writings were different interpretations of *one and the same event,* the death and resurrection of Jesus.[9] Today, too, the one and only saving event must be proclaimed in many different ways.

B. THE GOSPEL CAN ONLY REMAIN THE GOSPEL
IF IT IS NOT TAKEN IN ISOLATION

The whole question is seen more clearly if we now start to discuss the problem of the use of violence. The use of violence can certainly not be derived from the Gospel. And yet people who believe in the Gospel have used violence for centuries and in many different ways.

Violence has often been available to serve the very aims which seemed most beneficial at each period to the church's particular political partner. The crusades in the Middle Ages and the religious wars of the seventeenth century are typical examples of this combination. If today, in our age of internationalization and of church responsibility for oppressed groups in Asia and Africa, the same combination were to be used as in the past, it would obviously imply that the church should now, for example, support the violence of the African liberation movements—and this has also been proposed. But such a step can never be derived directly from the preaching of the Gospel. It is clear that the active use of violence must be motivated in some other way.

And yet at the present time only relatively small attempts are being made to arrive at a clear and conscious understanding of this question. This contrasts with earlier times when there was thorough reflections on these matters. In the process, as far as I can see, the same elements of the Christian faith were identified in each case: God as the Creator of life, the destruction of man as the power hostile to God, the law and reason as positive factors which could constitute a common platform for cooperation between Christians and non-Christians against the forces of destruction and which were thus on the side of God's creative will. These elements of the Christian faith are consciously passed over in silence today. The Gospel—or the message about Christ—stands alone and, it is believed, should stand alone.

But the following practical measures are all retained: political means of coercion, demonstrations, strikes, etc.; declarations, manifestos and other documents, which are obviously pagan—but reasonable!—are used, cited and accepted by Christians. If one then asks how documents of this sort can express what is good if everything good is supposed to come from the Gospel, one regularly receives the same answer: somehow or other the Risen Christ and His Word are behind all of these pagan documents. Another answer, but one which is seldom heard, is this: all men are created with reason and when they are faced with a form of destruction they can say and do something reasonable together about this destruction. That this is not the answer given is a unique characteristic of the twentieth century.

The reason for this is quite clear: it lies in the "German Christians" of the Third Reich and in their abuse of the first article of the Creed.[10]

However, the question which we now have to ask is not really a question of the use of violence and the motivation for it. Our question relates to the *Gospel*. Can the Gospel really remain the Gospel if it is taken in isolation? If everything that God does for us must be derived from the Gospel and *only* from the Gospel, is then this one Word God's Gospel, that is a joyful message of liberation, the message of salvation and redemption?

1. Creation and the Gospel

If one studies the Old Testament with a view to obtaining information about what the non-Israelites knew about God and his will, one finds almost nothing. But if one reads the same writings with the question of what they say about God's activities in the world, then the answers pour out of the text and then the text also speaks of the activities of the non-Israelites: God gives life, God directs the history of the nations, God governs Pharaoh and the king of the Persians, just as he also controls the birds, the stars, the springs of water, and so on. There would be no point here in quoting individual references from the Old Testament: that would create the impression that these things are only said here and there, whereas the Old Testament *as a whole* speaks of this God.

It is particularly important that precisely this faith in God as the Lord of all nations is the starting point for the prophetic criticism of their own *nation* (Amos 5:7-24; 9:5-10; Isaiah 10:5-12; 40:21-31).[11] Thus we find here a faith in God, the Creator of the world, a faith which is critical of the nationalism of the people chosen by God himself. If the faith in creation is exploited in the twentieth century in a way which furnishes arguments in favor of nationalism, then this is an unbiblical use of the first article of the Creed as a doctrine of *creation*. Such a doctrine of creation is no real doctrine of the Creator or of creation.

Why is *this* criticism not levelled against the "German Christians?" Why are they allowed to persist in their misguided idea that their

doctrine of the Creator as a doctrine of creation results in the position of the "German Christians?" These are questions to which one
can find no answer.

But if one asks a different question, "Why is it so important to
talk about creation?," then there are plenty of answers.

First, creation means that God acts directly *in the world,* and that
means for all men. The thing that the Old Testament prophets were
always proclaiming—that God is the Lord of the nations and that
He governs and directs everything—is clearly expressed in the doctrine of creation. The first article of the Creed means that Christians
in their worship of God can understand others, non-believers, and
that the goodness and reason of all men are *God's* goodness and
God's rule.

Second, creation which is in fact not a past but a present work of
God, means that God can work where men are strong and vital—not
only in weakness. This was a point of criticism in Dietrich Bonhoeffer's letter from prison: in the past, he believed, the church had not
adopted a "noble" attitude; instead it had looked for the points of
human weakness in order to express the power of God.[12] Bonhoeffer's
criticism is justified. But it is only possible to correct the church by
re-establishing the previously neglected doctrine of creation. Then
one can speak about God even when people are healthy, mature and
strong.

Third, the doctrine that man is made whole in Christ *presupposes*
that man is created by God and that forgiveness, redemption and
liberation are here not being given to a stranger. All the terms which
are used in the New Testament to describe the type and nature of
the gift given by Jesus presuppose that man, who was created by
God, is now to be saved from some kind of destruction: he receives
life which saves him from death, forgiveness which saves him from
guilt, freedom which saves him from slavery, etc. None of these
terms can be reduced to meaning that a being without knowledge,
an empty being, is now receiving the revelation. But it is this last
idea that is modern, indeed it is the only really modern idea; it is a
"positivism of revelation."

Here the most important point is the third. We are in fact dealing with the Gospel and its purity. The joyful, the "eu," is lost if
the Gospel is taken in isolation. The transmission of knowledge to
an ignorant person—this form of the Gospel—places the listener in a
situation in which he can only accept the word about God as a state-

ment but cannot receive it as joyful news about his own salvation. Just for the reasons mentioned here creation and the Gospel, the first and second articles of the Creed, belong together—and in this order.

2. The Law and the Gospel

And yet we have still not mentioned *the law* in this connection. The fact that the preaching of the Gospel to the nations (and not only to Israel) is a proclamation of the forgiveness of sins is made clear at many points in the New Testament (Luke 24:47; Acts 10: 43; 13:38). Paul presents the same point of view in all his main letters and in so doing expressly assumes that the Gentiles and the Jews are equal, that both lack the righteousness of good works although God demands it of them, that the whole world is *guilty* before God (Roman 3:19f), indeed, that the law of God is also at work among the Gentiles (Roman 2:14f).

This fact of God's universal demands is clearly based on God's *creative acts*[13] both in the missionary preaching to the Gentiles in the Acts of the Apostles (Acts 14:15-17 and 17:26-31) and in Paul's writings (Roman 1:18-32). As the Creator of the world God requires obedience from every individual.

We in the twentieth century have all learned the opposite order, "The Gospel and the law," and have been more or less influenced by it. The Gospel, it is said, is "the first word"; this first word issues in activities which the church carries out or promotes in the world. For the churches established by the Reformation the new order means a rejection of their normal ethical approach (which saw secular faithfulness in relationships with one's neighbors on working days as *the real* act of a Christian). For the Catholic church, too, (because it is also strongly marked by the new Protestant approach) the modern order means a rejection to a certain extent, namely a rejection of the traditional doctrine of "natural law."

Both of these doctrines—the Reformation doctrine of one's vocation and the Catholic doctrine of natural law—have been exploited for conservative political interests and ends; this cannot be denied. But the image of Jesus, the Good Shepherd, the children's friend, etc., has also been exploited in the same way. No one concluded from this that because of abuses of this kind the second article of the Creed or Christology should be abandoned or set aside. Instead they proceeded quite rightly to find *another* interpretation of the image of Christ. But as soon as one merely touches on the doctrine of creation, as soon as one merely mentions the corollaries to *this* point, one regularly meets the same reaction: *here* the interpretations do justice to the basis (that is to the first article of the Creed). This is what happens in politics when reference is made to creation!

Both the World Council of Churches' conference on Church and Society in Geneva in 1966 and the Second Vatican Council with its decrees on social questions can be cited as examples of the trend mentioned here. A kerygmatic theology, based on the Gospel, from which conclusions should be drawn about the activities of Christians in society has become a general theological phenomenon and holds sway both in the World Council of Churches and in Vatican II. We shall come back to these phenomena later on. The only question we are asking here is that of the purity of the *Gospel* in this "structure of activity." The Gospel stands alone; it must bear everything and motivate everything. Apart from the Gospel God does nothing—or rather: no thought is given to this; one acts as if God had stretched only *one* hand down to the world, just one—the message of Jesus Christ.[14]

As a consequence two realities are distorted. The world is not God's world, not by its very nature; it "becomes" God's world by means of preaching. The individual is not spoken to by God as an individual; rather, the word addressed to him is in fact a divine instrument sent out to change the *world*. When the Gospel speaks to the individual, the individual is not its goal.

In the New Testament and for the Reformation the Gospel means that unmerited justification is given and given without any conditions. As soon as any sort of condition is introduced into the offer of the Gospel, the preacher really abolishes the Gospel and sets the law up on the throne.

It is true that the man who listens and unconditionally receives the Gospel is incorporated into Christ by the "yes" of faith and is thus incorporated into love for the world and for all his fellow human beings—and this does not imply a limitation of sheer grace. But if the Gospel which the individual hears and which is intended *for him* is the only bridge between God and the world, if what God does for the world can only pass over this bridge, then the Gospel ceases to be a joyful message for the individual. This view of the political goal is a limitation of the *grace* which was here intended as a gift to the individual. This is especially clear if the individual is weak, sick, and dying.

C. UNDERSTANDING THE GOSPEL

What has been said so far could perhaps be understood as meaning that the Gospel has no social or political consequences. But this would be a misunderstanding. The preaching of the Gospel does indeed shatter social barriers. But the social effect is not the whole of the Gospel.

It is easier to understand what is meant if one divides the analysis into parts, first concentrating historically and exegetically on *understanding* the Gospel in order then to be able to analyze in greater detail *the proclamation of the Gospel today* and the tasks which this represents.

1. The Gospel shatters social barriers

In the New Testament the "Gospel" can be found in two different social settings.

Jesus uses the word "Gospel" for the message which he proclaims in a Jewish context and which, along with the healing of the sick, initiates the coming of the Kingdom of Heaven (Mark 1:15; Matthew 12:28). Everywhere in the synoptic reports as well as in the Gospel of John one can see how this coming shattered social barriers. Tax collectors, prostitutes and sinners, rejected by the society of that time, were chosen by Jesus. Indeed, as he preached this joyful message, he stated clearly and unambiguously that all of these outcasts would reach the Kingdom of Heaven *before* the children of Israel.[15]

Paul uses the same word "Gospel" to describe a joyful message with another structure. This also entails the coming of salvation through Jesus Christ but it concentrates first and foremost on God's saving act in the death and resurrection of Jesus. The social barriers which were broken down by the preaching of the Gospel in this case were different barriers; they were social barriers like those in Galilee and Judea, and they were also barriers set up by the law—but they were different. Now the dividing wall between Jews and Greeks, between "circumcision" and "foreskin" was broken down (Roman 1:16f; Galatian 2:14; Ephesian 2:17). The wall which Jesus wanted to shatter with his Gospel did not exist in Asia Minor, Greece, and Rome. But there was another wall against which Jesus had not fought.

Both of these walls were social and external in nature; one could see these walls with one's eyes. They also divided people from one another before God—or rather: they claimed that they were able to divide people from one another before God. The Gospel maintained

that this division was an illusion and that all people, whether bur-
dened with guilt or pardoned, were equal before God. Wherever the
Gospel was heard and accepted the social barriers were also visibly
torn down: people came together in faith and built up *one* fellowship.[16]

In this context one detail is of special importance for us. Among
the sayings of Jesus no authority is given to the Apostles to break
down the dividing wall between circumcision and foreskin. They
were commissioned to preach the Gospel and that is all. To recognize, discover, and unmask the obstacles to the Gospel, whatever
might destroy the purity of the Gospel, was their own concern.

If Paul had been able to quote Jesus on the question of circumcision, he would certainly have done so during the conflict with
Peter in Antioch. But he was not able to do so, neither could Peter
(he only had "the tradition" because there were no Greeks present at
the meals taken with the earthly Jesus). The criterion is therefore
simply this: "the truth of the Gospel" (Galatian 2:14). But that is
enough; with that one can break down fences and even walls.

This is also revealing for the understanding of the Gospel at the
time of the Reformation. The New Testament contained no word
about monastic vows, no word about letters of indulgence. Luther
had first slowly to discover *himself* that these institutions were obstacles for the free grace of the Gospel, as Paul also had first to discover
for himself that the dividing line between circumcision and foreskin
was something which the Gospel could not tolerate. The Reformation came about slowly because it proved to be difficult to recognize
everything at once and—above all—to unmask it.

Conclusion: *the Bible does not say who in a particular situation is
the enemy of the Gospel.* This conclusion is of decisive significance
for the preaching of the Gospel today.

2. The Gospel is more than the shattering of social barriers

The shattering which we have been discussing here takes place on
two fundamentally different levels. The battle in which the preaching of the Gospel is engaged is basically a battle for man's freedom
before God. If many people accept this freedom, then established
barriers which were clearly visible in earlier social orders in the
world can be torn down and disappear. This applies to many dividing lines, e.g., to those between pharisees and tax collectors, Jews and
Greeks, slaves and free men, monks and married people. Here and

there secular legislation has later even prohibited the maintaining of such dividing lines. But freedom *of conscience before God*, which is brought about by the Gospel, cannot be created by any such secular legislation.

Now, from another vantage point, we have come back again to the two realities: God's world and the individual. By means of its laws the state can cause external barriers to be broken down visibly. This breaking down can very well be a good deed of the secular authorities, a gift from God, just as bread, sunshine and rain (whether or not the Gospel is preached) are also good gifts from God. But freedom of conscience before God is something which only the individual—and no state—can have. And the individual can receive this freedom only from the Gospel, only free, only gratis, through faith alone.

Thus the Gospel is more than the shattering of social barriers. The positive line running from the preaching of the Gospel to its visible social effect is quite clear.[17] The weakness of traditional Lutheranism is that it has often obscured this positive link. But, as the Creator, God can give visible gifts which he does not give by means of the preaching of the Gospel, but in other ways. It is a weakness of modern ecumenical theology that it often obscures this freedom of God, the Creator.

The "more" to which we are referring here can be given only to the individual and to him alone. Freedom of conscience, liberation from guilt before God, independence of the law, are gifts which cannot by nature ever be given to a society or a state but only to a person.

And this "more" also opens up an eschatological future; freedom, innocence, and independence of the law are realities which cannot be totally realized in an earthly society but which—as absolutes—are meaningful if they are given before death in the form of affirmation and promise. They embrace the victory over death. The man who hears and believes knows in faith that no power can harm him.

It is quite logical that the man who is dying or weak, who cannot perform any deeds and is therefore of no use in changing the world, is the one to whom the Gospel is really addressed. This situation is reversed by political preaching today; the preacher addresses the powerful, the rich and the strong in order to convert them to an attitude of "identification," as it is called: they are to "identify themselves with the lowest." The paradoxical thing about Jesus' preaching is that he speaks directly to the lowest and the least and gathers precisely *those*, the weeping, hungry, and poor. This is the true church which hears the promise and thus already owns the future.

The other kind, the prophetic preaching addressed by Amos and Isaiah to the powerful in order to change society and the state, is not, strictly speaking, the preaching of the Gospel—it promises no bliss—but judgment, and it regularly and consciously uses *threats*. This is right for political preaching: it starts with creation; it speaks to man at his *strong* points and it uses the means of the law and of judgment. If one wishes to use the term "identification" in politics at all, one does have to start with parenesis and exhortation but also with a recognition of the fact that the rich man will finally have to be compelled by the use of force and legal power to identify himself with the poor man.

And at this point compulsion is a good thing. The aim of the exhortation is to change society. One is not defiling the exhortation if one turns one's eyes from the addressee, the strong man, and sets the distant goal, the transformation of society, in the center.[18]

But it is a defilement of the Gospel if one sees other goals beyond the addressee, if he becomes a "means to a social end." The poor man is the final goal of the word that is preached, just as the criminal at Jesus' crucifixion was the final goal of the promise. There are places where the Gospel has to be preached quite individually and in this sense "asocially." If the social effect is introduced at this point the Gospel is abolished.

D. THE PROCLAMATION OF THE GOSPEL TODAY

1. *The social effect is a part of the effective preaching of the Gospel*

The sinner is the final goal. He should not be used in order to change society. But, in a society in which one is not allowed to declare that the sinner is just, the mere preaching of the Gospel itself constitutes a major social change.

It is clear that the church today, if it wants to support the poor at all, must direct a polemic goad against its own nation. This was not the case four hundred years ago; then its own country was often poor. It was also not the case in the nineteenth century; the country was richer then but this relatively greater wealth had to be paid for by the poverty of many of the nation's workers. Now, however, the wealth is distributed and the voters of our relatively rich countries believe that it should be distributed further—but distributed among *us!* The churches are gradually setting themselves apart from these nations, not only in legislation, education and the like but also in their judgment of what is "just."

This process will certainly go further. It is a product of the Gospel, a genuine outcome of the classical shattering of social barriers. But what has all of this to do with the heart of the Gospel, with the declaration of the sinner's justification? Surely a former National Socialist, whom no one declares justified and who is very well aware that he has done wrong, is a better parallel to the despised tax collector whom Jesus loved? Yes, this is true; the church is not as strong as Jesus; it has first to wait for public opinion: and when that opinion has developed, only then can it speak up.

This was also the case in the fourth and the sixteenth centuries. The role of the emperor and the roles of the kings of the national states have been taken over today by international political organizations whose declarations, manifestos and statements perform the same function now as did the laws and wishes of the head of state in the past. This should be a warning sign to those who all too readily support the use of violence by liberation movements in distant parts of the world: their violence is fundamentally no different from the old kind, which was certainly necessary in the context of the state but which can in no way be justified by arguments from the preaching of Jesus—not even today.

The critical question which we have to ask in the contemporary situation is related to the new, almost total *secularization of the church*. It is no exaggeration to describe this secularization as almost total. The possibilities which the Christian faith provides in order to interpret an event in the *world* are primarily related to the first article of the Creed. So if this possibility is consciously set aside another article of the Creed must fill the gap. And, strangely enough, in our century the second article of the Creed, christology, has acquired this role which for it is quite new.

But this second article is identical, word for word, with the condensed *Gospel,* beginning with the annunciation and birth and ending with the ascension.[19] And the Gospel is the church's specific message, which brings the church into being and is preached by the church. This Gospel now bears the responsibility of supplying an interpretation of what happens in the world. That means of necessity that the church is secularized. The less the church relies on God's ability to act in the world, the more worldly such a church must become: it must then itself fill the empty space which it has created by taking God out of the world.

Why have we come to this hopeless point? It is important to see that the term "creation" was used to describe finished results. When Luther in his Small Catechism was trying to explain the meaning of "Creator of heaven and earth," his long explanation (it is ten times as long as the first article) did not once contain the word "earth" nor once contain the word "heaven." My birth, my food, drink, sleep, breathing, the fact that my life is "preserved" (= legal protection) and the fact of "lodging" and "clothing" (= our life together in families and social groups) —these are the real content of the dogma about God as the "Creator of heaven and earth."

If Lutheranism had stuck to this emphasis (which is clearly biblical), two mistakes would never have been made. First, there would have been no confrontation with Darwinism because the first article of the Creed has nothing to say about geology or zoology. Second, there would have been no confusion with a romantic nationalism, because the basic "elements of life" to which Luther refers can be found everywhere in the life of mankind, in all races and nations.

But, what is more important, for Luther God is the Creator *now;* the creation is something that is happening and not something that is already over—it happens in the same way as in the Bible where God is constantly giving life (Psalm 104).[20] That is probably the greatest change in the Christian's emotional attitude to the term "creation": the Christian today finds himself confronted with something which has been created and remains just as it was created, an "order," a status quo. This is why any change, life, or feeling for others can only come into the rigid structure from *Christ* and from the *Gospel.* In the biblical and Reformation faith in God, the Creator, there is no rigid status quo. If this status quo were to exist, God would be dead. But he is alive, and *he does not rest;* he is alive throughout the world. Maintaining the status quo can be seen as resistance to him, that is, as an attempt to keep what is one's own without love.

The birds do not do this, neither do the apple trees; only man does this.[21] The world is God's world, just as it is. Therefore Jesus can also see an example of his sacrificial death in a grain of wheat. Man's special position is first a result of his being the only one appointed to be the master of the rest of creation and therefore having a higher destiny than all the rest, and second of his being the only one to have departed from his destiny and therefore being more impure than all the rest (because of *man's* sin the earth is "cursed"). For this reason the Gospel, the message of *salvation*, is also not preached to the animals or the plants but only to man. However, God's acts in creation give all living beings earthly, bodily life in the same way. This is one of the main points of the Sermon on the Mount (Matthew 6:25-34).

What Jesus wants to bring about by means of this sermon is a *lack of anxiety*. God takes care of the world, so man does not need to do so. These are words from the Bible from which the church today shies away—but in the Bible they are still central and very meaningful, including politically meaningful, words. Indeed they are really the only words which can provide the basis for the actual political activity of the church—and that also means the leftwing, radical, political activity of the church. God himself takes care of the world; he sends socialism, workers' movements, strikes and the like, and he does so *without using the church*.

Precisely this fact which we always come up against whenever we examine the social and political activity of the Catholic or of the Protestant church, namely the Christian support for actions and programmes which have been developed *outside* of the church and beyond the reach of the preaching of the Gospel, this fact is made comprehensible by the belief in creation. Creation as such is mobile and flexible; it does not become rigid order or a status quo; it does not have to "fetch" its flexibility from a single source, from the Gospel. God is a living God in all of his works.

The curious conclusion that Christians who believe without any anxiety in God, the Creator, will become indifferent and leave their social responsibilities to others, is totally unfounded. If it is *God* who gives the sunshine without the Gospel being preached, this surely does not mean that the consequence should be indifference to the sunshine and the light of day—the Christians are the ones who can rejoice about it! The same applies to children, health, and so on —they are all God's gifts! The person who believes in the Gospel goes out into the world and breaks down social barriers there as well; he does this together with other people. In politics today this fellowship with *others* is the really decisive point.

Here Lutheran theology probably has a job to do. Both in the World Council of Churches and in Vatican II a christocratic tendency appears from time to time.

The choice of subjects for the Second Vatican Council could have brought about a revival of the doctrine of "natural law" on the Catholic side, because this doctrine is the social and political expression which the doctrine of creation assumed in scholasticism under the influence of Aristotle.[22] Today the doctrine of natural law could lay aside its Aristotelian dress. Its new content could be more firmly based on and influenced by the Old Testament. But this has not happened; Vatican II avoided the terminology of natural law.[23] Why? Probably because the doctrine of natural law had become tied to a politically conservative attitude.

The same thing happened again in 1966 in Geneva, one year after the end of the Council. The Conference on Church and Society uses the expression "status quo" almost exclusively to describe bad conditions as a whole and can hardly imagine that the overthrow of the status quo could spring from any source other than the Gospel. Thus the church is set in the center and given a role which is not its own to play.[24]

It is right that the preaching of the Gospel should shatter social barriers. But when it does so it is addressed to the indivdual who, his faith having been strengthened, is sent out into God's world, into a world in which God creates new things by using reasonable people in all groups and thus also visibly breaks down barriers.

2. *The social effect is not the whole of the Gospel*

In the chapter about understanding the Gospel we saw that what is proper to the joyful message, the declaration of the sinner's justification, is defiled if the social effect is seen as the *goal* of proclamation. Then the effect of the Gospel is that of a law. It impels the listener to perform works, and this impulsion is seen as the essential function of preaching.

Therefore the social effect is not the whole of the Gospel; the Gospel is "more," indeed this "more" is even the essential function of the Gospel. But this means that the individual, namely the individual who is listening at this very moment, who is hearing the word with his own ears, *he*—alone and in isolation—is the real goal. We find a public activity with so "small" a goal objectionable. But we find the same objection to Jesus' activities as doctor and redeemer. That the Lord of the world who is to judge everyone should stand still before *one* man and heal him or talk for hours by the well with *one* woman is without parallel in the messianic expectations of Israel.[25] Measured by its social effect such activity is madness.

It is equally foolish that God should have become man when he wanted to save mankind. If God speaks through the man, Jesus, he speaks in only one language (he has to be "translated" into the other languages of mankind), and at each time he can only be in one place (he has to reach the other places of the world by "sending," that is by mission). But this is the impractical way in which God acts when he is seeking the individual. The whole Gospel is just a story about an individual, Jesus Christ, and about what happened to him, a story which itself is intended for individuals. To this end preaching exists.

Now, if this is the essence of the message, what then is the essence of the situation today? There are certain characteristics which can already be identified now, although it is true that it is seldom possible clearly to recognize the situation in which one lives and exists. The generation which is growing up now will know less about texts from the Bible than the older generation. The Gospel is again being heard as if it were new. The older generations had usually received the Christian faith as part of the heritage of their childhood; they had perhaps also rebelled against it and, at their "conversion," they were able nostalgically to remember the old phrases. These are factors which determined the traditional, emotive, evocative style of preaching.

To preach in this way in the future will be senseless. And today this kind of homiletic tone already constitutes a weakening of the proclamation. It is our task now to offer something new to the people who listen, that is to introduce Jesus Christ to the listeners, to speak more or less as Paul spoke on the Areopagus.

This does *not* mean that we have to talk like the gnostics about an unknown god. God may be unknown in the sense that his saving plan (= His work in Jesus Christ) is only now being preached. But God has already been at work in the experiences of the listeners; this is the decisive point of the Areopagus speech (Acts 17:23-31). One cannot live as a man at all without living in God and without sensing the Creator and his will. But he is known as redemption, as forgiveness for the individual, only in the Gospel of Jesus Christ.

This same factor, a relative estrangement from the Gospel, will also bring about greater variety, openness and tolerance *in* the churches. When the whole of Europe acknowledged Christ in one form or another, the differences between the forms could have a divisive effect. Reformed, Lutheran and Anglican were names for different confessions which penetrated the legislation of the different nations—nations which were often at war with one another. This sort of variety has to be divisive; it cannot exercise a unifying function. But if a large number of people in Europe does not confess Christ at all, then the decisive difference suddenly becomes another one: it runs between the "yes" and the "no" to Christ.

Within the large group of people who all say "yes" there are naturally also differences. But they also existed between the four evangelists, big differences in fact. The Johannine writings in the New Testament do not once mention the word "justification" although they describe salvation in Jesus Christ in detail. They use other terms: life, light, truth, and the like. Whereas the Letter to the Hebrews, which also sees redemption in the same decisive events as Paul or John, namely in Jesus' death and resurrection, uses quite new expressions for *its own* description of the same redemption which are not used by anyone else in the New Testament: a rigidly structured doctrine of Jesus Christ as the High Priest who sacrifices himself. All of these New Testament writers said "yes" and did so in different ways.

The same thing is happening today. And the recurrence is connected with the fact that the outward setting of the church is gradually becoming the same as it was then. In a setting where people say "no" there is a group of *confessors,* of those who say "yes." The little story of the German Catholic and the Swedish Lutheran in the dining car between Malmö and Stockholm is typical of the situation today. They grasped that they were one and suddenly the foreigner on the other side of the table said, "Jesus Christ be praised."[26] Behind this encounter in the dining car there is a new experience of fellowship which did not exist fifty years ago. The other travellers do *not* say "Jesus Christ be praised"—that is the point. Those who do say it may be different, but they are profoundly one.

This experience of fellowship signifies unity, just as in the early church. The various towns—Antioch, Ephesus, Rome, etc.—had their own particular ways of thinking and terminologies without these dividing them from one another. The external minority situation gave them their unity. The specific features of each place did not penetrate into any legislation and could therefore not be felt anywhere to be a compulsion on people in other places. Today we shall soon be in a similar cultural situation. Then the various ways of thinking and terminologies which people normally use to express their human experiences will suddenly become *positive* factors which have to be accepted *for the sake of unity.* The Gospel must quickly take the form of these differences in order to be able to give them a uniform content.

This content implies an eschatological future for each individual. The content cannot be immediately expressed in social terminology; it cannot be identified by observing effects of a social kind. The Gospel does certainly shatter social barriers but its real effect is different —otherwise the word would not be *Gospel,* that is justification without works, the washing away of the sin of the listener.

Today in particular this aspect of the word which is preached needs to be emphasised. For today, as we have seen, the church is understood as the means and instrument of divine change to re-create the world. The introduction of the church at this point is a bit of justification by *works.*

To exhort the world and demand that it change itself, then to maintain that this can be brought about by the church, and finally to state in one's confession that one is oneself the church—this is a dangerous series of statements in which self-righteousness, disguised as responsibility, feels at home. As we have already observed, we cannot expect to find the enemy of the Gospel named in the text of the Bible. The preacher has to identify the enemy with his own eyes and then to unmask him. The "ecclesio-centric" doctrine about changing society is *the* enemy of the Gospel today. For by means of this doctrine Christians declare themselves justified—and justified precisely by their external impact, i.e., by works.[27]

It is amazing that the New Testament was able to place direct emphasis on the ability of the Gentiles to perform good deeds and that the Reformers (at a time of general church adherence and when there were hardly any pagans in Europe!) tried still more strongly to underline this ability, whereas we in the twentieth century have been able to evolve a doctrine of the Gospel as the only source of good external works which is more exclusive than ever before in the history of the church. And this at a time when we are shamed by insights in the practical field of politics, at a time of well-founded church obedience, of belated following in the steps of the Marxist atheists!

It is in fact true that the individual can understand the Gospel for precisely this reason; he understands it as a result of the general pressure, as a consequence of a general—and justified—accusation: after all he is a man and he has ignored the suffering of his fellowmen and brushed it aside. The Gospel is preached in God's world, in a world which is God's creation and which is governed by God. Demands do not only come from the Gospel; they are there before the Gospel and we are aware of them. But when the Gospel is preached to this world of God's, the person to whom it is addressed is the individual and his conscience.[28]

Thus the Gospel has a goal which is invisible. But as soon as the conscience of the individual stands before God, the eschatological dimension is also there. I stand before God with my own life, and my works do not help me. From a "social" point of view as well, every person has received more than he has given: from the very beginning life itself is given—it is "granted" to us to live. We have never given as much to the people whom we have met as we ourselves have received as purely external gifts. This is our sin as we face every coffin. "Our sin is that we are still living."

Into this conscience there comes the image of the man who was completely sinless but was executed as a criminal; indeed, this conscience becomes aware of his voice which does speak about barriers but this time not about the social kind of barriers which the man who listens has to break down by his own effort in the world. Here it is primarily a question of a barrier which I have erected myself and which I cannot break down.

Since my whole life—what I have received and what I have given—is under judgment before God, my relationships with my fellow men are included in my sin. The individual's social relationships can never remain untouched when the Gospel enters his conscience.

3. The Individual

Sociologists of religion have discovered that the number of people who pray is much greater than the number of people who attended services. The content of the individual's prayer is often related to his everyday life. Members of the family pray for one another when they are a long way apart and cannot help one another. These people who pray sometimes have very unclear concepts of God, from a dogmatic point of view, indeed, they even reject the traditional expressions of belief in God—and yet they pray! When human existence is in danger, an appeal is made to the same mystery as is the source of the life that was "granted."

This appeal is a combination of many aspects of life: sin, the will to live for and love a fellow human being. But there is one thing which is always present: there is a conception of human existence and therefore also a conception of the threat to life contained in the present situation. Then, if a preacher of the Gospel really reaches the listeners of his time, if there is a link between the content of his words and the needs of their hearts, this is always connected with the fact that the preacher himself can sense the "threat" (= that human existence is in danger) in such a way that the appeal from his heart and the appeal from the hearts of his listeners is basically the same appeal. Basically, because there are always differences even in the same family or in the same social group at any one place.

But there are certain types of "threat" that are feared by almost every person at a particular time. And these types change, as Paul Tillich has demonstrated.[29] There was a great fear of the last judgment in 1650 and very little in 1950. The situation is the reverse for the fear of death, of the act of dying: this has increased (probably because death is understood as the "absolute end"). God's world in the form of man's world has a history. *Therefore the Gospel also has a history.* No Reformation would have taken place at all if the fear in Martin Luther had not found an echo or struck a chord in the hearts of the people of Europe in the sixteenth century. The same applies to other periods of church history.

The Gospel, and this cannot be repeated often enough, is as such a story, the story of an *individual* and of his life, beginning with his birth and continuing through temptation, fear and death, and pointing with healing and forgiveness to the future. It would appear that this limited life has something to *give* in every age—whatever form the "threat" may take as one generation follows another—it can speak to the hearts of every age. The church may become boring but the story (= the Gospel) does not.

In the history of the Gospel proclamation as a human factor, a factor determined and therefore limited by its time, has the task of making real the story of an individual, the individual who is alive for ever to the hearts of the individuals alive at any particular time. It is impossible to bring something home in this way without an interpretation of man's existence. But the best interpretation is often done unconsciously: the preacher simply interprets himself and his own life—and thereby the life of his listeners.

The history of the Gospel is a part of the history of man's existence. And in both of these "histories" the individual is determinative. What is relevant to man is expressed in his appeal to God, and

GOD'S WORLD AND THE INDIVIDUAL

in this appeal, in this prayer, there lies the destiny given to him by God in creation which became flesh, not in his own human existence but in the existence of another, in Jesus Christ, about whom the Gospel speaks simply and especially through preaching. Thus Christ is included in creation, as the classical doctrine of the trinity has always pointed out. Christology is profoundly interlinked with anthropology.

The bridge between creation and incarnation, between anthropology and Christology, is not to be seen in the incarnation's being a gift of knowledge from above given with a positivism of revelation, by means of which the previously indecipherable chiffre of man's existence becomes comprehensible. Rather, creation is in itself already decipherable and comprehensible; as such it already possesses destiny, ethical demands, and awareness—but it *cannot be accomplished;* it is always subject in various ways to a "threat" and has to make an appeal.

This is why the human existence of each person is open for *incarnation,* that is: for what is told in the Gospel and then (building on the story) given by preaching (and by baptism and communion).[30]

Man can receive this gift of incarnation only as an individual. "Political" preaching quickly disregards the individual even in its external mode of address and concentrates its attention on society. Political preaching in this sense is an abolition of the Gospel in its very approach: it does not give righteousness; it demands it.

On the other hand, the individual is not an *individual* without the whole of his life. If he tries to come before God without the world, for which he is responsible before God, without his works (= what he has done *and* what he has neglected) and without remembering anything (= without his conscience), before God he is not an individual. The conscience is concerned with works and judges them before God. The conscience also does this in the hearts of those people who never use the name of God and who do not know the name of Jesus Christ. Indeed, conscience does this in all people and in all cultures, and does it because man is created.[31]

Of course, conscience is not concerned about the same works in all cultures, nor about the same works in different periods of church history! After all, man is not an object; he has a history. But in the course of his history with all its changes there are certain constants of human life which are always present: birth, fear, sin, love, hope, trust, destruction, death. And therefore he can never find himself in a situation in which the Gospel, as the story of an individual and his struggle with these same constants, could be meaningless.

But it is a difficult task to uncover the meaning fully and to open up the Gospel so that it speaks clearly. *This is what preaching is for.*

This will already have made clear that preaching has to be repeated and that the repetition cannot be a matter of reciting texts of sermons from an earlier period. The Gospel has to have new interpreters, living voices for the grace which searches out and justifies, in each generation.

But one thing is not yet clear: namely what should be done today in order to avoid the unhappy division between social preaching, on the one hand, and "orthodox," so-called central preaching, on the other.

The individual stands before God *with* all of his social relationships and not without them. The parable of the last judgment does not separate the individual from his works when it sets him before God; rather, his fellow men are there, too, as they always are in the judgment of the conscience. Sin as a religious concept is a social concept although the individual comes before God in a strictly personal self-examination and can only examine his own life.

But here judgment and grace are the same. The person who hears the Gospel, who receives forgiveness and who is accepted by God—just as he is—can freely re-engage in relationships with his fellow men. He does not make God's world flexible and mobile because it already *is.* It is in fact God's creation which could not exist at all unless God created it and gave it shape every day anew. The believer does not give the world its flexibility but he enters the world with courage and confidence. And this implies a new creation by God.

For not everything that causes movement is good. The idea that the status quo is always bad and that change always means a change for the better is unrealistic. Many of the things that move are a threat to human existence and there are situations in which almost any change entails a destruction of humaneness: there even a little bit of status quo would be a gift from God! The believer enters this world of new creation and threat with courage and confidence. That means that he shapes his own situation in love and freedom.

This also affects his fellow men. Sin is something which is expressed socially—in the suffering and torment of the sinner's fellow men. Righteousness (= forgiveness and grace) is something which is experienced as a relaxation and liberation in the life of one's fellow men as well. Individual ethics, in the sense that the individual is concerned with himself and his virtues, do not exist in Christianity. All Christian ethics are social ethics, and this is also what Luther said.[32]

And yet these social ethics concentrate primarily on *the* social relationships which each individual experiences with his fellow men. Thus each individual will be involved in a different field of social ethics. The "changes" which take place in all of these fields are the most important ones before God and they remain hidden until the last judgment. There is normally no word about them in the newspapers.

In addition there are common socio-ethical tasks which are carried out publicly and for which people have to be brought together by appeals and manifestoes. No one should believe that it is possible to bring together only Christians for public, common tasks of this kind. When human rights are violated and whole groups suffer many people recognize that injustice is taking place. Here Christians and non-Christians often work together. The outward success of such activities is first and foremost a success for the oppressed and deprived, not for the activists.

This at least should be the goal of the activists. The less that is said about the church in such cases, the better.

—*Translated by* MARGARET A. PATER

NOTES

All biblical quotations have been taken from the New English Bible.

1. For further discussion of this see L.-O. Armgard, *Antropologi*, Lund and Copenhagen, 1971, pp. 60-64.
2. Cf. E. Käsemann, *Exegetische Versuche und Besinnungen* I, 4th edition, Göttingen, 1965, pp. 214-223, and Vol. II, 2nd edition, Göttingen, 1965, pp. 262-267. See also W. Bauer, *Rechtgläubigkeit und Ketzerei im ältesten Christentum*, Tübingen, 1934, pp. 238-242.
3. On Acts 15 cf. C. S. C. Williams, *A Commentary on the Acts of the Apostles*, 2nd edition, Edinburgh, 1964, pp. 31-33.
4. See H. Dörries, *Konstantin der Grosse*, Stuttgart, 1958, pp. 31-34.
5. The details are very interesting in E. Peterson, *Frühkirche, Judentum und Gnosis*, Freiburg i.Br., 1959, pp. 58-63.
6. G. Wingren, *Man and the Incarnation. A Study in the Biblical Theology of Irenaeus*, Edinburgh and London, 1959, pp. 167 f. It is significant that uniformity was only introduced in this area in A.D. 325.
7. See e.g., D. Löfgren, *Die Theologie der Schöpfung bei Luther*, Göttingen, 1960, pp. 200-204.

8. In this the Conference on Church and Society in Geneva in 1966 constitutes an important turning point. See the message of the conference in *World Conference on Church and Society, The Official Report*, Geneva, 1967, pp. 47-50.
9. Cf. A. M. Hunter, *The Unity of the New Testament*, 2nd edition, London, 1944, pp. 20-33.
10. This also applies, for example, to Americans. After 1945, Germany influenced almost the whole world in an amazing way. One example of this is the review of my book, *The Flight from Creation*, Minneapolis, 1971, in the journal *Interpretation*, 1972, pp. 368-372, by H. P. Santmire.
11. Cf. Th. C. Vriezen, *Theologie des Alten Testamentes*, Wageningen and Neukirchen, 1957, pp. 300 f.
12. D. Bonhoeffer, *Widerstand und Ergebung*, E. Bethge, ed., 6th edition, Munich, 1955, pp. 232-236.
13. Cf. G. Lindeskog, *Studien zum neutestamentlichen Schöpfungsgedanken*, Uppsala and Wiesbaden, 1952, pp. 180 f.
14. This question was discussed by a research group on "Creation and Redemption" in "Societas Ethica" in 1968. Representatives of Catholic and Protestant theology worked together in the group. The minutes, which have been mimeographed but unfortunately not printed, were carefully written by K. Bockmühl (sixteen pages).
15. See J. Jeremias, *Jesu Verheissung für die Völker*, 2nd edition, Stuttgart, 1959, pp. 37-39.
16. Cf. here also E. F. Scott, *The Epistles of Paul to the Colossians, to Philemon and to the Ephesians*, 9th impr., London, 1958, pp. 167-175 (with its reference to Acts 21:28).
17. This positive line is emphasized particularly by D. von Oppen, *Das personale Zeitalter*, Stuttgart and Gütersloh, 1967, pp. 37-41.
18. H. Ivarsson, *Predikans uppgift*, Lund, 1956, pp. 158-163, gives a detailed account of the use Luther made of this type of sermon.
19. Likewise the language of the first article has certainly been modeled on Genesis 1:1.
20. D. Löfgren, *Die Theologie der Schöpfung bei Luther*, Göttingen, 1960, pp. 37-45.
21. Luther's interpretation of Matthew 5:43-48 is very instructive at this point. Nature is morally better than man. See W.A. 32, pp. 403-404 (Interpretation of the Sermon on the Mount 1532).
22. Cf. here B. Schüller, "Katolsk moralteologi," in *Etik och kristen tro*, G. Wingren, ed., Lund, 1971, pp. 100-111.
23. One proof of this can be found in the list of contents in K. Rahner and H. Vorgrimmler, *Kleines Konzilskompendium*, 2nd edition, Freiburg i.Br., 1967, pp. 733 f.
24. The theological analysis of "social change" is typical in *World Conference on Church and Society 1966, The Official Report*, Geneva, 1967, pp. 198-202.
25. This is one of the main points in E. Billing's presentation of the preaching and acts of Jesus; see e.g., *De etiska tankarna i urkristendomen*, 2nd edition, Stockholm, 1936, pp. 390-393.
26. O. Nivenius, *Tjäna Herren med glädje* (= Serve the Lord with gladness), Lund, 1970, pp. 77 f. (This document is the pastoral letter of the new bishop to the diocese of Lund.)
27. The way in which the passage about the last judgment (Matthew 25:31-46) is understood and exploited today, partly as the central eschatological text

for the church and partly as the church's program for social reform, is symptomatic.

28. This is also Luther's point of view. Cf. H. Olsson, *Schöpfung, Vernunft und Gesetz in Luthers Theologie,* Uppsala, 1971, pp. 505-507 and 562-570.

29. The best example in modern theological literature is P. Tillich, *The Courage to Be,* New Haven, 1954, in which different expressions of human fear are analyzed with great insight.

30. What L.-O. Armgard says about Løgstrup in his doctoral thesis of 1971 about life in creation as life under a "threat" is important here. The consequence is a different relationship between Christology and anthropology from the usual one; see Note 1, pp. 212-229.

31. Cf. C. A. Pierce, *Conscience in the New Testament,* London, 1955, pp. 66-74, 85 f., and 111 f. What Pierce says in this study of the New Testament and what Olsson says in his work on Luther in 1971 (see Note 28) is often identical even in the expressions used although no contact between Olsson and Pierce can be established. Luther's thoughts about the conscience are taken from the Bible and at the same time rooted in personal experience.

32. See H. Olsson, *Grundproblemet i Luthers socialetik,* Lund, 1934, p. 9.

II.

CREATION AND GOSPEL
IN THE SCRIPTURES

Chapter 3

Creatio, Continua et Nova
(Creation, Continuing and New)

"Creation" is a theme to which the Bible makes many references, in both testaments. "The new creation" and related topics occur, though with less frequency, in certain parts of the Old and New Testament scriptures. These twin themes have had their ups and downs over the centuries, arousing fresh interest periodically. Today both emphases are in vogue and attract attention as more than a backdrop or dénouement for the gospel in history. They have integrity in their own right. The history of God with his world includes creation and spans the aeons of time till the new creation. The very transmission of the gospel is intertwined with statements from the Christian community about creation and new creation.

There are good reasons why these twin themes have come into their own again in the 1970's. God as creator, "maker of heaven and earth," is, of course, basic to all theology and life, in Christianity and in most world religions. Credal affirmations about "the Father Almighty, maker of heaven and earth, of all that is seen and unseen," continually hold the theme before all believers, spanning the centuries. The doctrine of divine creation impinges not only upon God and the world but upon anthropology and all of life, time and history, the question of evil, and ultimately (or initially) the gospel of redemption.[1] Theologizing reflects vogues; Christian faith and piety may emphasize now the Son, now the Spirit.[2] If the 1970's have brought a new interest in Jesus (the "Jesus people," various fruits of the "New Quest" in the form of another wave of "lives of Jesus") and revitalized interest in the Spirit (charismatic, Pentecostal movements), this decade has also produced fresh concern about the creation (even if, in some quarters, the Creator God is reputed to be "dead"). From the christocentric, even christomonistic interests of the preceding decades, a shift has come, back to creation, at times however connected especially with Christ. From preoccupation with ecclesiology, emphasis has shifted to the world. The "flight from creation" which could be observed at many points[3] has reversed itself; there is a new engagement with the world of creation.

It can be claimed that such "worldly Christianity" follows inevitably not merely from inner developments within Christian thought but also from the growing interest in our "one world" over recent years and in the universe beyond earth's atmosphere, as well as from the amazing development of the natural sciences in recent years. Some totally new sciences have emerged since World War II; even older, established sciences are said to have doubled their accumulation of data in the last fifteen years! Along with this is the fact that most of Christendom has transcended old battles about evolution; we are ready to move beyond the "Bible-Babel" controversy, and Christians working in both biblical studies and the natural sciences, as well as systematic theologians, generally, have shown the way. Finally, to the list of factors giving impetus to the new interest in creation we may add the ecology movement, born of concern about the world and its dwindling resources (and specifically the charge that Genesis 1:28 in the Judaeo-Christian tradition has led to the plundering of "spaceship earth"),[4] as well as developments in the ecumenical movement, ever since Joseph Sittler's address to the World Council of Churches assembly at New Delhi in 1961, where the "call to unity" sought to outflank old impasses by staking out the whole realm of humanity and nature as the arena of "Christic grace."[5]

"New creation" has come into its own in a variety of ways. The theology and sermons of Paul Tillich ("the new being"); the existential understanding of Bultmann about what the rebirth of the individual believer means ("anyone in Christ is a new creation," 2 Corinthians 5:17); a widespread emphasis on the church as God's new creation or the new humanity bringing the good news of newness to all God's world; and all theologies of hope—these factors served to popularize the new creation theme. If the First Vatican Council can be said to have paid particular attention to the doctrine of creation, Vatican II can be claimed to have employed, effectively and in the spirit of our age, the terms and images of new creation.

Thus, the themes are before us, on every side. That makes it all the more necessary to examine what the scriptural witness is and what it implies about creation/new creation. For, just as the gospel must be recovered in every generation by fresh examination of the evangelical witness in scripture, so what the Bible says about creation and related themes must be re-examined periodically in order to recover what may have been minimized or overlooked previously and to discover how the Bible helps us speak more effectively in the emerging situations which we face. This is so not simply because the world addressed by faith today is constantly changing, but because biblical scholarship is never static; new discoveries and new times bring new insights and even new methodologies. At the least, examination of creation in the scripture will serve to remind us that in the biblical view it is not simply a matter of something at the beginning (*creatio originalis*) but a continuing process (*creatio continua*), thus introducing the whole range of what has traditionally been called God's providence. We may also find light on what "new creation" means more precisely, for even everyday Bible translations pose the problem at 2 Corinthians 5:17: is it, "*he* (the believer) or *it* (the world) is a new *creation*"? or does the Greek mean "new *creature*" (*Schöpfung* or *Geschöpf*)?

But how shall we go about examining and correlating the biblical evidence? Here we confront the methodological crisis which faces biblical studies, hermeneutics, and systematic theology today. A traditional approach has been to elevate into prominence, knowingly or unconsciously, some particular passage which dominates "the biblical view of creation (or 'new creation')." Usually this has been Genesis 1, the logical candidate for the task because it occurs first in the canon and is well known, or John 1:1-18 (the Logos prologue, with its points of connection for Western philosophy), or, more recently, the "Christ hymn" of Colossians 1:15-20. Here the biblical material is often brought into more or less direct relationship with what the systematic theologian does in expounding the meaning of a doctrine for today.[6] A second possibility, identified by some as *the* method of "biblical theology," shows greater awareness of the total biblical witness and seeks to integrate all relevant materials within the framework of "salvation history." A schema is assumed, stretching as the "plan of God" from before creation to the consummation, into which each biblical passage is built as a unified whole. Here theology becomes recapitulation of the biblical data within a pattern of time and history (Cullmann).[7] Against the approach of heilsgeschichte is the charge that it "homogenizes" the Bible and forces everything under salvation and Christ.

A third method seeks meaning, not in terms of a pattern of history or a doctrine developed from certain passages, but by looking for what the key verses have to say to the present, particularly in their understanding of existence for man. Such an anthropological interpretation, speaking to man's self-understanding, often is recast in terms of some current philosophy, e.g., existentialism (Bultmann's program of demythologization). In criticism of all these approaches a widely heeded analysis of contemporary biblical theology[8] urges that the work of the student of the Bible is to be primarily descriptive. He is to concentrate on "what it meant" in its historical context, leaving "what it means" today to others, the systematician, existentialist, or preacher—priest. Here, any unity must come, not from the fact that the same God is assumed as lord of Israel, the Jews, Jesus, and the church, or from a common denominator of anthropology ("Christology is the variable, anthropology the constant"),[9] but from "the ongoing life of a people cultivating the traditions of its history in the light of its self-understanding"[10]—with the proviso that much of Israel's faith and "election-consciousness" is transferred and applied to the new Israel, the church. This "descriptive" approach would avoid the task of choosing for itself what, within the witness of scripture understood in its life-context, is pertinent today. It runs the twin dangers of assuming both the ability of the exegete to work without presuppositions (*Voraussetzungslosigkeit*)[11] and, over the long haul, his willingness to do this without the "pay-off" of relevance.

So far as our immediate topic of creation new creation is concerned, a further problem in the face of all these methodologies is the specific relation of "creation" and "redemption" or, as it has sometimes been posed in the history of theology, "nature" and "grace." Traditional approaches, the method of existential interpretation, and certainly all theologies of heilsgeschichte have alike assumed the centrality of salvation. Redemption is taken as basic to an understanding of the category of creation. But some strands of the Bible, it is claimed, do not approach the matter in quite that way. Sermon passages in Acts like 14:15-17 (about the God "who made the heaven and the earth and the sea and all that is in them," who "did not leave himself without witness," but "gave you rains and fruitful seasons") or 17:22-31 (Paul before the Areopagus, about the God who made everything, that men might "feel after him and find . . . 'him whose offspring we are' ") do not fit in with the usual kerygma of redemption by the death of Jesus. In the Hebrew scriptures the issue is even more acute, for psalms and other passages suggest at times a view of God active in nature (rather than in history), who reveals his prowess in the heavens, the hills and seas, stars and the regularity of the seasons (Psalms 104; 8; 19:1-6). Given the fact that much of the world in biblical times thought in such terms of God in nature, some examples of this emphasis are to be expected in scripture. Was the attitude perhaps more widespread than our records suggest? Have our very methods of analysis wrongly subordinated "creation" to "redemption," or robbed it of its vitality as an independent theme? That question has been posed by investigators seeking a description of biblical religion, and even by some who want to hold to a framework of heilsgeschichte but nevertheless to give creation a larger place.[12] Thus, in contrast to "the God who acts in history," the "God who is," in nature and the world, has been stressed by some.

In the face of this welter of approaches and debates we propose to follow a methodology which is emerging increasingly in biblical studies today and which does justice to key aspects of each approach noted above: the "tradition-history" method (Traditionsgeschichte). In essence it is nothing more or less than tracing out each tradition which has left its imprint in the Bible's witness, in this case on creation, from the time it first appeared in oral form until it was written down (in a source document) or was finally redacted in the form we have it in Old Testament or New. It is assumed that these traditions will be examined against their pertinent backgrounds in the world of the day (Religionsgeschichte) and will be set forth descriptively, as far as possible.

This task will be carried out so as to arrange the Bible's statements on creation in a roughly chronological order. It must be admitted, however, that we shall be engaging ourselves in this task with an eye to seeing what the scriptures say about creation/new creation for today, both in terms of content and of how the biblical witnesses went about developing their statements. Accordingly, we cannot be unaware of the fact that over the twenty centuries since New Testament times this biblical material has been interpreted and reinterpreted in creeds, dogmas, liturgy, theology, and piety. We cannot escape knowing that certain passages have yielded existential or heilsgeschichte emphases, and we must look for the possibilities that the intention of a passage may have been to speak along just such lines. The fullest possible picture of the biblical traditions gives modern man a richness to digest, and a series of "points of contacts" to apply the biblical messages for today. Space allows us to present only some of the results of such an investigation, but they rest on the method just sketched.

Specifically, we shall lay out in Part I the biblical evidence of creation new creation from the point of view of Traditionsgeschichte. Fortunately an immense literature from recent scholarship is available,[13] and so we can try to sketch this material in brief outline. Then, in Part II, we shall seek to list the points, in the form of theses, which have struck us and other investigators about this mass of material. The theses put forth conclusions which are both the fruits of biblical theology and pointers for the theological tasks today. Enough illustrations will be given for each point from the biblical material sketched in Part I to provide an idea of what each thesis is founded on, without undertaking a detailed exegesis of every verse involved. Thus we may be able to see where the Bible speaks anthropologically of God and creation, and where a pattern of salvation history emerges. We seek to describe a process over the centuries which make up the biblical period, a process from which we may gain a clearer idea of which stages are especially relevant today. Amid these many testimonies to creation—initial, continuing and new—in scripture, we can look for repeated emphases and the realities to which they witness, which, when synthesized, help us in speaking on creation/new creation today.

I.
The Biblical Traditions about Creation and New Creation

All of Israel's neighbors, of course, possessed myths, legends, hymns, and narratives about the beginnings of the world.[14] These foreign influences are apparent already in what is probably the oldest reference in the Bible to God as "maker of heaven and earth," i.e., Genesis 14:19, 22. The context, where Abram gives tithes to the king of Salem (Jerusalem), Melchizedek, after the battle of four kings versus five, and the linguistic details there—including reference to "[Yahweh] God 'Most High' " (i.e., El Elyon; some versions even omit specific reference to "Yahweh")—all point to features from Ugaritic literature and a Canaanite emphasis on creation. The guess has been hazarded that this creation motif was applied to Yahweh—

Israel's God of the exodus, the pilgrimage through the wilderness, and the conquest—by the foreign priesthood of the Jebusites, which David had installed in the place of the house of Eli when he took over Jerusalem as his capital city (I Samuel 2:27-36; 2 Samuel 8:17; I Kings 1-2, Abiathar of the old priesthood supported Adonijah; Zadok, a Jebusite, supported Solomon and supplanted Abiathar).[15]

This reference to Yahweh as creator[16] provides occasion to introduce the question of how big a role creation played in Israelite thought, and how early, and the debate which has swirled around these points. To be sure, Egypt, out of which the Israelites came in the exodus; the desert peoples, no doubt, among whom some of the Israelite tribes had dwelt; and the nations to the east, such as Sumer, Akkad, and Babylonia—all these, like the Canaanites, had creation stories and cults that worshiped nature gods. Indeed, there was a common ancient Near Eastern theology (with local variants) concerning creation. Israel, however, seems to have centered her traditions and credo around (1) the exodus, (2) the Sinai experiences and the giving of the Law, and (3) the patriarchs. To what extent were creation-theology and creation-cult a part of her life, the way they were among neighboring peoples?[17]

We know that these creation-theologies of the ancient Near East shared a common worldview involving a sacred "mountain of God," a center for the universe or "navel of the earth," an underground river watering the city of God, a notion that the temple symbolized in microcosm the cosmic features of the universe, and a role for the king as representative of the deity. We know, too, that some of the Old Testament psalms and other passages reflect the same sort of imagery (e.g., Psalm 46) and that there are scattered references in the Bible which may reflect the Near Eastern myth of a battle at creation between the victorious deity and the forces of chaos, a battle the victory of which is celebrated each year in a cultic way at the New Year's festival, enacted by the king and bringing fertility to the land for another year. At least such a chaos battle theme is demonstrable for Babylon (the *Enuma Elish*)[18] and other nations, while references like Isaiah 27:1, 30:7, Habakkuk 3, or Ezekiel 29:3-5 may reflect an Israelite version of the primeval battle against a monster from the deep named "Leviathan" or, in Israel, "Rahab."

The exact details of such a creation myth with its ritual will probably never be settled, especially the questions of the extent to which the Israelite New Year festival incorporated the theme and its practices and of the degree to which most Israelites embraced such a creation emphasis. It would be foolish to deny that some in the nation must have been enamored of the general theme and must have shared its concern for nature and a nature god. It seems likely that Jerusalem, from the time of the temple which David planned and Solomon built (about 950 B.C.), with its Jebusite priesthood replacing the earlier priesthood from the cultic centers of the tribal confederation, knew a "Zion theology," as we may call it.[19]

"Zion theology" emphasized "throne and temple," that is the fact that God had chosen (elected) the house of David and the site of Mount Zion (cf. 2 Samuel 7:11; Psalm 132:11 ff.; 2 Samuel 24). In hymns of praise, creation was mingled with the themes of redemption by Yahweh and the gift of the law, cf. Psalms 89 (vv. 3-4, 19-37 on David, 5-13 on creation), 74, 77, 24. At times poetic compositions could be borrowed from the surrounding world (Psalm 104, on "continuing creation," parallels much of the Egyptian "Hymn of Akhnaton"), by more or less "Yahweh-izing" their contents (in 104, cf. vv. 1, 31-35).[20] Such hymns celebrated at times the kingship of Yahweh: he has become king (by his creation victory); he becomes king (enthroned again each year); he will become king (at the end of the universe—here we approach the idea of a "new creation," understood eschatologically); cf. Psalms 93, 97, 99.

It is possible that, while such a Zion-theology stressing creation developed at Jerusalem, there was ironically no parallel emphasis in the Northern Kingdom after the monarchy had been divided.[21] This might suggest that Israel remained truer to the older traditions of the exodus, which were without a creation emphasis, than Judah did. To what degree the average man in Judah embraced creation themes from the ancient Near East in their Jerusalem form is hard to say. One can guess, however, that some (e.g., among the prophets) opposed the emphasis and others (especially those who were involved in the temple cult) were swept along by it. At times creation may even have seemed to become a major or independent theme, just as in surrounding lands. But the evidence is mostly indirect.

The prophets, for example, prior to the exile, provide by their general lack of references to creation, a side to the picture which has been much debated.[22] Some of the two dozen or so allusions to creation in their extant writings can be set aside as later insertions and dated after the exile, when the concept of creation became a more frequently used category (e.g., Isaiah 17:12-14; 27:1; 34:11; Nahum

1:3-4). At times the prophets, as noted, do seem to reflect an Israelite or at least common Near Eastern creation-battle myth. Jeremiah, in particular, contains interesting phrases that reflect the creation story which was later to be recorded in what we know as Genesis 1. Does the reference to the earth as being "without form and void" (Jeremiah 4:23) provide a source for Genesis 1:2, or did Jeremiah know an early version of the myth which the Priestly writer was to incorporate in Genesis, or do both draw upon a common source? Similarly the Book of Amos contains snatches of a hymn setting forth God's work in nature but insists, with regard the creator "who forms the mountains and creates the wind," that as a polemical refrain puts it: "*Yahweh* is his name" (4:13; 5:8-9; 9:5-6).[23] A final illustration of how difficult the phrases in the prophets are to interpret comes from Hosea 8:14, in the accusation "Israel has forgotten his Maker." This sounds like creation language, but it may refer to the way in which Yahweh created Israel in the exodus events. It is always important to ask how creation references function. Often they undergird an ethical appeal (e.g., Malachi 2:10, "Has not one God created us . . .?", although here the context is the covenant and the reference to Israel), or the judgment theme (Isaiah 30:7; Habakkuk 3).

Another area besides the cult and reflections of it in the prophets where creation may have been a theme is that of wisdom literature and the international "wisdom movement" common to the ancient Near East. Clearly, in the later centuries, wisdom writings allude to creation, sometimes using the theme in support of ethical exhortation. It is likely that some wisdom traditions were of much earlier origin and included references to creation: cf. Proverbs, the Book of Job, and Ecclesiastes (e.g., Proverbs 3:19-20; 8:22-31; Ecclesiastes 3:11; 12:1, 7; Job 3:1-10; 22:12-14; chap. 37; 38:22-39:30).[24]

Thus far we have suggested that, while the exodus and related themes were formative of Israel's basic outlook, creation emphases appeared in cult and its literary forms and in wisdom literature, with occasional reflections in the prophets. This is the general picture for the tenth to sixth centuries B.C. However, the famous judgment of Gerhard von Rad, that "in genuinely Yahwistic belief the doctrine of creation never attained the stature of a relevant, independent doctrine" but was "inevitably related, and indeed subordinated, to soteriological considerations" (including the theme of judgment as well as salvation)[25] seems to be correct, even if it is in need of modification at points.

Perhaps the Old Testament approach to creation most interesting for theology today is that taken about 950 B.C. by the so-called J Writer in the "Layman's Source" incorporated in Genesis 2-3.[26] The period during which the temple cult in Jerusalem was taking shape was also a time of fresh international influences setting in motion that which in Israel has been called "the Solomonic enlightenment," a "humanistic" era during which old practices were giving way to new. The appeal to ancient cultic centers and institutions (like the "holy war") and even traditions (including the exodus theme itself) no longer carried the weight it once did. How does one speak of God when all is changing? The J Writer, avoiding the way of cult, accepted the new secularism and, still using the old traditions of exodus, Sinai, and the patriarchs, put together an epic that depicts God at work in the human heart and in everyday life as well as in the great events of history. The Yahwist (J), true to the times, includes creation in his account, but in a cultless, "secular," demythologized version, the intent of which is to explain how the human situation came to be the way it is. Yahweh created; man is the center of the creation; evil and sinning are a part of reality; God comforts and cares for man. There is probably a polemic against Canaanite nature and fertility cults (perhaps specifically against serpent worship). The lord who sends rain, however, is not Baal but Yahweh, who, in his love, even amid man's adversity, extends and keeps his promise. Many aspects of the Yahwist's views—his "secularist" view of man as God's creation, the anthropological emphasis, the stress on sin—were not to be picked up and developed for centuries.

The exile in Babylon after the fall of Jerusalem in 586 marks something of a watershed in Old Testament thinking about creation. If before the exile we have treatments of creation only to a limited extent in Zion-theology, wisdom literature, the prophets, and J, after 586 we have development in new and more extensive ways. For during the exile the remnant of the people of God was thrown into despondency. Old promises and appeals lost their luster; a new exodus, not just memories of the old deliverance from Egypt, was needed to sustain hope. The exiles were forced in Babylon to rub shoulders with a culture in which creation theology was a powerful factor. All around them there were reminders of the lordship of Marduk, won in a chaos battle at creation and celebrated annually at the New Year's festival by splendid processions, setting the rhythm for all life in Babylonia.

In this situation, between 550 and 540 B.C., a prophet, the "Great Unknown," arose, whom we call Deutero-Isaiah. His "Book of Comfort" (Isaiah 40-55) picked up not only the old themes of exodus and of election but the topic of creation as no Israelite had ever done before. He sought to awaken praise for God and hope for a new exodus back to Palestine. In so doing he employed creation imagery, both directly and subtly. So pervasive is his appeal to creation that it has even been argued that Deutero-Isaiah substitutes "creation-faith" for the exodus tradition as a basis for the "new things" being promised.[27] If so, creation, not past redemption by God, would be the foundation for his message. But we must remember that if Babylonian ideas of creation do stand behind what is said, the very creation category involved was already one of redemption and victory over forces of chaos at the beginning. Creation is then a "deus victor" motif. Moreover, Second Isaiah does not seem interested in "protology" (what happened "at the beginning") but in what applies now (creatio continua, actually with reference to the imminent future, a re-creation or new exodus). Hence a recent monograph argues that the proper theme in Deutero-Isaiah is not "creation" replacing or separated from "redemption," but rather "creative redemption" or, one may suggest, "redemptive creation," where "creation" becomes a "wondrous redemptive act of Yahweh, bringing to Israel a new national existence and a new prosperity of unprecedented scope, with 'creative' repercussions . . . even upon the cosmos," though cosmic re-creation is only occasionally hinted at.[28]

In due time came a series of returns from Babyon for some exiles, and even the restoration of a temple and cult life in Jerusalem. For this situation a Priestly School of writers (P), between 550 and 450 B.C., put together a document which included and actually began with a creation account, preserved in Genesis 1:1-2:4a. Cult and cosmos are its themes. Century-old ancient Near Eastern traditions are used but purified, with new structure imposed on the old materials and with a clear theological perspective. The power of Yahweh's word and man in the image of God as high point in God's creation are stressed. This Priestly Source tends to trace things back to earliest times and to ground institutions in creation—e.g., the sabbath. Whereas Deuteronomy 5:12-15 roots observance of the sabbath in the exodus ("remember that you were a servant in the land of Egypt, and Yahweh your God brought you out thence . . ."), Exodus 20:11 (P) traces it to creation: "remember the sabbath day . . . for

in six days the Lord made heaven and earth. . . ." For all the formula-like character of Genesis 1, it must be remembered, however,
that P's finished redaction is really a hymnic confession which purges
most of the mythic backgrounds in order to sing of Yahweh alone as
creator. The grandeur of the Priestly creation account and the position it was given by redaction at the beginning of the Pentateuch has
stamped it in the minds of many as "the" account.[29]

The return to Judah and restoration of temple life, with confession of Yahweh as creator and redeemer, did not turn out to be all
that most Israelites had expected. The road back was rocky, existence
difficult, the Second Temple of Zerubbabel shabby compared with
that of Solomon. New voices, often of apocalyptic tone, had to speak
further words of hope. From them, in the period between 537 and
450 B.C., come two oracles tremendously important for our theme.
At Isaiah 65:16b-25 a prophet whom we call Trito-Isaiah takes a description of what salvation is going to be like (no tears, no death;
access to God), reflecting the *shalom* of the original creation (v. 25,
cf. Isaiah 11:6-9) and presents the whole as a promise of God: "Be-
hold, I create new heavens and a new earth" (65:17). It sounds as
if God's new redemptive acts for Israel will have repercussions
throughout the universe, but a careful examination of the parallelism in vv. 17 and 18 and the references to the people of Jerusalem in
vv. 20-24 show that the intent of the author is really to speak of the
redeemed community as a new creation. This is "Zion-theology" in
the form of future promise. Later on, another passage (66:22), used
the same promise of a new heaven and new earth to ground the expectation, vividly described in 66:18-24, of punishment for the
wicked and eternal sabbath for the righteous.

Thus, in early days, Israel's spokesmen for God appealed to Yahweh's redemptive acts in the Exodus as a basis for faith. At times
Yahweh's power was viewed as extending to the beginning of things
at creation. The language of creation and appeal to what he had
done there creative-redemptively was, in the case of Deutero-Isaiah,
made part of the foundation of future expectations, God's prowess
being extrapolated into the time to come. In apocalyptic literature
that future hope is itself made the basis for further promises. This
goes a step further when, in a much later apocalyptic document in
the intertestamental literature, II Esdras (4 Ezra), scepticism about
God's acting in this present world in any form is so great that the

appeal must be made to a future age; for existing creation is so corrupt that an appeal to it would be of no significance.[30]

Space does not permit us to elaborate the developments which took place in the period between the testaments regarding belief about creation and hopes for a new creation, except to say that the theme is a more frequent one in the Apocrypha and Pseudepigrapha, for the rabbis and Hellenistic Judaism (especially Philo), and at Qumran.[31] Just as the exile created new emphasis on the theme, so did the period of the three centuries or so before Christ. In particular, all the Greek speculations about "the beginning"[32] began to be known to Jews, at least in the Diaspora.

What about Jesus? In his teachings he took over the normal Jewish view derived from the Old Testament traditions of God as creator. But contrary to much late Jewish thought of God as transcendent and remote, a Lawgiver and Judge, Jesus saw the Father as a God near at hand, caring for men. "Providence" was not Jesus' central message, but it was a genuine part of it (Matthew 6:26-34), as were trust in this Father and obedience to his will (cf. Mark 10:5). The so-called "nature miracles," like Mark 4:35-41, whatever their exact background, are really creation stories reflecting Jesus' basic trust in the creator.[33]

Accordingly, when the early church first began to include something about God as creator in its basic preaching, it was not untrue to Jesus' message. In the initial period after the resurrection the apostolic kerygma did not include any reference to creation. Jews simply assumed that Yahweh was lord of the world. Only when the message began to be addressed to Gentiles, who did not know the one God as maker of all things, was it necessary to add to the christological kerygma a section about the creator and his provident administration of the universe. Often material on this theme must have been taken over from Jewish missionary preaching to the Gentile world and from synagogue worship forms.[34]

A key step in Christian development of the creation theme came in the pre-Pauline Hellenistic Jewish and Gentile church when Jesus Christ was given a role in creation as God's agent or mediator and eventually as creator himself. Probably the oldest example is the little creed, now embedded in 1 Corinthians 8:6, which Paul quotes. Beside the phrase used in the synagogue, "One God . . . from whom are all things and for whom we exist," some Christian juxtaposed the

basic confession "Jesus Christ (is) Lord," and the result was a binitarian statement which in its parallelism gave Christ a role in creation: we believe in

> One God, the Father,
>   from whom are all things, and for whom we exist,
> and one Lord, Jesus Christ,
>   through whom are all things and through whom we exist.

Hebrews 1:2b-3 reflects a similar credal formula about "the Son,
through whom God created the world . . . who upholds the universe
by the word of his power." Christian faith, having experienced the
power of Jesus, wanted to confess his lordship with regard to the
foundation and sustentation of the whole world.

The most enthusiastic extrapolation of Christ's lordship in creation no doubt came in the Hellenistic Christian church at times of
worship, particularly in sacramental celebrations, when the Spirit led
believers to acclaim Jesus as lord over "all things" in the three-story
universe, "from the beginning." Jewish speculation about wisdom's
role in creation (cf. Proverbs 8:22-31; Sirach 24), Greek philosophy,
and perhaps gnostic thought supplied phrases and ideas; the experiences of faith supplied the motive power to praise a "Christ over
the cosmos." Philippians 2:6-11, Colossians 1:15-20, and John 1:1ff.,
it is widely agreed, contain hymns, now somewhat revised, of such
origin.[35] Obviously the experience of redemption through Christ is
here the origin of what is said about Christ in creation. It remained
for later centuries to take these hymnic doxologies as ontological assertions; the New Testament writers were to make different use of
them (see below).

The role of Paul and his epistles[36] with regard to creation was first
of all that of a transmitter of these early Christian assertions about
Christ as mediator of creation. Paul agreed with them and regarded
Christ as therefore preexistent, with a role in creation, original and
continuing (1 Corinthian 8:6). Secondly, from his Jewish background Paul used creation themes to speak of Christ as the "last
Adam" (1 Corinthian 15:45-49) or as "Adam to come" (Romans
5:14) from heaven, crucified and risen, whose image we shall bear,
whose imprint or "mind" dominates the community confessing him
as lord (Philippians 2:6-11; the reference to the cross in v. 8`is a
Pauline addition to make central the theology of the cross). Paul
even knew the idea of *creatio ex nihilo,* a theme which seems to have
appeared in Judaism first in 2 Maccabees 7:28; this theme of "crea-

tion out of nothing" Paul reflects in what is probably a credal formula cited in Romans 4:17, where it parallels the resurrection, thus making the resurrection a "new creation."

Further, Paul describes his own conversion as nothing less than a new creation for him (2 Corinthian 4:6, actually quoting Genesis 1:3 about his "enlightenment"). Romans 5 uses the story of Genesis 1-3 to show man's situation under sin (and hence now, in contrast, as redeemed by Christ). Such a connection between sinning and creation had been previously suggested in the J Writer (Genesis 2-3) and developed in 2 Esdras (4 Ezra). Romans 8 employs apocalyptic language (8:19-22) to make the point (8:17) that Christian existence invoves sufferings now and the *hope* of glory; it is not yet "all-glorious" but is still life "under the cross." To decide upon a much debated question: in Romans 8 "the whole creation" to which Paul refers probably involved "every created thing," inanimate as well as living, in the apocalyptic material which Paul quotes; but Paul's own application (8:17, 23ff.) shows that his interest is in *man,* Christian man, and not in non-Christian humanity or the animal world, let alone inanimate objects.[37]

Paul it is who brings to the fore the theme of "new creation"[38] in two monumental references in Galatians 6:15: "Neither circumcision counts for anything, nor uncircumcision, but a new creation," and 2 Corinthians 5:17: "if anyone is in Christ, he is a new creation" (RSV). In each case the translation "new creature" is to be preferred, and the reference is to the Christian believer, reconciled and justified (2 Corinthian 5:21), baptized into Christ (cf. Galatians 3:27-28), a part of the new community, the church (Galatians 6:16), which lives ("walks") under the cross (Galatians 6:14; 2 Corinthians 5:19, 21). The reference to new creatures is not individualistic; a community is assumed. The background in the Old Testament prophets about a "new heart" or "new spirit" given in order to "walk in Yahweh's statutes" (Jeremiah 31:33-34; Ezekiel 36:26-27) does not seem sufficient to account for Paul's expression. Apocalyptic language about the "new heavens and new earth" has been claimed as the background, but if so, we must remember that even in Isaiah 65 and 66 the intent of such language was to speak of the redeemed community. Furthermore, in the two Pauline passages there seems to be no reference to an apocalyptically renovated cosmos. "New creation" refers to a totally new relationship for God's creatures, i.e., persons redeemed through Christ. The most likely background continues to be that of Jewish proselyte baptism, where a convert was spoken of as a "new creature."

The other New Testament epistles after Paul continue to use Jewish—Old Testament expressions about God as creator (1 Peter 4:19; Ephesians 3:9), as did Paul himself (cf. Romans 1:20, 25; 1 Corinthian 10:26). The interpretation suggested above for "new creation" is borne out in the Deutero-Pauline literature; cf. Colossians 3:10 and Ephesians 4:24; 2:10, 15—the "new man" is created after the image [Christ] of its creator [God] by baptism and is set into the new community to do the good works of God. James 1:18, 1 Peter 1:23, and Titus 3:5 also belong here as baptismal references. Most significant is the way the author of Colossians has taken the older Hellenistic Christian hymn (1:15-20) and interpreted it by (1) clearer reference to the death of Jesus on the cross (insertion of v. 20*b*), by (2) defining the "body of Christ" not as the cosmos (as the hymn suggested), but as the church (v. 18*b*), and (3) above all by asserting that Christ permeates the world precisely as the church carries out evengelism as a missionary body, under the sign of suffering (1.21ff.). As the author interprets the hymn, cosmological speculation is given up in favor of practical working of the church in the world.[39]

Of course the apocalyptic side of our theme so prominent in late Judaism was not lost in primitive Christianity. Revelation 21 picks up and develops the thought of Isaiah 65 about a new heaven and a new earth. There will be no more sea, death, night, etc. (all the traditional ancient Near Eastern images are there), but, unlike Trito-Isaiah's hope, this will not be earthly Jerusalem restored but a new preexistent entity, coming down from above. However, in common with Isaiah 65, Revelation 21 focuses not on a new universe but here solely on the redeemed. When 2 Peter 3:13 speaks of "new heavens and a new earth in which righteousness dwells," it is reminiscent of Isaiah 66:22. The aim is to hold fast to a future hope, the parousia, and what is promised is a "home of justice" where the righteous will dwell while the wicked perish. Apocalyptic promise here sustains a rather narrow hope which, however, has its values for keeping hope alive and counterbalancing a gnostic "wholly realized eschatology" and devaluation of the Creator's world.

Finally the Gospel of John.[40] There is far less of cosmological interest here than is often supposed. The "world" God loves (3:16) — and judges, because it is in darkness—turns out to be the world of persons, faced with decision for or against the Light. Christ is already presented as the Light in the Logos hymn of 1:1ff. An earlier hymn, the contours of which can still be discerned, lies behind the passage— a hymn that was originally cosmological, in vv. 1-5 in its references to creation (R. E. Brown), or throughout (Bultmann). This hymn (vv. 1-5, 10-12b or parts thereof) and a confession from the Christian community (vv. 14, 16—if verses 14 and 16 were part of the original hymn, then the whole must have originated in Christian circles, for only a Christian group would say "the Word became flesh and dwelt among us") have been augmented by prose comments on John the Baptist and some explanatory comments. The whole, as it stands, can be read from the standpoint of salvation history (Brown) : vv. 1-4, creation; v. 5, the fall; 10-12b, Old Testament Israel's history; 14a, the incarnation; 14cd, the transfiguration. Or it can be taken to speak of "new creation," with Christ as the agent of eschatological sonship (J. A. T. Robinson; E. Käsemann). Or the passage can be given a creation focus: the Logos who created and who was light and life was always in the world (Bultmann), but then "creation" is also "revelation" and "soteriology," for the Logos unites cosmological and soteriological functions, and to receive him is to become a child of God (1:12; cf. 3:1-21, by being born from above; new creation!). Creation and redemption thus coalesce into a redemptive creation and creative redemption.

Such is the biblical data in outline. What are we to make of it?

II.

Theses about Creation and New Creation in Scripture

We have outlined a multiplicity of witnesses in both testaments to the Creator and creation, initial, continuing, and new. However, the very richness and variety sketched above—and all too briefly at that, as many exegetes, historians and students of the history of religions might claim—threaten, some may feel, to make our findings unusable for faith today or for dogmatic constructions about creation. Yet this variety—some even use the term "biblical pluralism"—is precisely what current research stresses. Claus Westermann warns: ". . . it is not possible to ground a doctrine of creation on the Bible which overlooks these differences and presupposes that there is only *one* valid presentation of creation in it."[41] Both "this" presentation and "that," and many more, are in the Bible, and it will not do to ignore some, to homogenize them to an ideology, or to declare some "false" and others "true." The initial task is always to outline the historical development of the "multitude of quite different, essentially divergent presentations of creation."[42] Westermann follows this statement with his own sketches of the Priestly, Jahwistic, and Deutero-Isaianic pictures of creation. We have suggested three or four such pictures in ancient Israel, three more after the exile, plus half a dozen or more strata in the New Testament. But do these dozen or fifteen biblical theologies of creation not share certain features in common?

All of them, we have seen, like the references to "new creation," share this: they come from the believing community (Israel in the Old Testament, the Christian *ekklēsia* in the New), and that means a community which believes itself redeemed by the action of Yahweh (in Christ). From the experience which the group has had of deliverance, sustenance, and fellowship, it finds itself wanting to speak of the lordship of its God in wider realms: the world as now experienced, the beginnings of the world (protology), and the outcome or final results of God's dealings with that world (teleology, eschatology). Faith projects its enthusiasm and testimony back to the beginning of things and forward to the fulfillment. Note that the believer (or the group of believers) witnesses in so speaking to that which he has not seen—for no one was present at the creation, from Israel or the church—and to that which no one has yet seen occur save as faith envisions it, clasping its hopes and trusting the One who reveals his truths to it.

We have seen, too, that language and ideas often common to the world of religions can be taken by a particular faith and used to speak of what its lord has done or will do. In particular we have observed that language appropriate to "beginnings" (creation terminology) can also be employed to state what God has done redemptively and to express the hope about what will follow (cf. especially Deutero-Isaiah). Hence there arises speech about a "new creation," asserting the glory of the *novum,* in contrast to the old, often in evocative terms. For Old Testament Israel this expectation of new heavens and earth occurred with apocalyptic longings. For the Christian community it was seen as not only future but also as actualized in baptism and life under the Crucified One. In Paul's use of the term *kainē ktisis,* attempts which might develop to "spiritualize" or view solely as individualistic the new creaturehood in Christ are precluded by the corporate and perhaps even ontic overtones in the Apostle's thinking.[43] And the desire to concentrate the new in the present, so that any future aspect is set aside, is countered by the continuing use of apocalyptic vision and categories and the appeal to life as existence under the cross, marked by suffering. In such ways the New Testament avoids the impression that "all things" may be "already realized" or that the cosmos is transformed by man or for him already. Creation continues, also for the transformed new people in Christ.

Over the centuries there have, of course, been all sorts of attempts to combine, simplify, apply, and interpret what the Bible says about creation and new creation. All of us know examples of how this subsequent tradition history of the theme in the Christian church has produced extreme misunderstandings (often based on a part of the biblical witness taken in a one-sided way) and fruitful syntheses (capturing for a time a balance of what the Bible says).[44] It cannot be stressed too much that each one of these endeavors was speaking to a specific situation of its own and reflects the insights and liabilities of outlook in that day; likewise that each subsequent presentation since New Testament times has usually prided itself on basing what it says on at least some aspect of the Bible's witness.

The first mandate in *The Shepherd of Hermas* picked out the thought of 2 Maccabees 7:28, so as to enjoin, "Believe that God is one, who created all things . . . out of that which does not exist . . ." (Mandata 1:1). The ancient church stressed Stoic and Platonic thought, but also wisdom-logos concepts from later Judaism in constructing its cosmology. Later systematicians were to distinguish "first creation" (where matter was made out of nothing) and "second creation" (when out of this matter the world was made) and to attempt to find these stages between the verses in Genesis 1. The Middle Ages were to produce an "apocalyptic anti-Aristotelianism" in response.[45] The Reformation sought to develop the fullness of scriptural references and, of course, stressed Christ. In the nineteenth century it was essential to come to terms with the rise of natural sciences. Space permits only these broad references to remind ourselves of how the history of the doctrine of creation was unfolded in Christian theology.

In broad terms it may be said with reference to new creation that at least three main avenues of interpreting have been followed. First of all, since some of the biblical references are apocalyptic in nature, an apocalyptic line of interpretation has emerged at times. The "new heavens and new earth," i.e. the new creation, is to come by a mirac-

ulous act of God, effecting and changing the world we know, which
is often regarded as hopelessly corrupt. In most cases this divine intervention is taken to be imminent—it will soon come to pass. The
apocalyptic interpretation has had its particular attraction in dark
times, be they in the second century or at the fall of Rome, around
the year A.D. 1000 or towards the end of World War II.

A second way of understanding "new creation" has been to trans-
pose the theme into ontological terms. A transubstantiated host be-
tokens the kind of change God can bring about, here and now for
the future. And so, since the Christ event, the whole cosmos has been
viewed at times as changed in its very structures. New creation is said
to be "christically" with us or soon to come to pass.

Those who repudiate the apocalyptic and ontological understand-
ings of new creation have a third way of interpreting it: existentially,
as a new situation for the believer, who is justified and open to God's
future. Gone is any fantasy world of apocalypticism or notion of
ontological change; what happens is that one's self-understanding is
made new.

The third position just sketched often seems to ignore creation as a
category; the first two are likely to concentrate on "world" as well
as, or instead of, "self." In all three approaches, of course, there may
or may not be particular concentration on the church as the "zone
of hope," apocalyptically, ontologically, or as the community of those
in the new existence.[46]

Being aware of all these problems of unity and diversity in scripture and of the long line of theological interpretation since New
Testament times, can we now sketch out any conclusions from the
biblical witnesses about creation/new creation for today?

The following theses are an attempt to sum up, for discussion and
further use, some of the main conclusions noted in working through
the exegetical materials, contentions hinted at in Part I above. It is
hoped that they may provide not only content but suggestions for
speaking about these themes today. Within the framework of this
volume they provide a further insight into the history of God's dealings with his world; they form a backdrop for the (likewise pluri-
form) witnesses to the gospel in the scriptures, in their historical
settings; and they illustrate how the biblical community at various
times in its more than a thousand-year history down to the close of
the New Testament asserted its identity in making assertions about
creation and new creation.

(1) *What the Bible says about creation—and* this holds all the more for *new creation—is a statement of faith.* In the light of its redemptive experience, which constitutes it as a community of faith, the group speaks. Faith expresses itself regarding God and things now, things past, and things to come. Creation passages are statements confessing God with regard to beginnings and the foundation of all things. "Creatio continua" is such faith given expression about existence currently and over the years. The idea of "new heavens and new earth" reflects faith in this same God extended to the future. To talk of being a "new creature" is, of course, the witness of faith to one's own transformation.

In passages considered above, examples are provided by 1 Corinthians 8:6, the binitarian credo about the Father and Christ in creation; Romans 4:17; the hymnic assertions in John 1 (where the community which is mentioned in the first person plural of vv. 14 and 16 affirms that "all things were made through the word," Jesus Christ) ; and perhaps Genesis 1. For my part, I should call all the passages outlined in Part I statements of faith in one way or another, and a number of them really creeds or fragments of a credo.

Westermann seems to disagree when he writes that in the Old Testament there is no statement or confession of faith about creation or the creator: "a) speaking about the creator never became part of a 'credo' in Israel; the summaries of Israel's faith were limited from beginning to end to the *'historical* credo' (G. von Rad) . It is first with the Apostolic Creed of the Christian church that speaking about God the creator is united in a confession of faith with speaking about God's saving acts. b) The other fact is that the Old Testament never speaks of faith in the creator or in creation."[47] Point b) I take to reflect the centrality of redemption and God as redeemer in the Old Testament. Point a) may reflect a distinction which Westermann suggests between creation (as a "universal work") and (salvation) history (to be discussed below, in thesis 8) . But is he right that it is only in the Apostles' Creed that God the creator and his saving acts are spoken of together? The kerygma of the early church seems to have done this already in pre-Pauline times, and surely in 1 Corinthians 8:6 we have a credo about the creator. Probably late Judaism had already taken such steps, to say nothing of the great confession in Nehemiah 9:6-38. Indeed, even for Genesis 1 opinions vary; von Rad speaks of the chapter as presenting "declarations of faith that concern existence of man here and now."[48]

There is thus good reason to regard what the Bible says about creation as statements of faith. And the very variety of situations in which faith spoke then may be helpful to us today in giving testimony in our times, which are like some of the biblical situations. It does not take much imagination to parallel the age of the Yahwist with our secularized, "religionless" seventies.

(2) *Talk about creation—and also new creation—in the Bible is usually in the mood of praise to God.* Hymns, slogans which embody the contentions of faith, and even at times narratives or revamped myths which are expressions of the faith of the community, give vent to the group's acclaim for him who made it what it is, its world, its past and its future. Hymns obviously have this quality, as witness the psalms with their ejaculations, "Praise Yah." Creeds regularly have a doxological aspect. An acclamation of Christ such as Colossians 1:15-20 could arise only in an atmosphere of worship. Even a formula-like narrative like Genesis 1 carries beneath its surface a feeling of awe and laud for God. "The basic theological tendency in all speaking about the creator and creation is to call the creature to reverence toward his creator and to the acknowledgement of God as the creator."[49] Or again from Westermann: ". . . the whole wealth of biblical statements concerning Creator and creation stand in conjunction with the praise of God."[50]

One may hazard the guess that "new creation" as a term for Christian believers, even though it may have derived from Jewish baptismal use, first became common coin in Hellenistic Christian circles of enthusiasts who likened their status to the moment of creation itself, "when the morning stars sang together and all the sons of God shouted for joy," and spoke ecstatically of God.

(3) *These doxological statements of faith about creation employ the language and insights of the world of the day,* reflecting at times what might be called the "scientific" view of the time. In the Old Testament, creation accounts and hymns employ Canaanite (Genesis 14:19, 22), Egyptian (Psalm 104), Babylonian (Genesis 1-2), and general ancient Near Eastern motifs and vocabulary (cf. "Zion theology"). In the New Testament we can find Stoic details, Platonizing concepts, and possible gnostic themes in passages like 1 Corinthians 8:6, Hebrews, John 1, and Philippians 2:6-11. The world of religions of the day served as the quarry whence materials for faith's assertions about the world were hewn. In most instances a case can be made that the materials borrowed reflect the common or advanced

scientific view then widespread. The parallel implication would be for faith today to avail itself of current scientific insights in making statements about the world.

(4) *Creation talk in the Bible* does not, however, seek to elucidate what current opinon or science holds; it *employs this vocabulary and these insights to set forth God and his glory* (answering the "who" question of creation) *and God's purpose, plan, or will, especially with regard to the high calling and response intended for man* (the "why" of human creation). Beyond the doxological acclamation of God by faith, there lies in statements about creation a further interest in man, not simply in himself but as made for God, with a purpose in the divine plan. Genesis 2 begins on the level of most ancient Near Eastern accounts: man is placed in the Garden "to till it and keep it" for God (2:15). Genesis 1 heightens the idea of a stewardship over the earth and of man as God's vice-regent (1:26, 28), but it also insists that man is "in God's image" (something never lost, according to P) and is to live within the structures of life God has provided. The Psalms and other passages carry this line of thinking further (e.g., Psalm 8:5-8) until it reaches the height of a grand argument in Colossians and Ephesians: in the plan of God man is called in Christ to be conformed to the image of God (seen in Christ), to work according to his will, bringing about reconciliation among men in the world.

(5) Clearly *New Testament faith sees Christ as having a role in creation* just as he does in redemption. To Old Testament statements about God as creator *addenda* are provided, naming Jesus Christ as agent or mediator in creation (1 Corinthians 8:6; Hebrews 1:3-4) or, eventually, as creator himself (John 1; Colossians 1:15-20).

(6) *In a remarkable number of biblical statements about creation the concern is with man in his existence.* Without invoking the argument that all statements about God are inevitably likewise statements about man, we can see from the texts themselves that the Bible's talk concerning creation is remarkably anthropological. The passages seek to account for man's situation in the world and set it forth with regard to his ties to God (Genesis 1) and his inclinations toward self and disobedience (Genesis 2-3). There is virtually no speculation in the Bible about God "in himself" or about a "time before time" or the "state prior to creation." Indeed, statements about the "how" of creation are both rare and reserved. In the New Testament we can notice an anthropological side to statements about creation such as

1 Corinthians 8:6 (". . . we live for God, . . . we exist through
Christ") and John 1 (creation is briefly touched on in order to
heighten the significance of the presence of the word and light, from
whom we receive life and through whom we believers become children of God). In our interpretation above "new creation" turned
out to reflect completely anthropological lines. Apropos this sixth
thesis, on anthropology, Westermann even makes a distinction between Old Testament accounts about the creation of the *world*
(most of Genesis 1) and the creation of *man* (Genesis 2), the older
account being the one about the creation of man.[51] Though the
redactoral arrangement in Genesis has put these in an order which
makes the world the larger frame of reference for the part about
man, we are suggesting that the anthropological side is more prominent than many later theologies traditionally have made it.

(7) *Many of the creation references in the Bible are directed* not
to "beginnings" (*creatio originalis*) but *to the ongoing process of
God's care for and preservation of his world* (*creatio continua*). First
Peter speaks for a great deal of the Bible when it urges trust in God
as "a faithful Creator" (4:19) who "cares for you" (5:7). A number
of the Psalms, not only those which deal with "nature" (104; 19:1-6)
but also the "enthronement psalms" (93, 97, etc.) with their references to Yahweh's continuing reign, express this theme. Even the
credal formulations and narratives which speak about creation "in
the beginning" also reflect a concern for God's continuing goodness
or bounty in nature or rule in the ordering of the world (cf. Genesis
1; Genesis 2, with its glance beyond Eden to later conditions; Hebrew 1:3-4). Deutero-Isaiah's use of creation imagery is oriented to
"now," not to "back there" in the beginning.

"Continuing creation" has become a sort of theological stock-in-
trade. Any "sharp differentiation between creation and preservation," it is said, "has no basis in the biblical witness"; they belong
together (Regin Prenter, citing Psalm 104:29-30).[52] Westermann,
however, offers the critique that *creatio continua* says too much and
is a contradiction in terms because "creation is something absolutely
unique"; "preservation," on the other hand, he claims, "says too
little" (God's work is more dynamic than just "preserving").[53] These
criticisms are worth bearing in mind, for "creation" stands in a class
by itself, *"in principio,"* and "new creation" can be compared only
to it, not to continuing preservation. But the terms are well en-
trenched and have the merit of suggesting a continuity of the One

God's actions in the beginning and in subsequent events up to the end. Prenter and Westermann are agreed that "because God is the creator, *all* that happens is effected by him," in nature and in history.[54]

A corollary of God's continuing activity whereby the Creator upholds his universe and works in its history as well as in nature is that his purposes can be served not only by an "elect people," but also by events in the natural order and by pagans. One need only recall how often in the Bible the God of continuing creation and redemption is said to work through disaster in nature, a hostile army, or even, in Deutero-Isaiah, a pagan king who serves as God's anointed (Cyrus; Isaiah 45:1). Having thus noted a certain intertwining of nature and history in God's ongoing work, we now come to the debated area of creation and redemption.

(8) *Language about God's creative work, initial or continuing, can also be used reflectively by faith to describe redemption, past, present, or future.* We have seen, especially in Deutero-Isaiah, how creation motives can be used to speak of deliverance by Yahweh about to be performed. We concluded that "creation faith" is one of many motives in the presentation of "creative redemption," not an independent topic or a substitute for "faith in God's redemptive work." In the case of "new creation" we discovered that creation terminology was a natural means of describing the change to a new status for the redeemed believer (2 Corinthians 4:6; Galatians 6:15; 2 Corinthians 5:17); this might be described as "redemptive creation." Apocalyptic material sometimes uses creation imagery to describe what will be "at the end" (*Urzeit gleich Endzeit;*[55] cf. Isaiah 65:25; Revelation 21), when all is consummated. Creation accounts themselves sometimes reflect language about a battle and a victory (conflict with chaos; Psalms, passages in the prophets); creation is a redemption from chaos.

All of this evidence suggests that creation and redemption are not competing categories, but intertwining activities of the same God. Creation language can be used in the service of redemption; redemption is a meaning of creation, past, present, and to come. "Creative redemption" is a helpful term to describe this unity. But the point seems to stand that it is the redeemed community which uses this language in all these cases. We have indicated possible occurrences where "creation" as a theme might have become detached from the redemption matrix (e.g., in cult and myth stressing a nature God, in wisdom tradition, in speculations about cosmic Christology), but it is hard to avoid the conclusion that the Lord being spoken of is he who redeemed Israel at the exodus or who raised up Jesus from the dead and made him Lord. To this extent von Rad's judgment about creation and redemption stands.

Westermann[56] seems to offer a qualification by insisting that no attempt is made in the Old Testament "to fully integrate the statements about creation into the acting of God in history" (*pace* von Rad). He distinguishes creation and God's universal work in Genesis 1-11 from the "special" or "salvation" history of God with his elect people in Genesis 12 and following. So it is that Genesis 1-11 reflects so much more material from other religions and cultures than do the more "Israelite" parts of the Bible. Strictly speaking, of course, this distinction would have to be extended so that certain of the Psalms, and "Zion theology," often only lightly "Yahweh-ized," would be counted among the "universal" parts of scripture. In the New Testament such "universal" and non-heilsgeschichtlich passages are harder to locate, since precisely those portions which are broadest in outlook (Colossians 1:15-20; Matthew 25:31-46) are the most christological ones. This distinction between a universal history (and God's acting to bless) and a *salvation* history (his acting to *save,* for his particular people) is worth noting. It is an alternative to too simple an equation between creation and redemption and to christologizing too completely God's universal work. God carries out his treatment of "all men" in a way that is distinguished even in the manner in which the Bible talks of it from the way in which he deals with his elect people.

(9) *Faith's talk about God's work of creative redemption can also be extended to the future,* so as to speak about the last times, eschatologically, as being like the first creation or, better yet, a new creation. This point has already been suggested, and can be illustrated by a host of apocalyptic passages in Deutero-Isaiah (who with some justification has been called "the father of apocalyptic") ;[57] Trito-Isaiah; and John the Seer, the author of the New Testament apocalypse. The power of God, exhibited in past redemption and creation, was an inevitable point of reference, especially in dark times. It thus became the basis for future hope for a time when God would do new wonders, the dream of "new heavens and a new earth."

(10) *In the New Testament, in the light of baptism[58] into Christ, early Christian experience of redemption at times takes the specific*

form of the self-understanding of believers as new creatures (kainē ktisis, Galatians 6:15, 2 Corinthians 5:17) . This new creation which they are involves a new outlook concerning their fellowmen and God''s world, but not (at least in these passages) elaborate cosmological speculations and certainly not assumptions that the new aeon has totally arrived (especially for the as yet unbelieving world) or guesswork about apocalyptic timetables. What, then, is life as God's new people like?

(11) *These believers "in Christ" are the first fruits and the nucleus for the new age to come,* the kingdom where the Lord Jesus reigns, the realm of the Father which is to be. Christ now reigns, who in Pauline thinking is alone the *imago dei.* (Contrast P, for whom man never lost the image of God; in Paul man participates in it only as he enters "in Christ" into fellowship with the Lord Jesus in the church.) The "new creatures" in Christ share in the first inklings of what is to come, but know of the fullness only by faith. They still live in the world, which is God's but which may bring them suffering. Cf. the Pauline passages treated in Part I, including Colossians 3:10; Ephesians 2:10, 15; 4:24; from them and from the total witness of scripture springs also a final point.

(12) *These new creatures* of God in Christ, as a community, i.e. the church, *have been set free to serve, to work and to transform* the tangled situations that exist, *in* and as *the church* under Christ, *in* and as part of *the world* under God's universal lordship. They look to their Redeemer-Creator, Christ, for strength, goals, and endurance, working out in trust the implications of their salvation, knowing that it is not of themselves, but of God. They look to God, their Creator-Redeemer, and know they hold a place with all men universally in his creation and help exercise a stewardship given to mankind.[59] Thus they are sons, stewards of grace in Christ, and children of God and stewards of his beneficence. Though "in Christ," they are still much like ancient Israel between the promise and its consummation. They continue to be *in via* in God's world, which provides the scope of theological reflection, seen under the aspect of redemption in Christ.

NOTES

1. All these topics are touched on in the recent standard study by Langdon Gilkey, *Maker of Heaven and Earth: A Study of the Christian Doctrine of Creation*, Garden City, 1959; paperback edition, 1965.

2. Curiously, in spite of impressions derived from later theology, the Bible only rarely connects the Spirit with creation; for possible examples, cf. Psalm 104:30; Genesis 1:2, though in both cases "breath" or "wind" may be the proper rendering (cf. Psalm 104:29 and for Genesis 1:2 the RSV note; also Job 33:4). At Ezekiel 37:9-14 the Spirit is connected with a new creation of life (vision of the dry bones). But by and large, creation/new creation are regarded as the work of God (the Father) or (in the New Testament) of Christ. Is the pneumatic emphasis, by its very nature, likely to be little interested in the created world?

3. Cf. G. Wingren, *The Flight from Creation*, Minneapolis, 1971.

4. The charge is made by L. White, "The Historical Roots of our Ecological Crisis," *Science 155*, 1967, 1207, reprinted in *The Environmental Handbook*, Garrett de Bell, ed., New York, 1970, pp. 20 ff.; discussion in *The Human Crisis in Ecology*, F. L. Jensen and C. W. Tilberg, eds., New York, 1972, pp. xiv-xv.

5. "Called to Unity," *The Ecumenical Review* 14, 1961-62, pp. 177-187. Professor Sittler's further views on Christology and cosmos can be found in "The Principal Problem for Protestant Theology Today," in *The Word in History: The St. Xavier Symposium*, T. P. Burke, ed., New York, 1966, pp. 60-68; "The Scope of Christological Reflection," *Interpretation* 26, 1972, pp. 328-337; and Chapter Six in *The Human Crisis in Ecology, op. cit.* (Note 4), pp. 95-103, which is primarily from his pen. As an example of work by the World Council of Churches, Division of Studies, see the draft study document by Hendrikus Berkhof, "God in Nature and History," in *Study Encounter*, Geneva, 1, 1965, pp. 142-160, with bibliography by P. Löffler, pp. 161-164; and the revised report under the same title in *New Directions in Faith and Order, Bristol, 1967*, "Faith and Order Paper No. 50," Geneva, 1968, pp. 7-31. For a general survey, cf. H. H. Ditmanson, "The Call for a Theology of Creation," in *Dialog 3*, 1964, pp. 264-273.

6. This I understand Professor Sittler to be doing, not only in his 1961 address at New Delhi but in more recent writings also: "to inquire how the intersection of some of these [New Testament christological images] with contemporary man's engagement with the natural world might draw christological thought into orbits of meaning coordinate with the magnitude of modern man's transactions with the modern world" (*Interpretation* 26, 1972, p. 328), especially on the basis of Colossians 1 and Ephesians 1 (p. 334). If this poses problems exegetically, in terms of the ostensive sense (what it meant for the biblical author), the possibility is held out that we seek the "nonostensive" sense, i.e., not "behind" the text, but "in front of it" (Paul Ricoeur), from the world of discourse of the reader today (p. 335). How does this differ from reading in new meanings "relevant" for our day, for which we condemn exegetes and theologians of the past?

7. Cf. O. Cullmann, *Christ and Time*, rev. edition, Philadelphia, 1964; *Salvation in History*, New York, 1967.

8. K. Stendahl, "Biblical Theology, Contemporary," in *The Interpreter's Dictionary of the Bible*, G. A. Buttrick et al., ed., New York, 1962, Vol. 1, pp. 418-432.

9. The phrase is H. Braun's, in "The Meaning of New Testament Christology," in H. Braun et al., *God and Christ: Existence and Province*, "Journal for Theology and the Church," 5, R. Funk et al., ed., New York, 1968, p. 115. Anthropology and "God as One or as acting" are rejected as common denominators for the Bible by Stendahl, *op. cit.* (Note 8), p. 423.

10. Stendahl, *ibid.*, p. 423, cf. 424.

11. Cf. R. Bultmann, "Is Exegesis without Presuppositions Possible?" trans. by S. M. Ogden, in *Existence and Faith: Shorter Writings of R. Bultmann*, New York, 1960, pp. 289-296. Compare Stendahl, *ibid.*, p. 422, section 4.

12. G. Lindeskog, *Studien zum neutestamentlichen Schöpfungsgedanken, I*, Uppsala, 1952, seeks to give creation a more independent role, though viewed from the standpoint of redemptive history. Vol. I covers Old Testament, New Testament, and intertestamental literature; Vol. II, on the rabbis and church fathers, has not yet appeared. English summary: "The Theology of Creation in the Old and New Testaments," in *The Root of the Vine*, festschrift for A. Fridrichsen, London, 1953, pp. 1-22.

13. In addition to Lindeskog, *op. cit.* (Note 12), and standard encyclopedia articles such as B. W. Anderson, "Creation," in *Interpreter's Dictionary of the Bible*, *op. cit.* (Note 8), Vol. 1, pp. 725-732, or: "Schöpfung," in *Die Religion in Geschichte und Gegenwart*, Tübingen, 3rd edition, Vol. 5, 1961, cols. 1469-90 (C.–M. Edsman, G. E. Wright, O. Michel, G. Gloege), cf. B. W. Anderson, *Creation Versus Chaos: The Reinterpretation of Mythical Symbolism in the Bible*, New York, 1967, with a good bibliography. T. Boman, "The Biblical Doctrine of Creation," in *Church Quarterly Review* 165, 1964, pp. 140-151; G. Lambert, "La création dans la Bible," in *Nouvelle Révue Théologique* 75, 1953, pp. 252-281; G. E. Wright, "God the Creator," in his *The Old Testament and Theology*, New York, 1969, pp. 70-96; and C. Westermann, "Creation and History in the New Testament," in *The Gospel and Human Destiny*, V. Vajta, ed., Minneapolis, 1971, pp. 11-38. Only the most significant of the specialized literature is cited below.

14. Cf. S. G. F. Brandon, *Creation Legends of the Ancient Near East*, London, 1963. Translations of pertinent documents are accessible in J. B. Pritchard, ed., *Ancient Near Eastern Texts Relating to the Old Testament*, 3rd edition with supplement, Princeton, 1969.

15. Cf. G. von Rad, *Genesis: A Commentary*, Philadelphia, 1961, p. 175. I. Hunt, "Recent Melchizedek Study," in *The Bible in Current Catholic Thought* (In Memoriam M. J. Greenthaner), J. L. McKenzie, ed., New York, 1962, pp. 21-29. J. A. Emerton, "Some False Clues in the Study of Genesis XIV," and "The Riddle of Genesis XIV," in *Vetus Testamentum* 21, 1971, pp. 24-27 and 403-439. N. C. Habel, "'Yahweh, Maker of Heaven and Earth': A Study in Tradition Criticism," in *Journal of Biblical Literature* 91, 1972, pp. 321-337.

16. The claim that the name "Yahweh" originally referred to a creation god ("he who causes to be") seems to me unproven. Cf. J. P. Hyatt, "Was Yahweh Originally a Creator Deity?" in *Journal of Biblical Literature* 86, 1967, pp. 369-377.

17. The creation emphasis is especially stressed in the writings of certain Swedish Old Testament scholars and the "Myth and Ritual" School. On a widespread common theology cf. M. Smith, "The Common Theology of the Ancient Near East," in *Journal of Biblical Literature* 71, 1952, pp. 135-147.

18. Cf. Pritchard, *Ancient Near Eastern Texts, op. cit.* (Note 14), pp. 60-72.

19. Cf. Anderson, *Creation Versus Chaos, op. cit.* (Note 13), pp. 64-68, 76-77, 102,

107, and 113; von Rad, *Old Testament Theology*, New York, Vol. II, 1962, pp. 46-48; and R. de Vaux, *Ancient Israel: Its Life and Institutions*, New York, 1961, pp. 325-330.

20. For the "Hymn to the Aton" of Pharaoh Amen-hotep IV (Akh-en-Aton), cf. Pritchard, *Ancient Near Eastern Texts, op. cit.* (Note 14), pp. 369-371. There is recent, brief discussion of Psalm 104 by L. E. Toombs in "The Psalms," in *The Interpreter's One-Volume Commentary on the Bible*, C. M. Laymon, ed., Nashville and New York, 1971, pp. 290-291.

21. The reason for claiming this is the apparent absence of a creation story in the E source associated with the Northern Kingdom, plus the fact that prophets associated with the north make little of creation, and psalms attributed to the north (Psalms 45, 77, 80, 81, 103, e.g.) stress the exodus rather than creation. If the Jerusalem temple embraced creation themes, the sanctuaries in the north might well have avoided them out of rivalry and loyalty to past tradition. On the other hand, if the kingdom of Israel was as regularly "pagan" and syncretistic as Old Testament references claim, we might well expect the ancient Near Eastern theology of creation to have been readily embraced in the north too.

22. Cf. A. D. Matthews, "The Prophetic Doctrine of Creation," in *Church Quarterly Review* 166, 1965, pp. 141-149.

23. See the analysis by H. W. Wolff, "Exkurs: Die hymnischen Stücke im Amosbuch," in his *Dodekapropheton 2. Joel/Amos*, "Biblischer Kommentar Altes Testament," XIV/2, Neukirchen-Vluyn, 1969, pp. 254-266.

24. Cf. von Rad, *Theology, op. cit.* (Note 19), Vol. I, pp. 151-152.

25. Von Rad, "The Theological Problem of the Old Testament Doctrine of Creation," trans. by E. W. Trueman Dicken, in *The Problem of the Hexateuch and Other Essays*, New York, 1966, p. 142.

26. Cf. O. Eissfeldt, *The Old Testament: An Introduction*, New York, 1965, pp. 194-204. Eissfeldt uses the term "Laienschrift" for a source (L) prior to J and E which contrasts with the "Priestly source." On the thought of J (and L), cf. P. Ellis, C.SS.R., *The Yahwist, The Bible's First Theologian*, Notre Dame, 1968, and H. W. Wolff, "The Kerygma of the Yahwist," *Interpretation* 20, 1966, pp. 131-158. Further, von Rad, *Genesis op. cit.* (Note 15), pp. 27-30, 72 ff.; and his essay, "The Form-Critical Problem of the Hexateuch," in *The Problem of the Hexateuch op. cit.* (Note 25), pp. 68-74.

27. Cf. P. B. Harner, "Creation Faith in Deutero-Isaiah," in *Vetus Testamentum* 17, 1967, pp. 298-306. Contrast, supporting von Rad's position on creation and redemption, R. Rendtorff, "Die theologische Stellung des Schöpfungsglaubens bei Deuterojesaja," in *Zeitschrift für Theologie und Kirche* 51, 1954, pp. 3-13.

28. C. Stuhlmueller, C. P., *Creative Redemption in Deutero-Isaiah*, "*Analecta Biblica*," 43, Rome, 1970, pp. 9 and 233. On Trito-Isaiah see K. Pauritsch, *Die neue Gemeinde: Gott sammelt Ausgestossene und Arme*, "*Analecta Biblica*," 47, Rome, 1971.

29. On P, in addition to von Rad's commentary on Genesis, in loc. on chapter 1, and Eissfeldt's *Introduction*, see W. H. Schmidt, *Die Schöpfungsgeschichte der Priesterschrift. Zur Überlieferungsgeschichte von Genesis 1, 1-2, 4a*, "Wissenschaftliche Monographien zum Alten und Neuen Testament" 17, Neukirchen-Vluyn, 1964; and C. Westermann, *Genesis*, "Biblischer Kommentar Altes Testament," I, Neukirchen-Vluyn, 1966- . In English, see especially Westermann's essay, "Creation and History," *op. cit.* (Note 13), and his two Calwer Hefte, 3o and 1oo, translated as *The Genesis Accounts*

of Creation, 1964, and Beginning and End in the Bible, 1972, in Facet Books Biblical Series, 7 and 31, Philadelphia.

30. Cf. W. Harnisch, Verhängnis und Verheissung der Geschichte. Untersuchungen zum Zeit—und Geschichtsverständnis im 4. Esra und in der syr. Baruchapokalypse, "Forschungen zur Religion und Literatur des Alten und Neuen Testaments," 97, Göttingen, 1969.

31. Lindeskog, Schöpfungsgedanken, op. cit. (Note 12), treats the period in some detail.

32. Cf. A. Erhardt, The Beginning: A Study in the Greek Philosophical Approach to the Concept of Creation from Anaximander to St John, New York, 1968.

33. Cf. R. Bultmann, Theology of the New Testament, New York, 1951-55, Vol. 1, pp. 22-26. A. Barnett claimed "providence" as Jesus' central message in "Jesus as Theologian," in Early Christian Origins (festschrift for H. R. Willoughby, A. Wikgren, ed.), Chicago, 1961, pp. 16-23. On the "nature miracles," see my Jesus in the Church's Gospels: Modern Scholarship and the Earliest Sources, Philadelphia, 1968; London, 1970, pp. 205-217, and the literature cited there.

34. Bultmann, Theology, op. cit. (Note 33), §9, pp. 65-92.

35. For the recent extensive discussions of this material, cf. J. T. Sanders, The New Testament Christological Hymns: Their Historical and Religious Background, "Society for New Testament Studies Monograph Series," 15, New York, 1971, and the literature cited there.

36. Note, specifically, in the extensive literature on Paul: L. H. Taylor, The New Creation, New York, 1958, dogmatically oriented and not always satisfactory; G. Schneider, Kaine Ktisis. Die Idee der Neuschöpfung beim Apostel Paulus und ihr religionsgeschichtlicher Hintergrund, Trier, 1959; H. Schwantes, Schöpfung der Endzeit, "Aufsätze und Vorträge zur Theologie und Religionswissenschaft," 25, Berlin, 1963; and J. G. Gibbs, Creation and Redemption: A Study in Pauline Theology, Leiden, 1971.

37. On Romans 8, cf. J. G. Gager, Jr., "Functional Diversity in Paul's Use of End-Time Language," in Journal of Biblical Literature 89, 1970, pp. 327-330; A. Vögtle, "Röm. 8, 19-22: Eine schöpfungstheologische oder anthropologisch-soteriologische Aussage?" in Mélanges Bibliques (Festschrift for Béda Rigaux), A. Descamps and A. de Halleux, eds., Gembloux, Belgium, 1971, pp. 351-366; idem, Das Neue Testament und die Zukunft des Kosmos, Düsseldorf, 1970, pp. 183-207.

38. In addition to the literature cited in Note 36 and the standard commentaries and word studies, cf. R. A. Harrisville, The Concept of Newness in the New Testament, Minneapolis, 1960, and P. Stuhlmacher, "Erwägungen zum ontologischen Charakter der kainē ktisis bei Paulus," in Evangelische Theologie 27, 1967, pp. 1-35.

39. On Colossians 1:15-20, cf. J. Reumann, research report in Christ and Humanity, I. Asheim, ed., Philadelphia, 1970, pp. 96-109; R. Harrisville, "The New Testament Witness to the Cosmic Christ," in The Gospel and Human Destiny, op. cit. (Note 13), pp. 39-63; and Sanders, Christological Hymns, op. cit. (Note 35), pp. 12-14, 75-87 (bibliography). Further, Eduard Lohse, Colossians and Philemon, "Hermeneia," Philadelphia, 1971, pp. 41-61.

40. Cf., with further literature cited there, R. E. Brown, The Gospel According to John i-xii, "Anchor Bible," 29, Garden City, 1966, pp. 3-35; R. Bultmann, The Gospel of John: A Commentary, Philadelphia, 1971, pp. 13-83; Sanders, Christological Hymns, op. cit. (Note 35), pp. 20-24 and 29-57;

J. A. T. Robinson, "The Relation of the Prologue to the Gospel of St. John," in *New Testament Studies* 9, 1962-1963, pp. 120-129; E. Käsemann, "The Structure and Purpose of the Prologue to John's Gospel," in *New Testament Questions of Today*, Philadelphia, 1969, pp. 138-167; R. Kysar, "Rudolf Bultmann's Interpretation of the ̲Concept of Creation in John 1:3-4," in *Catholic Biblical Quarterly* 32, 1970, pp. 77-85.

41. "Creation and History," *op. cit.* (Note 13), p. 14. Cf. also his remarks on "reality" and the medieval idea of God as *summum ens* (p. 22).

42. *Ibid.*, p. 18.

43. Cf. P. Stuhlmacher, "Erwägungen," *op. cit.* (Note 38).

44. For a brief survey, cf. G. Gloege, "Schöpfung, IV. A. Theologiegeschichtlich," in *Die Religion in Geschichte und Gegenwart*, 3rd edition, *op. cit.* (Note 13), Vol. 5, cols. 1478-1484; also L. Thunberg, "The Cosmological and Anthropological Significance of Christ's Redeeming Work," in *The Gospel and Human Destiny*, *op. cit.* (Note 13), pp. 64-89.

45. G. Söhngen, as cited by Gloege (as in Note 44), col. 1480.

46. On further aspects of these three lines of interpretation—apocalyptic, metaphysical and existential-subjective, cf. Harrisville, *op. cit.* (Note 39), pp. 52-57.

47. "Creation and History," *op. cit.* (Note 13), p. 17.

48. *Genesis*, *op. cit.* (Note 15), p. 46.

49. "Creation and History," *op. cit.* (Note 13), pp. 14-15.

50. *Genesis Accounts of Creation*, *op. cit.* (Note 29), p. 4.

51. "Creation and History," *op. cit.* (Note 13), p. 13.

52. R. Prenter, *Creation and Redemption*, Philadelphia, 1967, p. 199.

53. "Creation and History," *op. cit.* (Note 13), p. 23.

54. *Ibid.*; cf. Prenter, *op. cit.* (Note 52), pp. 194-195.

55. While the formula that "the last times will recapitulate the primeval times" (consummation = protology) is a handy one, it must not be overlooked that in some passages (even Revelation 21, for all its harking back to Old Testament details), *Endzeit* is "more than" *Urzeit*, just as Christ is "more than" the temple.

56. "Creation and History," *op. cit.* (Note 13), p. 15, cf. 16-17 and 22-24. For von Rad's view, cf. his *Theology*, *op. cit.* (Note 19), 1, pp. 126 ff. Westermann's stance is reflected in his commentary on Genesis and in other writings; cf. his *Schöpfung*, "Themen der Theologie," 12, Stuttgart-Berlin, 1971, especially pp. 165-175.

57. The phrase is attributed to H. Gese.

58. Cf. G. Bornkamm, "Baptism and New Life in Paul (Romans 6)," trans. by P. L. Hammer, in *idem*, *Early Christian Experience*, New York, 1969, pp. 71-86.

59. A reworking of the theme of "stewardship" seems to me in order, on the basis of both "creation" and "redemption" (God's universal work of blessing and his particularized work of salvation).

Chapter 4

The Historicity of the Scriptures and the Witness to the One Gospel

I.
The Reformation Understanding of the Scriptures

1. The two Reformation axioms

The Reformation began with a radical change in the understanding of the Scriptures. Whereas, for the medieval church, the Bible was just a part of the church's system of teaching which could only be interpreted rightly in harmony with the dogmatic tradition as a whole, for the Reformation it became the norm and critical counterpart of the Church's teaching. This change was a consequence of Luther's Reformation discovery: if the Gospel of God's justice, which he came upon in the Letter to the Romans, was the news of the forgiving love with which God approaches the sinner and not, as the church's tradition taught, the doctrine of God's retaliatory, punitive justice,[1] then the primary task of theology had to consist of setting this message of the Scriptures critically against the tradition which distorted and obscured it. As this approach was further developed, two main insights came to light which can reasonably be described as the basic axioms of the Protestant understanding of the Scriptures.

The first was the insight into the *historicity of the Gospel*. For Luther, the Gospel is not a doctrine unrelated to time and place but an event in which God acts in history. And this event has both a past and a present component: "So you see that the Gospel is a history (historia) about Christ, the Son of God and of David, who died, rose and was appointed Lord, and this is the shortest summary (summa summarum) of the Gospel."[2] According to this, the Gospel declares

God's saving acts in the past history of Jesus. But at the same time it is the present action of God because it takes place in the form of the word which is preached and which declares the salvation intended for the believer: "However, the Gospel can be and is nothing other than a proclamation of Christ, the Son of God and of David, who was God and man and who, through his death and resurrection for us has conquered sin, death and hell for all those who believe in him."[3]

The other insight which proved to be fundamental to Luther's understanding of the Scriptures is that into the *unity of the Gospel witnessed to by the Scriptures.* It is a more or less direct consequence of the first: for, if God's saving action which is contained in the Gospel can be clearly identified in history and declared to me in an equally unambiguous way, it follows that the outwardly different expressions of the Gospel in the Scriptures agree in essence and serve to interpret one another. It is not necessary to use tradition first in order to make sense of the Scriptures which as such are obscure; rather, under the guidance of the Spirit, the various statements in the Scriptures fit together for the Christian in such a way that he receives unambiguous, clear and intelligible direction. "This means that it (Scripture) is itself the clearest, easiest (facillima) and most intelligible, its own interpreter (sui ipsius interpres), proving, judging and shedding light on everything, as is written in Psalm 119. . . . Here it is clear that the Spirit gives enlightenment and teaches that insight comes only from the words of God. . . ."[4]

Even Luther was, of course, not able completely to maintain the tension between these two axioms. His well-known difficulties with the Letter of James were derived from the fact that the latter's doctrine of justification constituted a real, irreconcilable contradiction of Paul's: "There is a contradiction between 'Faith justifies' and 'Faith does not justify.' If anyone can make sense of these together, I shall put my biretta on his head and let him scold me for being a fool."[5] Thus here Scripture did not interpret Scripture; the different statements in the Letter of James and the Letter to the Romans did not complement one another to constitute the unity of the Gospel. Only a radically historical interpretation could have been of help here because it would have shown that Paul and James both belonged to quite different historical settings and represented quite different traditions within the history of Early Christianity. Although Luther's approach did provide the systematic requirements for such an interpretation, the practical possibilities for really carrying it out were not yet available to the exegesis of the 16th century. Thus Luther and his criticism remained within the framework of the second axiom and he tried to demonstrate that James, according to objective criteria of content, made no contribution to the preaching of the Gospel and therefore fell below the (equally objective but not historically determined) norm of the apostolic.[6]

Post-Reformation Protestantism then made the second axiom completely absolute and relegated the insight into the historicity of the Gospel to the sidelines. Thus the Scriptures became an ahistorical compendium of doctrine from which the exegete believed that he could derive the eternally valid and binding truth of pure doctrine by an appropriate combination of various statements and loci. The question of the sense in which the one Gospel could be comprehended precisely by virtue of the historical imprints on the testimony of the Scriptures remained unanswered.

2. *The causes of the crisis*

Therefore the development of the modern historical awareness which began in the eighteenth century took the Reformation churches by surprise. A profound crisis began at that time which has now lasted for two centuries and the end of which is by no means in sight yet. It became quite obvious that the Holy Scriptures were not a self-contained entity, isolated from the rest of the world, but that their individual elements were influenced to a large extent by the concepts of the world and the religious and mythological presuppositions of the period when they were written. The inner unity of the Scriptures also became clearly no less questionable than their historical credibility. As historical criticism progressed, they disintegrated into a bundle of heterogeneous historical accounts, cultic and legal traditions, between which it was scarcely possible to identify any continuity either of thought or of language.

In the twentieth century this crisis was made more acute by the ecumenical dialogue between the churches. As the churches of different confessions came to know one another better, there was a growing recognition of the fact that the doctrinal differences between them were not mainly a consequence of deviations from the Scriptures but, on the contrary, of different uses of the Scriptures.[7] But what about the unity of the Gospel to which the Scriptures bore witness if it could be claimed to be the point of departure for widely differing historical traditions?

3. Attempts at a solution

There has been no lack of theological attempts to surmount this crisis. They all share the aim to establish a balance between the scientific understanding of the complex historical processes which have resulted in the emergence of the Holy Scriptures and the conviction that only a uniform Gospel can be the basis and norm of the church's faith. These theological endeavors, irrespective of the wide range of differences between them, can quite easily be reduced to three basic types.

Historical reduction. This refers to the attempt to use the methods and criteria of historical science to obtain a reliable body of basic data from the divergent material of the Scriptures and to identify it with the Gospel which is normative for the church. Beneath the quicksand of changing ideas, theologies and interpretations a search is made for the original rock which can still serve as a firm foundation today.[8] And it is appropriate to the historical emphasis in this approach that this original rock is sought predominantly in the earliest identifiable form of Jesus' preaching. Similarly, the theologians of the Enlightenment believed that they would find an answer to their question about the true and genuine heart of Christianity in the history and teachings of Jesus,[9] although, unknowingly and because they lacked adequate hermeneutical resources, instead of finding the historical Jesus they evolved an ideal image which reflected the taste of their particular period.[10]

Thanks to a more subtle method of investigation the Life-of-Jesus theology today will no longer succumb so easily to this danger. However, the problem which it essentially faces is that of continuity since, if the later preaching of the post-Easter church is *de facto* no use as a basis for continuity because it obscures rather than illuminates the authentic image of Jesus, it is necessary to identify a reliable constant which would make an encounter between man of the present and Jesus of Nazareth, who lived in a quite different cultural climate, possible and meaningful.[11]

Such difficulties can be avoided if, instead of making the historical Jesus the goal of historical reduction, the issue at stake is that of the oldest form of the Christian message and this is set up as the norm. The kerygma of the apostles, i.e., of those who were gathered immediately around the historical event of revelation, can then be taken as the basis of the faith and contrasted with any later preaching of the church. Thus W. G. Kümmel believes that any reflection on the normative witness of the New Testament should aim at distinguishing the three earliest forms of the New Testament kerygma, namely the preaching of Jesus, the preaching which interpreted the life and death of Jesus and witnessed to his resurrection in the early church and in Pauline theology: "If as a result of strictly historical theological study it can be demonstrated that a basically uniform proclamation is the result of taking these three oldest forms of the New Testament kerygma together, then we have identified a central message against which the rest of the testimony of the New Testament can be measured."[12] If the original apostolic tradition is thus something like the canon within the canon, the "rest of the testimony of the New Testament," for its part, is further interpretation by the church and of only secondary relevance.

This solution attempted by numerous different theologians proved to be so suggestive that it was adopted to a large extent by Section II of the Fourth World Conference on Faith and Order (Montreal, 1963) in its report on "Scripture, Tradition and Traditions."[13] One of the central statements of this report says, "Thus we can say that we exist as Christians by the Tradition of the Gospel (the *paradosis* of the *kerygma*) testified in Scripture, transmitted in and by the church through the power of the Holy Spirit."[14] The content of this Tradition is "the revealed truth of the Gospel"[15] and its criterion is that it came from the apostles. And it precedes the Scriptures in the same way as they existed before the interpretation which began in the post-apostolic period and which gave rise to the various church traditions, since "Tradition in its written form, as Holy Scripture (comprising both the Old and the New Testament), has to be interpreted by the Church in ever new situations."[16]

But there are serious objections to this approach, and they are of a both historical and theological nature. For example, the criteria used to effect historical reduction are anything but clear. It is just as difficult to separate the apostolic kerygma from the Scriptures as a whole as the preaching of Jesus, because early Christianity, for reasons which have still to be explained, declined to use Jewish rabbinical methods of transmission. Moreover, the category of the apostolic is clearly unsuitable as a category for historical criticism. Paul and his doctrine are never merely a counterpart to the church; rather, they represent the preaching of the church to a large extent when he comments on and interprets existing traditions and statements (e.g., Philippians 2:8; 1 Corinthians 11:26). And on the other hand it is very probable that non-apostolic writings in the New Testament, like the Letter to the Hebrews and the Gospel of John, have elaborated traditions which go back to the generation of the apostles. Apart from this, the terminology of Montreal is treacherous in the sense that it makes "Tradition" into a term which is set above the Gospel ("the Tradition" of the Gospel).[17] Thus the Gospel is basically defined as a complex of doctrinal and confessional statements which can be derived from the Scriptures by historical reduction, and this may do justice to the approach of I Corinthian 15:1 but not to that of Galatians 1:12. In other words, this reduction of the Gospel to a particular body of tradition does not take sufficient account of its nature as a powerful saving event which comes from God and is always intended for historical people. The testimony to the Gospel in the Scriptures is primarily, as we must demonstrate, a witness to an experience of salvation; but this can in no way be reduced to transmissible kerygmatic statements.

Selection with a view to a kerygmatic principle. Primarily theologians who have recognized the inadequacy of formal, historical criteria to define what the Gospel is, try to find a solution by adopting a method of criticism based exclusively on theological criteria. In doing so they follow on from Luther's second axiom mentioned above by trying to identify "whatever witnesses to Christ"[18] in the kerygma and historical diversity of the Scriptures and, on the other hand, by relegating to the sidelines anything which obscures the Gospel rather than helping to express it. Thus a "canon within the canon"[19] is created which may draw its essential emphasis—according to the judgment of the various exegetes—either from Jesus' proclamation of the Kingdom of God with its liberation of man, or from the Pauline doctrine of justification and his theology of the cross[20] or from the Johannine doctrine of incarnation. This is not only an elegant solution to the problem of the essential contradictions even in the earliest "apostolic" kerygma; it also appears to do justice to the nature of the Gospel as an event in words which directly affects and makes demands on man.

But this is at the expense of the historical wealth of the Scriptures! This in fact constitutes a revocation of the early church's decision about the canon which was taken in conscious opposition to the tendency embodied by Marcion toward a selection from the content of the testimonies handed down from the first generation.[21] Moreover, the question must here be asked as to whether such reduction corresponds to the intentions of the Biblical witnesses whose authority is invoked: did Paul or John try to formulate an eternally valid expression of the Gospel or were they not far more concerned to give expression to their experience of salvation for the benefit of certain historical situations by using the appropriate linguistic means in each particular case?

Integration of the Scriptures. A quite different approach predominates where there is a church-centered view of salvation history, as is the case primarily in Catholic theology. According to this view the unity of the Gospel is not to be found *in* the Scriptures but *beyond them,* namely in the church which embraces and embodies all the possibilities of Christian faith and life.[22] Here the historical diversity of the early Christian testimonies is not felt to be a threat to the unity of the Gospel. On the contrary, this view seems to make an unconditionally positive attitude to the results of historical-critical research really possible. The fact that there was a Palestinian and a Hellenistic kerygma in early Christianity, that the New Testament contains Paul as well as James, John as well as Luke, and the Letter to the Hebrews as well as Revelation, becomes evidence of the wealth of possibilities open to the church.[23] The church is able to put together the variety of testimonies and doctrinal statements contained in the Scriptures to create the overall unity which runs through them but had not yet been manifested. The dogmatic Constitution of the Second Vatican Council[24] on divine revelation also sees the place of the Scriptures in the church along precisely these lines: "This tradition which comes from the apostles develops in the church with the help of the Holy Spirit. For there is a growth in the understanding of the realities and the words which have been handed down. . . . For, as the centuries succeed one another, the church constantly moves forward towards the fullness of divine truth until the words of God reach their complete fulfillment in her."[25]

If the Scriptures thus provide all the possibilities available to the church, they are themselves nothing more than a function of the church which uses them to design its own future. "Her normative function for the future Church was exercised precisely *by* reducing to writing her *paradosis,* her faith, her self-constitution. Conversely, her production of the Scriptures came about precisely as the form in which she constituted herself the normative law for the Church's future course."[26] It is obvious that the insights of recent research into the history of the tradition, according to which the church's interpretation of the events of its own life constituted the initial stages of the development of the early Christian tradition, will fit into this view without any difficulty.

On the other hand, if this were true, it would be the definitive refutation of the Reformation view of the Scriptures, which maintains that the Gospel witnessed to in the Scriptures is a critical counterpart to the church and to the traditions at work within it. A Gospel that was only "a part of the expression of the life of the early church"[27] would find it difficult to exert a normative influence on the church of the present. And even the attempt to find the unity of the Gospel in the Scriptures would be a useless undertaking, because anything that the exegete might find would be at best fragments of the Gospel pointing to a future unity.

Such systematic logic should not, of course, affect the historian's judgment. He has cause rather to raise the critical question whether this approach does not ignore the fact that the early Christian witnesses who speak through the Scriptures were always concerned to express the whole of the Gospel in their particular situations and not merely a part of it, which would only be justified by an overarching whole. Irrespective of the potential diversity of linguistic media which precludes the absolutising of one particular linguistic expression of the Gospel, it is understood as an essential unity by the most important New Testament witnesses. The vigor of Paul's disagreements with the Judaisers in Galatia and the Gnostic enthusiasts in Corinth would be incomprehensible if it had only been a matter of a choice between different possible expressions of the church's life and not between the acceptance or rejection of God's saving acts!

This brief and necessarily simplified outline of the question may make clear that the real problem, the cause for differing positions, is that of the Gospel and its unity. The acceptance of the historicity of the New Testament as a document is shared today by almost all church traditions as a consequence of the widespread recognition of the results of historical-critical research. But it does certainly cause a crisis in the understanding of Scripture in so far as it renders an over-hasty identification of the Gospel with the New Testament, which has become Scripture, impossible and urgently raises the question what really constitutes the Gospel.

It is therefore also certainly no coincidence that the discussion of the canon, which has been conducted in recent years not only in the various churches but also at the ecumenical level, has not produced any notable results.[28] Hardly anyone today would disagree that the New Testament canon is a selection made according to very unclear criteria, of heterogeneous early Christian writings. However, the debate still continues on the sense in which this selection of the canon was suitable for giving the successive generations of the church access to the Gospel. But a decision on this is only possible on the basis of reflection on *what the Gospel is* according to the New Testament witnesses and *how it works.*

The following reflections will therefore also be devoted to this subject. Does the way in which the witness to the Gospel took place at the beginning of Christian history indicate any constitutive structural characteristics which shed light on the particular way the tradition was constituted, the final result of which we have before us in the canon of the New Testament? Thus we regard the New Testament as the outcome of a development, the inherent motive forces of which have to be identified.

II.

The New Testament as Witness to the Gospel in History

1. The Gospel which has become the Scriptures

"If a Christian about the year 100 A.D. had been asked whether his congregation had a holy and binding book of divine relevation, he would have answered the question proudly and unhesitatingly in the affirmative: the church possessed such books, the Law and the Prophets, known today as the Old Testament. For more than a hundred years, and even in Justin's writings about the middle of the second century, the Old Testament was seen as the only determinative and quite adequate holy book of the church, which the Jews who rejected the Christians were therefore wrong to invoke in their defence."[29] The New Testament was thus not considered as Holy Scripture, i.e., as a body of normative, sacred tradition to be placed alongside and of the same value as the Old Testament, during the period when the limits of its canon were being defined. In addition, since it is in no way self-evident in view of the way early Christianity was rooted in Judaism, attention must be drawn to the fact that there is also a complete lack of any beginnings of a normative interpretation of the Old Testament in analogy to that of the Pharisaic teachers of the Torah. The elaborate technique of the rabbis for memorizing and handing down and the way the disciples of Jesus treated their tradition are worlds apart![30] Even occasional references such as we find in 1 Corinthians 11:23 and 15:2 f., for example, cannot obscure this fact. Here Paul is referring to determinative traditions which are common to the whole Church and he even uses rabbinic terms for tradition (*paralambanein* and *paradidonai*), but in neither place are the traditions he mentions quoted literally; rather they are intermingled in an almost inseparable way with the apostle's own interpretation. And Paul is by no means the only one to take such liberties. To quote only one example, if one compares the various versions of the accounts of the Lord's Supper (I Corinthians 11:23-26; Mark 14:22-25; Matthew 26:26-20; Luke 22:15-20), the wide variety within the tradition, in this case a consequence of the liturgical needs of different congregations, becomes apparent. This free use of a tradition which was fundamental to the life of the church speaks in an unmistakable way.

The earliest testimonies themselves leave us in no doubt about the central impulse which determined the development leading up to the New Testament when they describe one of the determinative expressions of the life of the growing church with the words *euangelion* and *euangelizesthai*. Here, and not in the terms for tradition which are undoubtedly also present, we probably have the key to the history of the early Christian literature,[31] but this could of course only be demonstrated by a more detailed examination of the history of the terms.[32] Here we can only limit ourselves to a few references.

2. The structure of the Gospel of the Early Church

Deutero- and Trito-Isaiah above all constitute the *initial Old Testament basis*. Thus Isaiah 52:7 refers to the herald (mebǎsser; Greek *euangelizomunos*) who comes to the waiting inhabitants of Jerusalem to "bring good news (masmi ǎ Salôm mebǎsser tôb), the news of deliverance, calling to Zion, 'Your God is king.'" And in Isaiah 61:1 the prophet describes himself as the herald sent by Yahweh whose responsibility it is to announce comfort and deliverance to the people: "He has sent me to bring good news (lebasser; Greek *euangelizesthai* to the humble, to bind up the broken hearted, to proclaim liberty to captives and release to those in prison; to proclaim a year of the Lord's favor and a day of the vengeance of our God" (cf. Psalms 40:10; Psalms 68:11). The Greek Old Testament may lack the theological use of the noun *euangelion* and yet, as P. Stuhlmacher has recently demonstrated, the writings of post-biblical Judaism also supply evidence of the use of the noun *besorah* as a religious term (e.g., Numbers Rabbah 14:4; Sifrei Deuteronomy 32:4 pg. 307; Megillath Taanith 12; General Rabbah 50:2), and this everywhere "in the sense of a liberating message of deliverance in general, of angelic messages, of revelatory preaching and, in an almost technical sense, of prophetic messages of salvation and disaster."[33]

Whether Jesus adopted this terminology and described himself in Isaiah 57:2 and 61:1 as the bearer of the eschatological message of comfort and salvation cannot be proved with certainty because there are varying views of the authenticity of Matthews 11:4-6 (Q).[34] But in any case *Gospel* as an established term can already be found in *pre-Pauline traditions:* thus the hellenistic Jewish Christian missionary preaching to the Gentiles is called *to euangeliou tou theou.* (I Thessalonians 2:2) and its accomplishment *euangelizesthai* (Acts 14:15; Hebrews 6:1). The main concern here—and it is important to emphasize this—as is made clear by the summary of the content of the preaching (I Thessalonians 1:9f), is not to impart information about certain facts but to announce an act of God that was taking place: God makes Himself known to the Gentiles as the One who has claims on them by calling them to leave their idols and confronting them with the reality of judgment and salvation. Just as in Isaiah 52:7 and 61:1, the addressees here are drawn into an eschatological event initiated by God.[35]

What made this event possible was, however, the history of Jesus; thus the *euangelion tou theou* becomes of necessity the *euangelion Iesou Christou.* The Gospel requires historical explanation, as can be seen above all in connection with the old creedal statement in I Corinthians 15:3b-5. Here the present is related to the past, not only by the review of the decisive events in the life of Jesus but, above all, by the deliberate use of the title "Christ" which claims that Jesus is the promised one who fulfills the history of Israel. But this history which is fulfilled by Jesus is precisely not set up as an object to be contemplated from a distance; rather it is explained as relating to the church of the present: thus the climax of the statement is its affirmation of the saving significance of the death of Jesus ("died for our sins, in accordance with the scriptures," v. 3) and its reference to the witnesses who make known the present power of the Risen One (". . . appeared to Cephas, and afterwards to the Twelve," v. 5b). Therefore the Gospel, according to I Corinthians 15:1-5, can basically be described as the proclamation of the historical saving acts which God performs for the benefit of the congregation. The individual historical reminiscences of Jesus' life, which are listed in 1 Corinthians 15:3 bf. and which may be based on more detailed reports and traditional accounts,[36] do not themselves constitute the "Gospel" but rather the act which brings people to understand that this past history relates to them and to allow it to become a powerful force to change their lives.[37]

We can see the *structure of the Gospel* most clearly *in Paul's writings*. The Gospel for him is God's eschatological saving action taking place through words by means of which past history shows itself to be effective in the present. These two aspects—the present eschatological event and the effect of remembering things past—cannot be separated; rather they are interdependent. This is made especially clear by the opening sentences of the letter to the Romans (Romans 1:1-7) : on the one hand the Gospel is seen here as a contemporary event in the sense of Isaiah 52:7: it is set in motion by God's choosing the apostle as his appointed messenger ("apostle by God's call, set apart for the service of the Gospel," v. 1) , and its achieves its aim by bringing about "obedience in all nations" (v. 5). But on the other hand the Gospel has a content, namely Jesus Christ and his history (v. 3f). In fact the Gospel only achieves its aim when the nations of the world in the obedience of their faith experience as their own the history which God has brought about and enter into it.

Thus a reminder of things past is certainly constitutive of the Gospel but their mere reproduction is not the Gospel. Paul refers back to a fixed body of catechetical material which he calls "tradition" (*paradosis:* 2 Thessalonians 2:15; 1 Corinthians 11:2).[38] It can probably be assumed that the content of this tradition included the tradition of Jesus (cf. e.g., I Corinthians 7:25; 11:23; II Corinthians 4:5; Romans 15:3) to a much greater extent than is immediately discernible from the apostle's letters. But he does not call this material "Gospel"; it only becomes the Gospel when it becomes an integral part of the saving event to the service of which the apostle has been appointed. Thus it is no contradiction for Paul to admit, on the one hand, that he depends on others for the traditions which he represents (Galatians 2:2) but, on the other hand, to claim that he did not receive his Gospel from men but "through a revelation of Jesus

Christ" (Galatians 1:12). Paul does not claim to be an apostle of Jesus Christ because he stands at the head of a line of tradition but because the exalted Christ has called him to be the bearer and exponent of a universal event (Galatians 1:1; 1:15f.).

This event does have a particular historical structure: Paul knows he is the bearer of the Gospel for the Gentiles (Romans 1:5 and 14; Galatians 2:7). This corresponds to the Gospel for the Jews on the other hand with Peter as its exponent. In what respects do the two forms of the Gospel differ? And is not their coexistence, which was legalised by the agreement between Paul and the church in Jerusalem, contradicted by Paul's own emphatic claim that there could not be "another Gospel" than the one which he proclaimed (Galatians 1:6)?

This much is probably certain: the difference between the Petrine Jerusalem Gospel and the Pauline Gentile Christian Gospel can hardly have resided in the historical material which each of them used. Both Galatians 2:7 and I Corinthians 15:3ff. indicate that there was agreement on this, indeed that Paul considered this agreement essential. The difference lay more in the way in which this material was expounded for the different historical addressees. The "framework of interpretation and meaning in which the statements about Christ the Messiah"[39] were seen and interpreted was different in each case. The Jerusalem Christians emphasized the Gospel as God's saving action within the historical setting of Judaism, and did so probably by proclaiming Jesus as the eschatological fulfillment of Israel's hope of salvation. Paul, because of his calling, had to approach the Gentiles in their historical setting; there the Gospel could only be shown to be a saving event by demonstrating that Jesus had started the eschatological victory over all barriers. As "the saving power of God" (Romans 1:16) the Gospel could only reach the Gentiles if it was a Gospel free of laws, which annulled all the human means of seeking and hoping for salvation and pointed only to God's unconditional concern for his creation in Jesus Christ.

Since part of the historicity of the Gospel is its interpretation for the particular situation of real men, there could therefore be no other Gospel for the Galatians than the Gospel free of laws which Paul had preached to them. Even though another Jewish Christian Gospel existed alongside it, that was of no significance for them. The only Gospel for them was the one which spoke to their situation (Galatians 2:6). To reject it—perhaps even on the grounds that the "other" Gospel was based on a more reliable tradition and was closer to the historical source—implied a denial of the historical form of the Gospel as a whole.

This makes it clear *that the Pauline doctrine of the law and of the justification of the godless is not merely a consequence of the Gospel but one of its integral parts.* The error of a number of modern exegetes[40] is an error already committed by the Galatians, who tried to find the Gospel in a complex of authorized, normative expressions of the tradition and believed that on this basis they could disqualify the Pauline proclamation of justification as an irrelevant addition.

On the other hand there is an historical fact, the importance of which can hardly be overestimated: that the "pillar" apostles in Jerusalem condoned the particular form of the Pauline Gospel for the Gentiles (Galatians 2:9) .[41] For this was at least an admission in principle that the Gospel could not be limited to a repetition of facts and doctrines but that it is, rather, an event which interprets itself to contemporary historical situations. This concession, which probably went far beyond the normal practice of the Jerusalem Christians themselves, can only have been possible because they remembered that it corresponded to the structure of Jesus' own preaching.

3. The preaching of Jesus as a basis for the structure of the Gospel

One of the salient characteristics of Jesus' preaching is that facts and interpretation are interwoven within it. It is not an objective communication but constitutes rather an event which speaks to people in particular situations and provokes their reaction. Its main emphasis is on the aspect of communication.

Thus, although Jesus proclaimed the immediate proximity of the Lordship of God, he refused to state the time when the eschatological events would begin (Mark 13:32) . Unlike the apocalyptic interpreters of history in his time, he did not give his followers a view of the world and of history in objectifiable facts and data but called upon them to be alert and obedient (Mark 13:35; Matthew 24:42-50) .

As was the case with the apocalyptic interpretations of history, Jesus also avoided the messianic expectations of his time. He did claim an authority for himself which almost demanded a Christological explanation, as for example in his interpretation of the law (Matthews 5:17) and in his claims on his followers (Mark 8:38) , and yet he resisted the demand for a visible justification of this claim (Matthews 12:38-42; parallel Luke 11:29-32): the only sign that the world around receives from him is "the sign of Jonah," i.e., the call to conversion! Thus there seems to be much to indicate that Jesus did not apply any of the contemporary messianic titles to himself (except perhaps the title 'son of man' but this appears in the possibly authentic passages not as a direct expression of sovereignty but enveloped in paradoxical enigmas, e.g., in Matthews 8:20; Mark 2: 28). From the very beginning he thus precluded any possibility of making his appearance into an objectifiable fact by fitting it into an existent category of interpretation. His identity is not discovered by anyone who wants to know something about him but only by those who are prepared to allow him to change their lives. Faith is the only appropriate attitude for men to adopt when they meet him (Matthew 8:10; parallels Luke 7:9; Mark 9:24).

Accordingly there is a striking predominance of the use of parables in Jesus' preaching. The parables of Jesus are forms of communication which have as their particular characteristic the fact that they do not impart certain obvious facts about the Lordship of God to the hearers but expect them to enter into a process of understanding and deciding, the outcome of which is quite open in each case.[42] Thus the choice of each image constitutes a presumption upon the addressee which he may reject. When Jesus, for example, compares God's acts with those of a Palestinian shepherd who devotes all his energies to looking for the sheep missing from his flock (Luke 15:4-7), this is a challenge to the hearer to accept this image as appropriate to the matter in question and to reject as inappropriate others which have influenced his attitude to it so far. If the communication process succeeds it is not because of the pungency of the image which can demonstrate something to the hearer but simply because the listener is prepared to accept that Jesus vouches for the appropriateness of the image with his activity and appearance. Thus the parable is intended to bring the hearer to see that the history of Jesus is right with reference to God and his acts.

If, as the Gospels probably report with historical accuracy, Jesus spoke about his death to his disciples (cf. Mark 8:31; 9:31; 10:33f.), the same thing must apply here. In the announcements of his passion, his death is not in fact presented as a meaningful fact of obvious significance but as an enigmatic, obscure event: "the Son of Man had to undergo great sufferings, and to be rejected" (Mark 8:31a). This event could be interpreted as the definitive failure of the history of

Jesus—and the disciples at first identified themselves with this interpretation (Mark 8:32; 14:50). Only for those who are prepared to start with God in interpreting the history of Jesus can this end become an event through which Jesus' mission reaches its goal.

4. Easter as the starting point of the Gospel

But Jesus did not only prefigure the structure of the Gospel by his preaching; by his history he provided it with its content! The sense in which this happened can be deduced from the testimony to the resurrection. The appearances of the Risen Lord made the witnesses certain that God Himself did not abandon Jesus to death; He did not disprove the history of this man but supported it by making it explicitly his own history. Jesus of Nazareth and the course of his life were set free at Easter from the ambiguity of all historical phenomena and subjected to a clear judgment of God. Hence one can really claim that the resurrection is the central and unsurpassable interpretation of the history of Jesus. Through it, God enables people to take their stand on the foundation of the history of Jesus in faith, action, and hope. In this sense the resurrection of Jesus is the starting point of the Gospel as a saving event.

We shall now develop this briefly to distinguish it from some frequent misinterpretations.

The testimony to the resurrection is not an attempt to provide historical proof for an observable fact belonging to the past. Such proof would be absurd from the point of view of our modern understanding of history which makes all events in the past subject to the criterion of possible analogy to the framework of reality known to us; even according to the judgment of the first witnesses it would not do justice to the nature of the resurrection. In I Corinthians 15:1-11 Paul in no way intends to submit a historical proof of the resurrection;[43] rather he wishes to demonstrate that there is a uniform witness to the resurrection event in the church which excludes interpretations such as those current in Corinth. Accordingly the oldest Gospel ends with the empty tomb (Mark 16:8): what then follows cannot be told as a past fact in Mark's view. It requires another form of expression, namely that of witness!

Similarly the testimony to the resurrection is not the announcement of a mere "that" of God's acts. It is not only a call to men to overcome the scandal of the cross and to relate it to their own existence as judgment and salvation from God.[44] Rather it is related to

Jesus' history *as past history* and, beyond that, to the whole history of Israel. For the event of Easter becomes a mere declamation if it does not reveal how God's acts bring the history of Jesus into force as a history affecting the world and thus at the same time open up this history in such a way that I can make my life a part of it.

While history is thus an integral part of the testimony to the resurrection, it must be emphasised at the same time that this can only be *interpreted history*. The testimony to the resurrection is in fact by no means synonymous with a mere inauguration of a reminder of Jesus of Nazareth and his history. When the first witnesses referred to the raising of Jesus, this was for them by no means a way of expressing their determination to continue to support the "concerns of Jesus" despite his death and not to allow them to become a lifeless past.[45] This would have been possible only if they had seen the "concerns of Jesus" as a doctrine independent of his person, a mere communication of facts about God. But since Jesus in his preaching had called people to reply on God's acts and because he had demanded above all that God should be believed with reference to his own behavior, it was impossible to preserve the memory of Jesus without simultaneously answering the question about God's final attitude to the course of his life and his history. As a mere memory the history of Jesus would be disproved by the cross.[46] When looking back it would simply appear as a history whose claim to God proved to be a utopian error because God allowed no room for it in the world. Thus the remembered concerns of Jesus would have neither time nor place in the world, a utopia which could at best be compared with existing circumstances as a "principle of hope" and a "wishful mystery."[47] But in reality, Easter authorizes an interpretation of the history of Jesus which reveals the place of this history in the world and in my life. This is precisely the interpretation provided by the Gospel when it announces God's eschatological saving acts through Jesus to the whole world.

*5. The Gospel as Witness to and Interpretation of the History of
   Jesus*
   The evolution of the Gospel writings. It was apparently only in the early church in Palestine, and even there only for a relatively short space of time, that people were satisfied with handing on the sayings and teachings of the earthly Jesus. The presumed remnant of this way of preaching, "Q," was in fact very soon relegated to second

place by the narrative Jesus tradition and was later absorbed by it in the larger synoptic Gospels (Matthew and Luke). Thus the *formation of the Gospel writings* came about, a form without parallel in the whole of classical literature. That which was already in evidence in the historical data of the kerygma in I Corinthians 15:3b-5 underwent a development as the Jesus tradition was elaborated: the recollection of Jesus' life and behavior was interpreted in the light of the resurrection and thus became "Gospel" (Mark 1:1; 14:9; Matthew 26:13). It would be difficult to deny that the investigation of what Jesus did and said during his earthly life played a certain part in motivating the early church to care for the tradition.[48] This interest in past history undoubtedly differed from that of the modern historian; the concern was not to reconstruct an image of the "Jesus of history" as a person who belonged to a particular period of past history; the question was rather that of the "earthly" Jesus, i.e., of the circumstances of an event which was certainly situated in the past but which was open to the present. Thus the church explains the background to the cross by collecting reports about Jesus' controversies with the representatives of Judaism (Mark 2:1-3, 6; 12:13-27) which show that the outcome of Jesus' life was not a chance fate but the necessary consequence of his activity in Israel. The interest in tradition does not depend here on individual historical coincidence but on the way that Jesus met his death because of a confrontation with the law (Mark 2:23-28). For this demonstrates that in Jesus the conclusive decision was taken about the whole history of Israel.

This attitude is most impressively demonstrated by the oldest account of the death of Jesus (Mark 14:43-16, 8). Here the historical details are almost unrecognizable beneath the layers of Old Testament motifs and references, most of which are taken from the psalm of suffering, Psalm 22.[49] By describing Jesus in this way as the righteous one who suffers, his death is shown to be the fulfillment of the way of obedience marked out by God for Israel.[50] This interpretation comes from the point of view of faith; it is made possible by Easter. But even if the facts which it uses will not stand up to a historian's analysis, it still reveals the meaning and aim of the history of Jesus in a way which would never be possible by making an exhaustive presentation of historically verifiable facts!

In the tradition of the Gospels the past history of Jesus is very often opened up to relate it to the life of the post-resurrection church. Here too the present is not simply projected back into the past: that Jesus did not found the church is just as clearly evident in all the layers of the tradition as is the fact that the way in which the group of disciples lived before Easter could not be continued after Easter in the church without a break (cf. Luke 22:35f.). But the Church does see itself as the fellowship made possible by Jesus' behavior. The fact that he was concerned with the despised and outcasts from the religious community of Israel (Mark 12:13-17; Luke 7:36-50; 19:1-10) is just as important to it as that he set up his unconditional life-for-others as the norm for the behavior of his disciples (Mark 10:38-45).

The Lukan account of the Last Supper (Luke 22:14-38), for example, can show us particularly clearly how this interpretation of the Jesus tradition was applied to the church.[51] Here the actual words of the Last Supper (v. 14-20) are set in the framework of a discourse of Jesus which is obviously geared to the situation of a congregation celebrating the Lord's Supper and discusses its problems: namely the danger of apostasy (v. 22f.) and the struggle for power among the leaders of the congregation (v. 25-28).

Christology as an interpretation of the salvation event. The growing church faced its biggest task of interpretation in the transition from the spiritual setting of Judaism to that of hellenism, i.e., in the preaching mission to the Gentiles—which probably first took place in Antioch. The spiritual home of Jesus and his disciples was the framework of Judaism under the influence of the Old Testament. Even though the knowledge of the Greek language was widespread in the Palestine of the time and there was no lack of influences from hellenistic culture, the frame of reference for all the branches of the early church in Jerusalem remained initially the Old Testament. Over against this, the transition to people who were not familiar with this way of thinking entailed the breaking of new ground. If, as Paul believed, the Gospel was really God's eschatological saving act which concerned all the nations of the world, the attempt had to be made not only to translate the Gospel outwardly into other languages but to interpret it in such a way that it could gain access to the thinking and questions of each recipient. The boldness with which this transition was made can best be seen by looking at the development of *Christology.*

For the oldest post-resurrection church Jesus was the Son of Man, i.e., it identified him with the person expected by apocalyptic Judaism as the eschatological mediator of salvation whose coming from

heaven implied the beginning of the last events. But this attribute
'Son of Man,' perhaps because it was too closely linked with apocalyptic ideas, very quickly gave way to the title *Christos.* And this
happened although Jesus himself had avoided the title "Christ"
(Messiah) according to all historical probability.[52] The outward reason for the adoption of this title was the fact that Jesus had been
crucified because he was accused of being a Jewish pretender to be
the Messiah (Mark 15:26). Why did the early church take upon
itself the risk of making precisely this title, which expressed Jesus'
abysmal failure in the eyes of its Pharisaic opponents, into a positive
description of Jesus' function? The answer can only be: because it
made it possible to situate Jesus' appearance within the framework
of Old Testament expectations of salvation! "The title expresses a
continuity between the task he had to fulfill and the Old Testament."[53] And this means that he is related to history. For people
who think in Old Testament Jewish categories the question of salvation is primarily a question of history. Where late Judaism was
awaiting an eschatological leader (e.g., Psalms of Solomon 17:32;
18:3 f.; IV Ezra 7:28; Manual of Discipline 9:10) he was hoped to
be he who would fulfill God's promise about the history of Israel as
given to the Kingdom of David (II Samuel 7:14). The church answers this question by proclaiming that it is precisely the Crucified
and Humiliated One who is the Christ; in him Israel's history finds
its saving fulfillment (1 Corinthians 15:3).

On the other hand, Paul's writings and the traditions which originated in the Gentile church lead us to make a striking observation:
here the title "Christ" has degenerated into a proper name; its previous main function has been transferred to an attribute that was
already to be found in the church in Palestine (e.g., Mark 1:11;
13:32; Matthew 11:27f.) but which only had a marginal function
there: Son of God *(uios theou)*. And this attribute is linked with a
scheme which appears at first sight to have little to do with the history of the earthly Jesus because of its mythical leanings: it refers to
the coming of the pre-existent Son of God into the cosmos, to his
incarnation and his final exaltation and installation as the Lord of
all authorities and powers (Philemon 2:5-11; Colossians 1:15-20;
Hebrews 1:3f.; I Timothy 3:16). Obviously by adopting this scheme
the Gospel was supposed to provide an answer to the questions of
the hellenists about salvation. What worried them was not the prob-

lem of history but that of the cosmos.[54] They saw themselves as prisoners of a system of authorities and powers and subject to the constraints of fate from which there was no escape. If these people had any conception of salvation then it could only be as of a power which would break open this prison from the outside and set them free. The confession *"Iesous Christos"* was not able to present the Gospel to the hellenists as the act of God which spoke to them and their situation; but this was possible by confessing Jesus as the pre-existent Son of God, who existed before the cosmos, whose incarnation had stripped the cosmos of its power and whose exaltation as Lord had forced all the cosmic powers to their knees so that now "every tongue [can] confess, 'Jesus Christ is Lord' " (Philippians 2:11).

The danger which this interpretation comprised was considerable: if, as was very possible with this scheme, the Gospel abandoned its reference to history, it could easily become a speculative myth or an individualistic doctrine of salvation. It all depended on the Son of God, to whom the pre-existence concept referred, not being misunderstood as an ahistorical symbol of the divine powers available to man but remaining the crucified Jesus of Nazareth. This is probably the reason why Paul corrected the pre-existence concept when he used it by linking it with a reference to the cross (Philippians 2:8; Colossians 1:22). That this by no means banished the danger of an enthusiastic, mythological Christology in the Gentile church is shown clearly enough by the situation in Corinth (I Corinthians 1:18-25; 15:12ff.). Therefore the fact is all the more impressive that the apostle in no way abandoned the pre-existence concept or retreated to a supposedly less dangerous Jewish Christian Christology which was dogmatically guaranteed by the early church in Jerusalem. To be the bearer of the Gospel for the Gentiles really meant that he had to be the interpreter of this Gospel in a new language comprehensible to the Gentiles. And interpretation always entails risks. Anyone who retreats to using a language without risks has to expect not to be understood any more.

6. Apostolate and Gospel

An important question which we have only touched on so far now becomes unavoidable at this point: is this freedom of interpretation not part and parcel of the apostles' special commission and thus restricted to a numerically limited group of people of the first generation? If we look at the statements of Paul, the only apostle whose voice comes directly to us from the New Testament, this question must indeed be answered in the affirmative to a certain extent.

Paul knows himself to be the ambassador of the Risen One (I Corinthians 9:1; Galatians 1:12; Romans 10:14f); this applied not only in the formal sense of the execution of his mission to the Gentiles but also to the content of the Gospel which he had to preach. Thus he understood his task as "priestly service . . . of the gospel of God" (Romans 15:16) and concluded from this, "I will venture to speak of those things alone in which I have been Christ's instrument to bring the Gentiles into his allegiance, by word and deed" (Romans 15:18). In this sense the apostle's words are no longer his own and what he says is the work of the Risen One for the sake of the church, an interpretation of the Gospel through which Christ interprets himself.[55] Following this line Paul is able to make the Exalted Lord the real agent of his preaching; Christ speaks through his ambassador, "Be reconciled to God!" (II Corinthian 5:19ff.; cf. Romans 15:15; I Thessalonians 4:1). This also applies to his ethical instructions when Paul establishes the link between the inherited words of the Lord and the particular present situation by virtue of the authority he has received (I Corinthians 7:10ff. and 16f.). The apostle's instruction makes the word of the Lord relevant in a way which is absolutely binding on the church.

If we relate this to our reflections on the resurrection as an empowerment to interpret the history of Jesus, it can be said that this empowerment applies primarily to the immediate witnesses in so far as they already have a part in this history. They are associated with this history and are therefore able to interpret it as their own. This applies equally to those who are disciples during Jesus' earthly life and to the former persecutor of Christians, Paul.

But of course it is not possible to ignore the fact that Paul also admits in so many words that his congregations possess the Spirit which provides the ability to interpret the Gospel for one's own situation (1 Corinthians 12:4; Romans 12:6).[56] And he expressly recognizes the ministries of prophecy and teaching side by side with the apostolate (I Corinthians 12:28). It is not least to the credit of the historical-critical analysis of the Gospels that it has provided us with material to understand how these early Christian prophets and teachers worked. Many anonymous hands contributed to the transmission and interpretative development of the Jesus tradition. But this all happened in the first generation more or less still under the supervision of the apostles. By virtue of their authority based on their link with the history of Jesus they had the possibility to reject inappropriate interpretations of the Gospel or—as we have seen in the case of Paul—to correct them. This possibility was no longer open to the next generation, for the apostolate came to an end with the death of its bearers. There is no sign in the New Testament of any attempts to continue or institutionalize it in the form of an office to guarantee the interpretation of the Gospel. This is the root of a problem which began to create serious difficulties for the church from the second generation and was only resolved pragmatically by the establishment of the canon which avoided the basic theological questions.

7. Witnessing to the one Gospel as a problem of the post-apostolic period

What norms were to govern the preaching of the Gospel after the death of the apostles and the final collapse of the expectation of the Second Coming? This question was not only raised by the non-realization of the Second Coming and the experience of the passage of time but above all by the development of separate groups which were no longer able to reach agreement even on basic questions. The stereotype warnings about false teachers (e.g., Acts 20:26ff.; I Timothy 6:3-10; II Timothy 3:1-9; II Peter 2:1-22) give us some idea at least of the extent of the crisis at that time.[57]

The attempts to resolve this crisis, which began to be made in the years around the turn of the second century, were by no means uniform. We shall try to outline the most important ones briefly.

The most wide-spread was the *traditionalist approach*. The various interpretations of the Gospel were systematically attributed to the authority of one of the major witnesses of the past. This can be seen, for example, in the strikingly large number of pseudonymous writings of that period, among which the Pastoral Letters are of special interest because they outline a hermeneutic programme corresponding to this approach: Paul was said to have left his Church the *paratheke*—this refers to a fixed body of teaching and interpretation— which it is to preserve unharmed (I Timothy 6:20; II Timothy 1:12) . Whereas the false teachers are always looking for something new and their teaching is the product of their own caprices (I Timothy 1:4; Titus 1:10) , what matters for the Christian is to "keep

before" him what he has "heard" and what has been "put into" his
"charge" (II Timothy 1:14). This guardianship is essentially the
task of the officials to whom the *paratheke* was entrusted at their or-
dination (II Timothy 2:2). But it naturally cannot be ignored that,
in the view of the writer, this also included *de facto* a certain
amount of interpretative exposition: he refers to pastoral exhortation (I Timothy 5:1; 6:2) and warning (II Timothy 2:25; 4:2).[58]
But this is not enough to obviate the impression that central importance for the church's existence is attributed here to the fixed expression of the tradition.

The *Lukan historical account* presents a much more flexible
variety of traditionalism. Here the norm of the Gospel is not a fixed
written body of traditional statements traced back to the authority
of the apostles but the witness of the apostles which refers back to the
history of Jesus. Luke writes his account in order to provide proof
by examining the historical material that the preaching which originated with the apostles and on which his church is based (Luke
1:2) is reliable (1:3) and, conversely, that the apostles (whom he
identifies in a historically inaccurate way with the twelve) are reliable witnesses and guarantors of this history because of their association with the earthly Jesus (Acts 1:21f.; 10:37).[59] Although this
clearly indicates the historical ties of the Gospel which constitute a
corrective to the threatened deviation into an ahistorical myth, it
also leaves the way open for another danger, namely that the Gospel
will become a rigid reminder of historical facts.

The position at the opposite extreme to all forms of traditionalism
is expressed in the *Gospel of John*. It shows the earthly Jesus interpreting himself directly to the present irrespective of any authorities,
institutions or traditions.[60] There is no mention here of a guarantor
for the history of Jesus, except the figure of the beloved disciple who
remains anonymous and whose authority consists only of really
understanding the history of Jesus (13:23f.); this means that he does
not restrict himself to factual evidence but is able to interpret the
meaning of this history (19:35ff.). Indeed, he therefore does not
even need the resurrection as a stimulus to interpretation (20:8f.).
Nor does the church appear as an historical counterpart to revelation; there is simply the group of the disciples who recognize the
truth of Jesus directly through the guidance of the Spirit (16:13)
and hear the voice of the Good Shepherd (10:16).[61] Whenever Jesus
speaks the listener is contemporaneous with him; therefore tradition

as a memory giving access to past events has no independent existence for him.

There may be many reasons why this conception remained a more or less isolated episode in the history of early Christianity. One of them at least must have been the fact that, by concentrating everything on the "now" of Jesus' appearance it distorted the problem of history which is related to differences in times and situations. The interpretation of the history of Jesus which emerges from the Gospel will only become a force which transforms my life if it speaks to me in my concrete setting in history.

Precisely this insight is the starting point for the interpretation of the Gospel adopted by the author of the Letter to the Hebrews, a Christian teacher from around the turn of the century whose name is not known to us.[62] He knew that the Christian life is lived in the movement of history and he therefore took upon himself to accompany the changing historical situation of his congregation with his words: anyone who limits himself only to the doctrines and traditions he has inherited will miss salvation (5:14; 6:4ff.). However, one can also not encounter the word at a timeless distance from one's own historical situation, but only by understanding this situation within the framework of the effect of God's saving action upon it "while that word 'Today' still sounds" (3:13).

Since this unknown teacher devotes himself to the task of interpretation with an intensity comparable only with Paul's, the temporal distance from the beginning is no problem for him. He knows that "in this final age [God] has spoken to us in the Son (1:2) and that these eschatological words of God were expressed historically in the preaching of the witnesses of the first generation (2:3) which is reflected in the creed with which the congregation is familiar (3:1; 4:14; 10:23). For him this takes the place occupied by the call of the Risen Lord for the men of the first generation, because it makes him part of the succession of interpretations which started at Easter.

III.

The New Testament as the Norm for Witnessing to the Gospel in the Church

The Gospel is *historical* in the sense that it expresses God's saving action in history as an event which changes men and the world; it is *one* in the sense that its content is the one Jesus Christ in whom

I am confronted unmistakably clearly with God's acts. These two
Reformation axioms were very quickly confirmed by the New Testament in the course of our considerations. But can they also, as the
Reformers believed, be applied to the New Testament in its written
form? In what sense does this book, with its many layers and lack of
uniformity, highlight the Gospel as the norm which governs the
church? We shall attempt to answer these questions by putting
together the individual observations we have made on the basis of
the New Testament evidence.

As Holy Scripture the New Testament is constantly reminding
the Church anew *that the Gospel is related to history* and at the
same time making clear to it *that it always encounters this Gospel
only as something beyond its control.*

The New Testament canon must not be understood as a rigid
basic principle, nor can the Gospel be identified with the canon as
a whole or with some of its individual parts. The church of the
second century did without historical and theological criteria to a
large extent, when defining the canon, by approving the writings
which were already accepted by the congregations. Its decision has
only to be seen as a fundamental *confession* of the limitation of the
need for normative testimonies in the early period but not as a
definition of the nature of this testimony. For we have seen clearly
enough that the question of the nature of this testimony was already
answered in different ways in the New Testament itself.

The fact that the New Testament canon places a variety of historical expressions of the Gospel side by side is an indication that
this Gospel is not within our control. In other words, it is impossible to identify the Gospel with certain kerygmatic formula, doctrinal statements or historical accounts. What we find in the New
Testament are in each interpretations of the Gospel for particular
situations. But this of course is not to say that the New Testament
canon is the basis of the "multiplicity of confessions"[63] because the
variety of testimonies it contains makes the question of the one
truth impossible.

The parallel existence of different historical interpretations of the
Gospel rather serves to prevent any individual church from considering this Gospel as its own particular doctrine and at the same time
means that in its own situation it can dare to submit to the Gospel
by means of which Christ brings about the unity of his Church in
defiance of the arbitrary power of all human institutions and the

claims to absoluteness of all human doctrines. Similarly, throughout the New Testament the Gospel is seen as something which challenges the church and keeps it moving but which is not in its possession. This is true although it does not require much exegetical effort to trace the individual traditions and kerygmatic statements of primitive Christianity back to their origin in the church. By entering the service of the Gospel these traditions share in its nature as an act of God! Thus at the beginning of the New Testament we do not find the church giving rise to traditions but God working for the church to come into existence through Jesus Christ.[64]

The crisis in the understanding of the Scriptures to which we referred at the beginning was undoubtedly caused by the historical-critical interpretation of the New Testament. While bemoaning the fact that it has called into question things that used to be definite and has relativized supposedly historical certainties, it should however not be overlooked that precisely this historical criticism may well also be able to provide means of surmounting the crisis. By laying bare the historical diversity within primitive Christianity it can save the Church from misinterpreting the New Testament as a law by which the church is bound to rigid doctrines and expressions of the life of a distant past. And it can give the church the courage to recognize the fact that the interrelation of witnessing to a past event and interpreting it for the present, as historical research reveals in the New Testament, corresponds to the nature of the Gospel, and to make it the basic structure of its own preaching.

But the New Testament must remain "the only norm, rule and guideline" for the church not only for the structure of its preaching of the Gospel but also for its content. And this authority over the content has three aspects which must not be viewed in isolation.

The New Testament writings contain the *first testimony* to God's saving action in Jesus Christ. Because the Gospel concerns the history of Jesus of Nazareth, the voices which witness to this history from an immediate temporal and spatial proximity are of special importance. The apostles constitute the basis of the New Testament as the appointed witnesses of the first generation. This is true although direct apostolic authorship can only be claimed with certainty for the authentic letters of Paul. Even the anonymous testimonies of the first generation can at least be considered indirect expressions of apostolic witness.

The New Testament gives us *access to the first phase of the pro-*

cess of interpretation undergone by the Gospel. The early church understood itself to be the outcome of the Gospel preached by the apostles. It "not only proclaimed what it had heard; it conveyed to another situation what it had heard with what it had experienced because of what it had heard."[65] This initial historical experience of living with the Gospel and the first expressions of forms of community based on the Gospel are of special importance to us. Even those who are sceptical about the basic possibility of comparing all historical processes must judge that here forms of historical living in obedience to the Gospel were tried out and that they ranged over a certain number of possibilities. But these should not be misunderstood as examples to be copied uncritically. The wrong ways and decisions of the first generations serve as models because they help us to draw up criteria so that we can share responsibly in the necessary process of interpreting God's saving action for the world of today: this applies for example in the case of how tradition is viewed in the Pastoral Letters or of Paul's political ethics. We are part of a succession of interpretations of God's action in Jesus, beginning with the witnesses to the resurrection—as the Letter to the Hebrews can teach us. Critical listening to what the first witnesses said can help us to find a language in which the saving power of the Gospel will show itself relevant to our age as well.

The New Testament constitutes *the beginning of the history of the influence of the Gospel.* It set in motion a process of understanding and interpretation which involves not only the Christian churches today but also—at least indirectly—the forms of society in the modern world which have been influenced by the Christian tradition. Of course it would not be appropriate to wish to limit the theological relevance of the Scriptures only to their function as the starting point of a general historical process,[66] because the Gospel would thus be merged with universal history and its nature as a saving event relating directly to man in his particular present would be ignored. But the Gospel, precisely because it aims at a concretion appropriate to the situation, does call upon the church to define its position critically in each particular historical situation. One of the most important tasks within this definition of one's own position will be the discovery of and reflection on the traces left in history by past generations as they interpreted biblical traditions.

—Translated by MARGARET A. PATER

NOTES

All Biblical quotations have been taken from the New English Bible.

1. WA 54, 185 f.; cf. on this point P. Stuhlmacher, *Gerechtigkeit Gottes bei Paulus*, Göttingen, 1965, pp. 19-23.
2. WA 10, I, 10.
3. WA, D Bibel 6, 6. Cf. also WA 12, 260.
4. WA 7, 97.
5. WA Ti 5, No. 3292a.
6. "Secondly, that it (i.e., the Letter of James) is intended to teach Christians and in the course of such long teaching it does not once refer to the suffering, resurrection and spirit of Christ; it mentions Christ a number of times but it teaches nothing about him; it only speaks about general belief in God. For it is the responsibility of a true apostle to preach about Christ's suffering, resurrection and ministry and to lay the foundation for this same faith. . . . And this is the true touchstone for judging all books, namely to see whether they promote Christ or not. . . . Anything that does not teach Christ is not apostolic, even if it is taught by Peter or Paul. And whatever witnesses to Christ is apostolic, even if it is done by Judas, Ananias, Pilate or Herod" (WA D Bibel 7, 384). Cf. on this point I. Lønning, *Kanon im Kanon. Zum dogmatischen Grundlagenproblem des neutestamentlichen Kanons*, Oslo and Munich, 1972, pp. 99-105.
7. Thus the report of Section II (Scripture, Tradition and Traditions) of the Fourth World Conference on Faith and Order states: "The traditions in Christian history are . . . expressions and manifestations in diverse historical forms of the one truth and reality which is in Christ." "Loyalty to our confessional understanding of Holy Scripture produces both convergence and divergence in the interpretation of Scripture." (No. 47 and No. 54, quoted from *The Fourth World Conference on Faith and Order. Montreal 1963*, P. C. Rodger and L. Vischer, eds., New York, 1964, pp. 52-54).
8. The expression is that of J. Jeremias (*The Parables of Jesus*, London, 1963, p. 11) who can be considered a major exponent of this program.
9. On the fascination which the criterion of historical unity constituted for the critical theologians of the second half of the 18th century, cf. W. G. Kümmel, *The New Testament: The History of the Investigation of its Problem*, London, 1973.
10. Cf. the famous criticism by A. Schweitzer, *Geschichte der Leben-Jesu-Forschung*, 6th edition, Tübingen, 1951, pp. 631 ff.
11. An equally interesting and disputed start has been made by H. Braun to outline the basis of Jesus' authority. He finds a constant in anthropology and therefore considers it possible for modern man in dialogue with the Jesus tradition to gain insight into certain basic experiences of human existence: here it is a question of the insight "that the Jesus tradition wishes to teach man to see himself as having received everything as a gift" (*Jesus. Der Mann aus Nazareth und seine Zeit*, Stuttgart and Berlin, 1969, p. 171.)
12. W. G. Kümmel, "Notwendigkeit und Grenze des neutestamentlichen Kanons," in E. Käsemann, ed., *Das Neue Testament als Kanon. Dokumentation und kritische Analyse zur gegenwärtigen Diskussion*, Göttingen, 1970, pp. 94 f. (referred to hereafter as "Das NT als Kanon").
13. P. C. Rodger and L. Vischer, *op. cit.* (Note 7), pp. 50-60.
14. *Ibid.*, p. 52 (No. 45).
15. *Ibid.*, p. 52 (No. 49).

16. *Ibid.*, p. 53 (No. 50).
17. *Ibid.*, p. 52 (No. 45); in criticism of this E. Käsemann in *Das NT als Kanon*, p. 350; "Strangely enough this procedure has in no way alarmed the Reformation confessions as it should have done; on the contrary it has met with agreement from many of their representatives as well."
18. See Note 6.
19. Concerning the history and difficulties of this term see I. Lønning, *op. cit.* (Note 6), pp. 16-30, who comes to the conclusion that here "the definite form of the word 'canon' represents the complete technical use of the term to describe the Bible whereas the indefinite form somehow implies a re-institution of the original meaning of the term."
20. Thus E. Käsemann, for example, says (in *Das NT als Kanon*, p. 405) that the justification of the godless is the heart of all Christian proclamation. "Since in it Jesus' message and ministry are presented as the message and ministry of the Crucified One and his glory and lordship are thereby unmistakably distinguished from all other religious statements, proclamation must be considered to be a canon within the canon; it constitutes the criterion for judging the spirits in general, including Christian preaching in the past and the present."
21. H. V. Campenhausen, *The Formation of the Christian Bible*, London, 1972, pp. 147-209.
22. Thus e.g., P. Lengsfeld, "Katholische Sicht von Schrift, Tradition und Kanon," in *Das NT als Kanon*, pp. 213 ff.
23. "The Catholic attitude tries to do justice, without prejudice, to every side of the New Testament: to be catholic, to be open and free towards the whole, all-embracing truth of the New Testament" (H. Küng, "Early Catholicism in the New Testament as a Problem in Controversial Theology," in H. Küng, *The Living Church*, London and New York, 1963, pp. 233-293).
24. From *The Documents of Vatican II*, M. Abbott, ed., London and Dublin, 1966, No. 8, p. 116.
25. *Ibid.*, p. 116 (No. 8).
26. K. Rahner, *Inspiration in the Bible*, New York, 1966, pp. 51-52.
27. P. Lengsfeld, *op. cit.*, p. 215.
28. A representative cross-section of this discussion is contained in the volume edited by E. Käsemann: *Das NT als Kanon* (see Note 12).
29. H. V. Campenhausen, "Die Entstehung des Neuen Testaments," in *Das NT als Kanon*, p. 110.
30. B. Gerhardsson (*Memory and Manuscript*, Uppsala, 1961) of course argues differently, but his attempt to describe the evolution of early Christian traditions on the basis of methods of transmission used by the Jewish Scribes has met with little support among scholars.
31. Thus G. Gillet, *Evangelism. Studien zur urchristlichen Missionssprache*, Dissertation, Heidelberg, 1924 (?), p. 175, quoted from Stuhlmacher, pp. 18 f.
32. J. Schniewind, *Euangelion. Ursprung und erste Gestalt des Begriffes Evangelium*, Gütersloh, 1927-1931; G. Friedrich, article on *"euangelizomai, euangelion*, etc," ThW II, pp. 705-737; O. Michel, article on Evangelium, RAC 6, col. 1107-1170, and, above all, P. Stuhlmacher, *Das paulinische Evangelium, I. Vorgeschichte*, Göttingen, 1968.
33. *Ibid.*, p. 152.
34. Authenticity is supported by, i.a., J. Schniewind (*op. cit.*, p. 25); G. Friedrich (ThW II, pp. 715 ff.); W. Marxsen (*The New Testament as the Church's Book*, Philadelphia, 1972, pp. 89 f.); R. Bultmann (*The History of the*

Synoptic Tradition, Oxford, 1963). However, P. Stuhlmacher (*op. cit.,* pp. 218-225) thinks that this may be a prophecy of the early church to establish the difference from the Baptist's disciples.

35. Stuhlmacher, pp. 258-266.

36. In this connection one might think primarily of stories about Jesus' passion and laying in the tomb and of reports about his resurrection appearances whose 'Sitz im Leben' was catechesis; cf. C. H. Dodd, "The Primitive Catechism and the Sayings of Jesus," in *New Testament Essays: Studies in Memory of Th.W. Manson,* Manchester, 1959, pp. 106-118; P. Stuhlmacher, *op. cit.,* pp. 275 f.

37. This agrees with Luther's statement according to which the Gospel is realized, "when the voice comes and says that Christ is your own in his life, teaching, acts, death, resurrection and everything that he is, has, does and can do" (WA D Bibel 6, 8).

38. L. Goppelt, "Tradition nach Paulus," in *Kerygma und Dogma* 4, 1958, pp. 213-233; J. Roloff, *Apostolat-Verkündigung-Kirche,* Gütersloh, 1965, pp. 83 ff.

39. P. Stuhlmacher, *op. cit.,* p. 280.

40. Thus, for example, according to E. Molland (*Das paulinische Euangelion. Das Wort und die Sache,* Oslo, 1934, p. 63) ". . . the doctrine of justification [is] not the content of the message of the Gospels but its theological consequence." But, against this, Stuhlmacher, *op. cit.,* p. 281.

41. Galatians 2:9 is probably a quotation of an official decision taken at the Council of the Apostles. Thus, in addition to other exegetes, most recently G. Klein, "Galater 2, 6-9 und die Geschichte der jerusalemer Urgemeinde," in G. Klein, *Rekonstruktion und Interpretation,* Munich, 1969, pp. 99-128.

42. E. Fuchs, *Hermeneutik,* 2nd edition, Bad Cannstatt, 1958, p. 221; E. Jüngel, *Paulus und Jesus,* 2nd edition, Tübingen, 1964, pp. 120-139; J. Roloff, "Anamnese und Wiederholung im Abendmahl," in *Erinnern-Wiederholen-Durcharbeiten. Zur Sozialpsychologie des Gottesdienstes,* Y. Spiegel, ed., Stuttgart, 1972, pp. 122 f.

43. Thus, however, R. Bultmann, *Theology of the New Testament,* London, 1952, Vol. I, p. 295.

44. *Ibid.,* pp. 47 ff.

45. Thus W. Marxsen, *Die Auferstehung Jesu als historisches und als theologisches Problem,* Gütersloh, 1964, pp. 34 f.

46. This is very well put by J. Moltmann (*Der gekreuzigte Gott,* Munich, 1972, p. 116): "The real criticism of Jesus' preaching is his history and his end on the cross."

47. Thus E. Bloch, *Atheismus im Christentum. Zur Religion des Exodus und des Reiches,* Frankfurt, 1968, pp. 226 ff.

48. Concerning what follows cf. J. Roloff, *Das Kerygma und der irdische Jesus. Historische Motive in den Jesus-Erzählungen der Evangelien,* Göttingen, 1970.

49. M. Dibelius, *From Tradition to Gospel,* London, 1934.

50. E. Schweizer, *Lordship and Discipleship,* London, 1960.

51. H. Schürmann, *Jesu Abschiedsrede, Lk. XXII, 21-38, 3. Teil,* Münster, 1957.

52. O. Cullmann, *The Christology of the New Testament,* London, 1959, pp. 111 ff.; F. Hahn, *The titles of Jesus in Christology,* London, 1969, p. 161.

53. Cullmann, *op. cit.,* p. 126.

54. E. Schweizer, *op. cit.;* idem, "Das hellenistische Weltbild als Produkt der Weltangst," in *Neotestamentica,* Zürich and Stuttgart, 1963, pp. 15-28.

55. J. Roloff, *Apostolat-Verkündigung-Kirche,* pp. 95 f.

56. L. Goppelt, *op. cit.* (see Note 38), p. 224.
57. On this cf. especially W. Bauer, *Rechtgläubigkeit und Ketzerei im ältesten Christentum*, 2nd edition, Tübingen, 1964.
58. J. Roloff, *op. cit.*, pp. 254 ff.
59. This program, as G. Klein has demonstrated ("Lukas 1, 1-4 als theologisches Programm," in *Rekonstruktion und Interpretation*, Munich, 1969, pp. 237-260), can already be deduced from the prologue to the Gospel, Luke 1:1-4. However, it is not quite clear to me how Klein can link the insights which he has gained here with the assertion that according to Luke the transmission of the normative tradition from the beginning is guaranteed by a principle of apostolic succession (*ibid.*, p. 260). The enquiry in which Luke is involved is aimed only at establishing the link between the first witnesses and the history of Jesus and leaves out of consideration the question of the transmission of the tradition.
60. In this connection cf. E. Käsemann, *Exegetische Versuche und Besinnungen* I, 2nd edition, Göttingen, 1960, pp. 180 f.
61. E. Schweizer, "The Concept of the Church in the Gospel and Epistles of St. John," in *New Testament Essays: Studies in Memory of Th.W. Manson*, Manchester, 1959, pp. 230-245.
62. Cf. my essay on this: "Kommunikation und Rezeption als Probleme eines frühchristlichen Lehrers," in *Die Predigt als Kommunikation*, J. Roloff, ed., Stuttgart, 1972, pp. 75-92.
63. Thus E. Käsemann, "Begründet der neutestamentliche Kanon die Einheit der Kirche?", in *Das NT als Kanon*, p. 131; but on the other hand G. Ebeling, "The New Testament and the Multiplicity of Confessions," in G. Ebeling, *The Word of God and Tradition*, London and Philadelphia, 1968, pp. 148 ff.
64. Not least for this reason the procedure adopted in Montreal of restricting the question of the normativity of the New Testament to the question of the tradition and its origin is problematic.
65. W. Marxsen, "Das Problem des neutestamentlichen Kanons," in *Das NT als Kanon*, p. 243.
66. Thus e.g., W. Pannenberg, "The Crisis of the Scripture Principle," in *Basic Questions in Theology*, London, 1970, Vol. I, pp. 1-14.

III.

THE PASSING ON
OF THE GOSPEL

Chapter 5

The Transmission of the
Gospel in the First Centuries

A thorough study of the transmission of the Gospel across the centuries of history would of necessity require us to deal with the entire history of the church, from its origins to our own day. Tracing the general lines of development, it might then be possible to give an exhaustive, overall response to the question. But even if such a study were possible from the historical point of view, it would require an immense amount of work and is hardly necessary for our purposes, which remain more systematic than historical.

Thus it seems judicious to confine our research to a more limited segment of the history of the church, a period which might be, if not exemplary, at least characteristic of the issue.

The first two centuries of our era are particularly relevant to our question. Indeed, there we can see how the first transmission of the Gospel came about; then how it spread, beginning from Jerusalem, throughout the whole Mediterranean. Never again was the history of Christianity to know such an extensive and rapid expansion as during this period. Characteristically, this transmission was effected in a variety of languages, beginning with Aramaic, and spreading finally to Greek, Latin, and even some eastern languages. The cultures into which the Gospel penetrated were equally varied; it affected the hellenistic Greek and Roman world, reaching down to the common people, slaves and merchants as well as intellectuals.[1]

This first two hundred years is significant for the Gospel's transmission, because it brings us face to face with the brute fact of the dynamic reality of the transmissions. Moreover, the ways in which transmission takes place point to a whole series of responses exerting influence upon the entire subsequent history of the church. For

while these first two centuries attest to an extraordinary expansion
of the Gospel, they also have a fundamental importance for us today
because they show us how transmission was thought through, and
how this led to the elaboration of norms for determining in the
future the conditions of a true and corect transmission of the Gospel,
as opposed to incorrect and falsified transmissions.

In other words, the first two centuries show us how the doctrines
of Scripture and Tradition, as well as their reciprocal relationships,
were born and developed.[2] The whole complex of questions thus
elaborated has perpetuated itself throughout history, in spite of different accents given to the one or the other.

For all these reasons, the study of early Christianity focuses on
a period especially rich and fruitful for our investigation and, therefore, can afford us a variety of interesting and valuable elements for
our systematic reflection.

Before we approach the subject, however, two preliminary remarks
must be made. First of all, it is necessary to try to pinpoint the meaning of the term "Gospel" for early Christianity. Was the word then
as ambivalent as it is today? Did it signify both the "content" of
the Christian proclamation (Jesus Christ and the salvation that he
brings), as well as the "container" (a writing that recounts the life,
death, and resurrection of Jesus of Nazareth)?

Next, it is necessary to question the meaning of the term "transmission." What phenomenon does the word describe? Does it represent a simple and easily understood process? Does it obey certain
general rules? A preliminary analysis is necessary to clarify these
questions.

1. *The Gospel to be Transmitted*

The Greek noun clearly means "Good News," and the verb "to
announce good news." The two terms, from the time of the first
Christians onwards, had a very particular technical sense which was,
however, derived from the colloquial meaning current in the Hellenistic world.[3]

With the exception of the Johannine literature, which uses
neither of the two terms, the verb "to evangelize" appears infrequently in the synoptics.[4] For Luke, who attaches a certain importance to the word, it signifies the activity of Jesus as messenger of
the end of time and of the coming Kingdom.[5] It also designates the
activity of John the Baptist as precursor of the Messiah[6] and char-

acterizes the activity of any and all missionaries who preach and announce the salvation given in Jesus Christ.[7] Since "evangelize" has as its content the proclamation of Jesus Christ, it is not surprising that the noun "Gospel" very rapidly became synonymous with preaching about Jesus Christ: to preach the Gospel, or to "evangelize," is the same thing as preaching Jesus Christ.

Hence the noun, infrequently attested in the gospel texts,[8] appears widely throughout Pauline literature, where it takes on a very precise meaning.[9] The Gospel is naturally the content of Christian proclamation. And this content is so very evident that it seems useless to Paul to spell it out, except on such solemn occasions as the beginning of the Epistle to the Romans, or in his defense of the resurrection.[10]

> Paul, a servant of Jesus Christ, called to be an apostle, set apart for the gospel of God which he promised beforehand through his prophets in the holy scriptures, the gospel concerning his Son, who was descended from David according to the flesh and designated Son of God in power according to the Spirit of holiness by his resurrection from the dead, Jesus Christ our Lord. . . .[11]

Thus Jesus Christ is none other than the content of the Pauline Gospel; he *is* the Gospel. Consequently, the Gospel becomes the power of life and salvation, a power which calls men to a decision of faith.[12] As an "apostle," Paul knows himself to be a recipient of the Gospel, and can even speak of "his Gospel." He is well aware that it is the same as that of the other apostles, but he feels a special responsibility.[13] Moreover, Paul brings up a very personal point concerning the Gospel which sets the Gospel against the Law: The Gospel, as the proclamation of Jesus Christ, offers salvation to him who believes, thus affirming justification by faith. Consequently, the Gospel is opposed to the Law, which seeks to gain salvation by works.[14]

This understanding of the Gospel as Good News of Salvation in Jesus Christ, as summed up in Jesus Christ himself, remained the basic notion of the early church. But little by little there developed a second meaning of the term "gospel" which ended up referring to a written account of the life of Jesus. And here one encounters Irenaeus' dialectic between "Gospel" and "gospel accounts," between "one Gospel" and "the four gospels."[15]

Hence it could be stated that every Christian author up to around A.D. 150 used the term "Gospel" in the sense of Good News, whether it referred to the proclamation of Jesus or to the Good News about Jesus.[16]

Clement of Rome alludes to Paul's letter to the Corinthians when he states: "What was the primary thing he (Paul) wrote to you 'when he started preaching the gospel'?"[17] It is clear that here we are dealing with the beginning of Paul's apostolic activity, and not with an allusion to a written work.[18]

Similarly, there is no doubt that the word refers to preaching about Jesus Christ when Ignatius of Antioch speaks of "taking refuge in the 'Gospel,' as in Jesus' flesh," and when he states that "the 'Prophets' . . . anticipated the gospel in their preaching."[19] The same is true for Polycarp, who speaks of "the apostles who preached the gospel to us,"[20] and whose martyrdom was "according to the gospel."[21]

The Epistle of Barnabas seems to have no knowledge of the canonical Gospel,[22] and the word designates the apostolic proclamation. As a matter of fact, the apostles are "to preach his Gospel,"[23] and have been given "authority to preach the Gospel."[24]

While all the witnesses cited up to now are clear and unambiguous, there are other texts which are less self-evident and which could be disputed, although it would be impossible to assert any of them refer specifically to a written gospel.[25] In the sermon called the second epistle of Clement, the following text is found: "For the Lord says in the Gospel: 'If you fail to guard what is small, who will give you what is great? For I tell you he who is faithful in very little, is faithful also in much.' "[26] Here we might well have an allusion to a written gospel, even though the quotation is not found in exactly this form in the canonical gospels. But it is equally understandable if the term simply means preaching. There is no special rule permitting us to go further and see here traces of a lost gospel.

The Didache could equally make us think of a written gospel. "You must not pray like the hypocrites, but 'pray as follows' as the Lord bids us in his gospel. . . ."[27] Certainly, the "Our Father" which follows could constitute a serious index of reference to the gospel of Matthew[28]; however, the expression "his gospel" makes it difficult to tie this writing to the Lord as if he were its author. Gospel here is synonomous with Christian preaching, revelation, tradition. It is self-evident that this tradition contains written elements, and hence the written gospels as well. But it is also clear that the author of the Didache, like many others of his time, placed the heading of "Gospel" over the entire Christian tradition, and not just a particular writing.[29] Other texts in the Didache referring to Gospel should be interpreted in the same way: "Now about the apostles and prophets: Act in line with the gospel precept";[30] "Furthermore, do not reprove each other angrily, but quietly, as you find it in the gospel. . . . Say your prayers, give your charity, and do everything just as you find it in the gospel of our Lord."[31]

Thus at the time of the Apostolic Fathers, the term "Gospel" generally meant the Christian proclamation. However, it seems equally possible that it also began to designate a written gospel, although we cannot say for certain. In any case, for Justin the term means unequivocally a written account of the life of Jesus, and the change appears to have had precedents. As a matter of fact, in his First Apology Justin writes: "For the apostles in the memoirs composed by them, which are called Gospels, have thus delivered unto us what was enjoined upon them. . . ." (Then follow the words of institution.) [32] The primitive title of the written gospels was "memoirs." Justin uses the word at least thirteen times, while he uses the word Gospel only three times to refer to a written account of the life of Jesus.[33]

With Irenaeus the situation becomes completely clear and unequivocal. The bishop of Lyon is absolutely sure about the nature of the one, unique Gospel which has Jesus Christ as its content, and which is the object of Christian proclamation. He knows and frequently uses the four written gospels. In fact the Gospel must be unique, since its content is Jesus Christ, who is himself unique. Thus the following affirmation of Irenaeus is perfectly clear: "All and each of them (the apostles) alike having the gospel of God. . . ." [34]

But while the Gospel is unique, it was still preached by many, and was even put in writing by certain of its proclaimers: "They [the apostles] first preached it abroad, and then later by the will of God handed it down to us in Writings, to be the foundation and pillar of our faith."[35] Hence there exist written versions of the Gospel, and even various editions of it.[36] It might then be said that while there is only one Gospel in the strict sense, there are a variety of written gospels. This plurality of "forms" and "images" of the Gospel does not threaten its unity[37]; it might even be said to confirm it.[38]

However, an important question arises: How many gospels should we accept? There are some who would increase the number of gospels; there are others who would seek to reduce the number to but one gospel.[39] Efforts to make the Gospel unique run the risk of being warped either by a profusion of forms and images, some even mutually contradictory, or by a false and artificial unity. Irenaeus found a middle way, the one given to him by tradition. He accepted four gospels; no more, no less. In order to demonstrate the necessity of a fourfold Gospel, he used a series of expedient and less than convincing arguments: The four gospels are analogous to the four points of the compass, to the four cherubim, the four beasts of the Apocalypse, etc.[40] In fact, the real argument is simply that if there are four gospels, it is because the tradition of the church transmitted four of them, and these four can lay claim to apostolic origin.

Thus Irenaeus definitely establishes a distinction between "Gospel," understood as the content of Christian proclamation, and thus also as the content of the tradition of the church, and "gospel" understood as an apostolic redaction of the life of Jesus, as a written account of the preaching of the apostles about Christ. It follows that the basic theological concept for the first two centuries, as for the rest of the history of the church, is the concept of the Gospel, of the Good News about Jesus Christ. It is this Good News and this Gospel which the church has the responsibility of transmitting from generation to generation.

2.   The Transmission of the Gospel

We are now faced with the question of what it means to speak of the "transmission" of the Gospel.

From the grammatical point of view, it should be stated that the term is loaded with a very special meaning. It expresses an aspect of the Tradition which insists on what might be called the act of transmitting (actus tradendi), active tradition (traditio activa), as opposed to the passive tradition (traditio passiva) or transmitted tradition (traditio tradita). In effect, what we are seeking to study here is not the content of the tradition, or the Gospel as such, but the manner in which the Gospel is communicated in history from person to person and from place to place. Is not this "transmission" a fundamental characteristic of the life of the church in history? The church exists only for one purpose; its organization and activities have but one end: to transmit the Gospel to all men, in all times and in all places.

When we seek to analyze the act of transmitting the Gospel, we see that this act can be broken down into three inseparable elements which reappear at each link of the chain. Paul very sharply defines them in 1 Corinthians 11:23 "For I received from the Lord what I also delivered to you. . . ." If transmission is to take place there must first of all be a reality to transmit. Paul has received something—here it is the words of institution of the Lord's Supper. In fact, this transmitted reality is nothing less than the Gospel. Second, there must be someone to receive this Gospel. Paul is here the receiver, the object of transmission. Finally, and this is the essential thing, it is imperative that this someone, the object of the transmission, becomes the subject of a new transmission, so that what has been received and believed is passed on to others who, in their turn, receive it only to transmit it again.[41]

On the basis of these affirmations the following remarks can be made:

The transmission of the Gospel takes place by means of men who cannot remain neutral to what they receive and transmit. They are seized by the Gospel and their existence is transformed. Under these conditions, transmission cannot be understood as a simple repetition, a pure retelling of a message from the past. To transmit means, in a certain sense, to interpret.

The men who transmit the Gospel differ widely. They come from different cultural and social *milieu,* they belong to different races, they speak different languages. Under these conditions, in order for the Gospel to be received and transmitted, the need arises for translations, and even new terminology. Thus the transmission of the Gospel in the first few centuries encountered problems such as hellenization of the Gospel, preaching to the cultivated classes, translation into such languages as Latin, Syriac, Coptic, etc.

Transmission of the Gospel even in a homogeneous milieu would still be varied and diverse, since individuals do not receive the Gospel in the same way, and similarly they do not transmit it in the same way. The existence of four canonical gospels clearly demonstrates the multiplicity of interpretations and different forms of transmission. Thus a variety of interpretations of the Gospel— sometimes divergent and warped—is found throughout history. Another way of saying this is that the history of the transmission of the Gospel encounters the problem of heresy.

In order that this manifold and diverse transmission should remain faithful to the one Gospel, and not slip from a legitimate pluralism to treason, it is important to specify norms. These norms would have the purpose of separating out the aberrations in transmission, avoiding errors, and safeguarding the unity of the Gospel. Consequently, the history of the transmission of the Gospel will necessarily run up against the problem of norms permitting the Gospel to remain faithful to its original object within the framework of a plurality of legitimate transmissions. The history of the transmission of the Gospel parallels the history of the formation of the biblical canon.

Thus an analysis of the notion of transmission permits us to single out the problems facing our historical research into the transmission of the Gospel in the first two centuries.

3. *The Transmission of the Gospel in Apostolic Times: The Apostles as Agents of Transmission*

According to the New Testament and the early church, it appears that the Apostles are the first links in the chain of Gospel transmission. They are in effect, the necessary intermediaries in any attempt to get back to Christ and have access to his revelation. In this sense we can say that the church is founded on the Apostles.[42]

Of course, the Apostles were not the only agents of transmission of the Gospel. Other persons could and did participate in its propagation. However, the Apostles represent a special category from a theological point of view: The Gospel they transmitted is worthy of faith; it is the measure of every other transmission. And this is what assures their importance.

It is true that the Apostles form a group with rather fuzzy historical contours,[43] but their unequaled position stems from the fact that they are witnesses of the resurrection, and thus of the central event of the Gospel. When Paul tries to justify his apostolic calling, he links himself precisely with the vision of the resurrected Lord: "Am I not an apostle? Have I not seen Jesus our Lord?"[44] Naturally the Apostles are not the only ones to have seen the risen Lord, as Paul witnesses in I Corinthians 15:5-8. But what characterizes them is the fact that they are the authorized witnesses of the Resurrection, those whose witness evokes faith and must be received in order to authenticate a true transmission of the Gospel.

The importance of the Apostles in the transmission process appears quite clearly in Luke. In the prologue to his gospel, he writes:

"Inasmuch as many have undertaken to compile a narrative of the things which have been accomplished among us, just as they were delivered to us by those who from the beginning were eyewitnesses and ministers of the word, it seemed good to me also. . . ."[45] The faith that Luke wants to evoke is founded on a transmission guaranteed by eyewitnesses to the events, eyewitnesses who later became servants of the Word; in other words, the Apostles.

The Johannine literature does not use the term "transmission"; nevertheless, it too recognizes the importance of eyewitnesses, of those who have heard, seen and touched and whose role is to transmit and to announce: "That which was from the beginning, which we have heard, which we have seen with our eyes, which we have looked upon and touched with our hands, concerning the word of life—the life was made manifest, and we saw it, and testify to it, and proclaim to you the eternal life which was with the Father and was made manifest to us—that which we have seen and heard we proclaim also to you. . . ."[46] The important thing is that these are eyewitnesses who transmit the Gospel of life, and this is what authenticates the transmission.

Paul, for his part, gives fundamental importance to the idea of transmission. The beginning of 1 Corinthians 15 is significant from this point of view: "Now I would remind you, brethren, in what terms I preached to you the gospel, which you received, in which you stand, by which you are saved, if you hold it fast. . . . For I delivered to you as of first importance what I also received, that Christ died for our sins in accordance with the scriptures. . . ." What Paul announces and transmits is the Gospel of the death of Christ, but it is also and above all the Gospel of the resurrection, as seen in the rest of the chapter. Paul is conscious of being a link in the history of the transmission of the Gospel, a history which begins with Christ, continues with the witnesses of the resurrection, reaches Paul and, through him, the Corinthians.

But Oscar Cullmann has pointed out that for Paul this line of transmission is paralleled by another line of transmission which comes directly from the Lord.[47] Indeed, in I Corinthians 11:23, Paul introduces his narrative of the first eucharist in these terms: "For I received from the Lord what I also delivered to you. . . ."[48] It is clear that Paul was not present at the institution of the Lord's Supper by Jesus; rather, he was informed by others, by persons who had been there, or who had been informed by intermediaries. But at the same time, Paul declares that he received this narrative from the Lord or, in other words, that the Lord had transmitted it to him directly. Thus there is both a transmission in the historical sense, and a direct transmission coming from the Lord. Apparently, we can conclude from this remark that the historical act of transmission, in order to have its full significance, requires that the Lord himself confirm the authenticity of the transmitted Gospel, and that he do this by direct intervention, thus making historical transmission a divine transmission.

This transmission must not stop at the conclusion of the apostolic generation; it must be perpetuated and remain the rule of the life of the church. Thus Paul declares to Timothy: "You then, my son, be strong in the grace that is in Christ Jesus, and what you have heard from me before many witnesses entrust to faithful men who will be able to teach others also."[49]

It must be pointed out that the transmission of the Gospel includes the transmission of the Old Testament. From the beginning this is an integral part of the apostolic proclamation. Indeed, the Gospel of Christ is not a spontaneous apparition like some gnostic myth; it was prepared for by the entire Old Testament history from which it issues. It is prefigured by the events marking the life of Israel, to which it gives significance. Hence the Old Testament is the promise of which Christ is the fulfilment. Indeed, the Old Testament Scriptures are inseparable from the Gospel, with the difference that they are really Scripture, while the apostolic proclamation, even if it includes written elements, remains essentially oral.

The account of the disciples on the road to Emmaus illustrates these considerations: "And beginning with Moses and all the prophets, he interpreted to them in all the scriptures the things concerning himself."[50] Hence the Old Testament is the only written or scriptural reference, in the fullest sense of the word when one is speaking of Christ and transmitting his Gospel. It is the prophecy and proclamation of Jesus Christ, the written substructure onto which the transmission of the Gospel can be grafted.

4. *Transmission of the Gospel in the Post-Apostolic Age:*
   The Reference to the Apostles

The end of the apostolic age—impossible to date exactly—changed nothing in the fact of transmission itself. It continued to be the Gospel's mode of communication, because in fact it belonged to the

Gospel, the very nature of which is to be transmitted since it is good news about salvation for all men in all times and in all places.

However, with the death of the last apostle, a new threshold was crossed; the first links in the transmission were no longer present. That transmission now had to continue in the absence of the apostles, who nevertheless remained the necessary intermediaries for getting back to Christ. At the same time, other links began to be added to the chain of transmission.

The Epistle of Clement of Rome to the Corinthians is important in this respect. It describes the progress of the Gospel which is given by God, passed to Christ, from Christ to the apostles, from the apostles to the bishops of the Church: "The apostles received the gospel for us from the Lord Jesus Christ; Jesus, the Christ, was sent from God. Thus Christ is from God and the apostles from Christ. In both instances the orderly procedure depends on God's will. And so the apostles, after receiving their orders and being fully convinced by the resurrection of our Lord Jesus Christ and assured by God's word, went out in the confidence of the Holy Spirit to preach the good news that God's Kingdom was about to come. They preached in the country and in the towns, and appointed their first converts, after testing them by the Spirit, to be the bishops and deacons of future believers."[51] It is therefore part of the nature and order of the Gospel that it be handed on first by the apostles, and then by those instituted by the apostles as bishops or deacons. And Clement insists on the continuity of this transmission: "Now our apostles, thanks to our Lord Jesus Christ, knew that there was going to be strife over the title of bishop. It was for this reason and because they had been given an accurate knowledge of the future, that they appointed the officers we have mentioned. Furthermore, they later added a codicil to the effect that, should these die, other approved men should succeed to their ministry."[52]

Evidently, one could now no longer appeal to the apostles as guarantors of a true and exact transmission of the Gospel. The question then arose: How, as one gets further from the apostolic period, is it possible to conserve the bond with the apostles, i.e., the only guarantee that the transmission is faithful?

The response to this question is simple: what was implicit in the earlier period must become explicit. In other words, the reference to the apostle which had no need to be formalized in the early days of the church had to be spelled out and affirmed. Indeed, in New

Testament times it was not particularly necessary to defend the authority of the apostles; they represented a living authority, an accessible guarantee of the Gospel. Thus, in the New Testament there is hardly any discussion of the apostles, except for Paul, who defends an apostolate challenged by some, and Luke, who seeks to emphasize the importance of the apostles in the earliest church. But once the apostles have disappeared, in order to justify the preaching of the Gospel, it became necessary to point to the apostles as preachers and as guarantors of the Good News. Hence we can see how the attempt was made to enter into the apostolic succession and to transmit the same Gospel as the apostles did. In other words, as the apostles died, it was felt necessary to make explicit the reference to their preaching, and from there to develop a theology of the apostolate.

Numerous examples can be cited of these references to the Apostles by the authors of this period. The full title of the Didache is characteristic, whether one takes the accepted version (*The Teaching of the Twelve Apostles*), or the variant (*The Lord's Teaching to the Heathen by the Twelve Apostles*). The claim of the author is simply to pass on the teaching of Christ as it was transmitted by the Apostles.[53] Similarly, the *Epistle of Barnabas* invokes the Apostles as preachers of the Gospel and those who possess the authority of the Gospel.[54] The same idea is found in Ignatius of Antioch, who affirms an identity of thought between the Apostles and the Lord,[55] thus demonstrating that the Apostles did nothing but repeat the preaching of the Lord, i.e., the same Gospel.[56] The same is true for Polycarp[57] and Hermes.[58] It is therefore possible to affirm that, for the apostolic Fathers, the apostle is seen to occupy a fundamental place in the chain of transmission: He is the necessary intermediary between Christ and the faithful, the passageway which permits us to return to Christ. The reference to the apostolate is necessary to justify the transmission of the Gospel.

But to be honest, if we insist on the importance of the Apostles, we also have to admit that not much is known about them. They have tended to become a collective body, an all-inclusive group with less and less individualized and distinct traits. They are "the Twelve," as the title of the *Didache* suggests, assimilating straight-away the twelve disciples into the Apostles. For Ignatius, they had become a group similar to the presbyterium, itself rather poorly individualized.[59] In fact, under the best of circumstances, not more than two of the apostles are known: Peter and Paul. The others remain almost completely clothed in anonymity.[60]

The reference to the apostles became more and more important in order to guarantee the transmission of the Gospel. But the question remained: How was the transmission of the Gospel to take place, since the apostles were no longer the direct agents of its transmission? From this point of view nothing had changed from the preceding period; the transmission of the Gospel was carried out essentially by word of mouth. It was basically a living Word that was communicated, and not a Scripture. It must be understood that the God of Christian revelation became flesh; he was a human person who came to dwell among us, and not a piece of writing. Moreover, the history of this period, in which the church is seen to live from the transmission of the Gospel without New Testament Scriptures, should remind us that we ought never to confuse Gospel and Scripture. It should remind us that the very nature of the church is to live from the transmission alone: by tradition alone *(Traditione)*.[61]

But while this transmission is above all oral, it is necessary to recognize that it can also be written, because the apostles or their disciples left written testimony of their preaching. Hence there are apostolic writings to be transmitted; there is a written transmission of the Gospel. But in reality this written transmission is but the brief, fragmentary and sporadic deposit of an essentially spoken witness. In general, Paul writes to churches where the Gospel had already been preached. And if Luke writes to Theophilus, it is in order to spell out in his gospel and Acts, the Gospel which had already been transmitted to his reader.

Very soon these apostolic writings came to be gathered into various blocks: the four gospels, the Pauline corpus. But between the years A.D. 100 to 150, A.D., this apostolic production had not yet been grouped into one work; it did not have canonical value; it was not yet "Scripture."

The transmitted Gospel included, however, a written portion which was firmly fixed: the Old Testament. As in the apostolic period, the Old Testament was Scripture, the only official book where a witness to Christ can be found, one that was incontestable even while it may have been difficult to decipher.

Thus the Christian authors of the post-apostolic period quote very infrequently the writings which make up the New Testament; but they make abundant reference to the Old Testament, which they naturally interpret in a Christological fashion. For the *Epistle of Barnabas,* the Old Testament no longer has any historical value; it has meaning only with respect to the Christ which it announces and prefigures.[62]

It is equally possible to appeal here to Irenaeus of Lyon who, while he lived somewhat later than the period in question, represented its spirit equally well. In order to prove the truth of the preaching of the Apostles, (i.e. the Gospel such as it was preached in the church of his time), Irenaeus does not appeal to apostolic affirmations, which would only lead to a vicious circle, but relies entirely on the Old Testament. Thus he manages to produce a christological demonstration uniquely in reference to Old Testament sources.[63] In *Adversus Haereses,* Irenaeus left clues which clearly show the importance accorded to the Old Testament, understood as Scripture, and to the christological key necessary to understand it:

> If any one, therefore, reads the Scriptures with attention, he will find in them an account of Christ, and a foreshadowing of the new calling (vocationis). For Christ is the treasure which was hid in the field, that is, in this world (for "the field is the world"); but the treasure hid in the Scriptures is Christ, since He was pointed out by means of types and parables. Hence his human nature could not be understood, prior to the consummation of those things which had been predicted, that is, the advent of Christ.[64]

5. The Crisis in the Transmission of the Gospel in the Second Century: Elaboration of the Written Apostolic Reference

The reference to the Apostles did not prevent the multiplication of interpretations given to the Gospel. Such a situation is understandable; every transmission of the Gospel is at the same time an interpretation of it. The Gospel is not passed along like an inanimate deposit, like a dead object or a relic of the past; it is a living reality, transmitted by way of living men who receive it, live it and witness to it in their turn. It is transmitted by means of men of greater or lesser intelligence, from different social backgrounds, with varying religious inclinations and personal experiences. Hence the innumerable possibilities of different interpretations, some indeed divergent, and even opposed to each other. Thus the second century saw the appearance of a considerable number of interpretation-transmissions of the Gospel, extending from those which seem most traditional to us to those which appear the most aberrant.

Naturally each of these interpretations appealed to the Apostles as their stamp of authenticity and truth. This much was essential, in any case, to obtain a sure token of credibility for those who refer themselves to Christ as the fundamental authority, and to his Apostles as intermediaries essential for getting back to Christ.

Consequently, every preacher of the Gospel claimed that his Gospel was assuredly that of the Apostles. Marcion, for example, refers himself to the apostolic authority of Paul. And his faithfulness to that Apostle goes so far that he wishes nothing less than to be the continuation of the one, true Apostle, Paul. In the name of Paulinism—the opposition of Law and Gospel, Justice, and Love—he rejects the Old Testament as the expression of the Law and Justice of the Demiurge, an expression opposed to the Gospel of Paul. This leads him to bring together a collection of apostolic writings of Pauline origin—writings naturally expurgated to meet the needs of his doctrine. This collection represents his written reference to the apostle and the norm of his doctrine.[65]

The same is true of the gnostics who, in most cases, sought to tie their doctrine either with the teaching of an apostle or with someone from the apostolic period.[66] But since in many cases this claim turned out to be a bit extravagant, the gnostics conceived a secret transmission, going back to the apostles and Jesus, a transmission that remained unverifiable. Thus Basilides refers himself to Glaukias, the interpreter of Peter, and hence, finally, to Peter himself.[67] Valentinus is supposed to have been taught by Theodas, himself a disciple of Paul.[68] The Carpocratians make reference to Mariamne, Salome or Martha; the Naassenians to Mariamne, to whom James, the brother of the Lord, was supposed to have handed on the true doctrine.[69]

But it was not only the heretics who referred themselves to the Apostles as guarantors of their doctrines; the orthodox did it as well. There is no real difference between these groups, except, perhaps, for the fact that the reference to the Apostles was first invoked heretically. Irenaeus is a remarkable example here. In fact, he shows on the one hand how the principal churches were established by the Apostles and, on the other hand, how the preaching in these churches is in conformity with the Gospel because of an uninterrupted succession of presbyters. For the Bishop of Lyon the guarantee of a true transmission of the Gospel is thus conformity with the teaching of the Apostles.[70]

Tertullian is equally explicit on this subject, and takes up Irenaeus' argument: The truth of a doctrine depends upon how well it is related to the Apostles.

> If this is so, it follows that all doctrine which is in agreement with those apostolic churches, the wombs and sources of the faith, is to be deemed true on the ground that it indubitably preserves what the churches received from the apostles, the apostles from Christ, and Christ from God.[71]

Hence, for all the Christian groups of the period in reference, the preaching of the Church, the oral part of the tradition, was connected with the Apostles. The fundamental claim of each and every one was to transmit only what the Apostles had transmitted.

This reference to the Apostles does not show itself only on the level of oral and spoken tradition; it appears also on the level of literature. In this period a variety of works appear, laying claim to apostolic authority for the purpose of making themselves acceptable to the Christian public. The number of gospel accounts put under the patronage of an apostle indicates the importance of the apostolic label for Christians of that time.[72] An equally large number of Acts are also found attributed to apostles,[73] as are numerous apocalypses.[74] All of this points to the importance of the notion of apostolicity as a source of authority for the transmission of the Gospel.

But since every one appealed to the Apostles as justification for the transmission of his Gospel, we witness a crisis. The reference to the Apostles was devalued because it was used wrongly and indiscriminately. But then we are led to ask the question: how can we distinguish true apostolicity from false, and that which is truly apostolic from what is not? The answer to this question determines the true transmission of the Gospel.

The problem is found posed by Papias of Hieropolis. Struck by the realization that very little was then known about the Apostles, he began a search for traces which might be found in their locality. Moreover, he investigated not so much written traces as living ones, oral traditions preserved by one or another of the forefathers. And the harvest of apostolic recollections which Papias includes in his "Explanation of the Words of the Lord" is highly interesting, judging from the report of Eusebius of Caesarea.[75] It is worth noting that around A.D. 150 not a great deal was known about the apostolic period beyond that which was contained in the written tradition. A number of traditions reported by Papias as going back to the Apostles, such as those related to millenarism, are seen to be aberrant or seriously mutilated.[76] It might simply be said that the transmission of the Gospel, even when it claims to go back to the Apostles, can dwindle, because little by little the memories of what the Apostles were like are lost. On the other hand, the transmission might also be expanded by adding to or deforming the original Gospel. Hence the crisis: Faced with all these claims of apostolicity, both diverse and varied, numerous and multiform, written and oral, all claiming to be transmissions of the Gospel, how is it possible to discern the authentic transmission of the one Gospel coming from Christ by way of the Apostles? With the onslaught of the crisis in the second century, the slogan of apostolicity risked being voided of meaning, since it could, in fact, justify any Gospel whatever!

The problem was therefore to specify the nature of true apostolicity, in such a way that it could serve as a base and a reference for every other mention of apostolicity. The formation of the New Testament canon was a response to the question posed by this crisis of apostolicity. In fact, in face of this multiplication of Christian literature and the claims of a large part of it to be apostolic, the formation of the New Testament canon, or the recognition of a certain number of writings as an apostolic and written form of the Gospel, helped determine the level of credibility and apostolicity of a good number of writings which had remained ambiguous. At the same time, the choice of a series of writings recognized as being of apostolic origin permitted the separation within the expanding and developing oral tradition of what was truly apostolic from what was not. The response to the second century's crisis of apostolicity was the formation of the New Testament canon: in other words, the recognition of a certain number of writings as authentically apostolic. These later became the criteria of all apostolicity.

In this way a collection of writings sprang up alongside the Old Testament, to which were attributed, little by little, the qualities of Scripture: inspiration and inerrancy—qualities which had never before in Judaism been applied to the Old Testament. Naturally, this process could not be realized in a day, nor everywhere at the same time. However, it should be pointed out that in this process of canonization local churches were led to make ultimately very similar decisions about certain secondary books. And it might be added that these decisions by local churches were so close to one another that the emerging New Testament coalesced into nearly the same fundamental form without any collective decisions having been made.

Thus the second century church gradually defined a New Testament canon and, in so doing, affirmed that this canon represented the apostolic Tradition *par excellence,* a tradition both essential to and constitutive of the church, a Tradition to which every transmission of the Gospel must be referred if it is to be correct and faithful. Without doubt, this is the most important contribution of the early Church to the transmission of the Gospel: to have spelled out the written, apostolic touchstone to which every ensuing proclamation of the Gospel must conform. The formation of the New Testament canon, the apostolic Scriptures, is the essential response of the second century church to the crisis provoked by the watering down of the apostolic reference. From then on, the church had a point of reference from which to legitimize the transmission of the Gospel. This Gospel is defined sharply enough to eliminate certain interpretations while at the same time it remains large enough to allow for the possibility of a number of others.

6. The Conditions for a Correct Transmission of the Gospel

The precision given to the idea of apostolicity by the formation of an apostolic Scripture was of fundamental importance for the church of the second century. However, the notion of apostolicity was developed in still other areas; even the idea of apostolic Tradition came to be more tightly defined.

Irenaeus of Lyon is once again a valuable witness. In his *Adversus Haereses,* he refutes gnosticism through Scripture. But the gnostics he dealt with refused that scriptural authority: "But when they are refuted from the Writings they turn around and attack the Writings themselves, saying that they are not correct, or authoritative, and that the truth cannot be found from them. . . ."[77] Where, then, is one to look? In the tradition, the heretics respond: ". . . the truth cannot be found from them (the Scriptures) by those who are not acquainted with the tradition. For this (they say) was not handed down in writing, but orally. . . ."[78] Hence, in order to defend the truth of the Scriptures—and here we must also include the New Testament Scriptures—Irenaeus was first of all compelled to establish the truth of his own tradition, and the error in that of the gnostics.

The tradition of the church is true because it goes back to the Apostles by way of a succession of presbyters. The criterion of the truth of the tradition is thus its apostolicity. And the argument used to establish apostolicity is the citing of lists of bishops or presbyters leading back to the Apostles. Here the theme of apostolic succession is seen to emerge. For example, Irenaeus gives several examples of apostolic succession: in the Church of Rome, the Church of Smyrna and the Church of Ephesus.[79] Conversely, the tradition of the heretics is false because, no matter what they say, it does not go back to the Apostles, but varies according to the proponents of each heresy. It is secret, unlike the transmission of the Gospel, which is open and aboveboard. It is varied and contradictory, proving that it does not come from a single source, and does not have its origin in the Lord.[80]

If, therefore, the tradition which comes from the Apostles is in the Church, and if the Scripture recognized by the church, and its interpretation, are true and correct, then Irenaeus can declare: "Let us turn, then, to the demonstration from the Writings . . ."[81]

The reasoning of Irenaeus shows first of all that his primary and essential interest is Scripture; this is the norm of truth, for it contains the apostolic witness. The appeal to the tradition coming from the Apostles is secondary in the sense that Irenaeus refers to it only when his adversaries do. The appeal to Tradition has an apologetic and polemical orientation.

However, tradition is important; it is the principle which permits the legitimization of Scripture; the principle which, since it is apostolic, assures that Scripture truly contains the apostolic message. In fact, tradition appears as another means of knowing the apostolic Gospel. The Apostles preached, and their proclamation has been transmitted through the preaching of the church.

As a matter of fact, apostolic Scripture and apostolic Tradition converge and are identical in essence. They are two different channels by which the Gospel of the Apostles comes to the church. Both in fact go back to the Apostles as the decisive and unequivocal authority for anyone wishing to know Jesus Christ.

But their function is not identical. When Irenaeus wants to establish a doctrine, he appeals to the written Scripture of the Apostles, and more generally to the Scriptures. He finds there the material for his theological reflection and the doctrinal elements necessary for the elaboration of his synthesis. As far as Tradition is concerned, Irenaeus uses it as a formal authority which serves to justify both his use of Scripture—since it is the tradition which gave him the Scriptures—and his interpretation of Scripture.

Thus the church of the second century, through the solidification of the apostolic witness recorded in the New Testament and the elaboration of a doctrine of apostolic tradition, gave itself the elements of legitimization, the norms which would permit it to assure for posterity a correct transmission of the Gospel. Scripture and apostolic tradition relate to each other reciprocally. The written apostolic witness, in order to be understood, needs a *living* apostolic witness in the church. The orally preserved apostolic witness, in order not to go astray and to remain faithful to itself, needs constantly to be referred to the written apostolic witness. For the church of the second century, the faithfulness of the Gospel transmission consisted in the harmonious relationship between these two forms of apostolic witness: Scripture and tradition.[82] Clearly, two dangers threaten the transmission of the Gospel: First, the isolation of Scripture, cutting off its historical roots, and making the written apostolic witness a thing sufficient in itself. This is the risk of docetism, the Protestant temptation. The other danger consists in isolating the tradition, enlarging it and, finally, seeing in it an autonomous source of revelation which would permit it to develop independently. This is the Catholic temptation. But the correct interplay of these two elements allows a faithful transmission of the Gospel.

Having arrived at the end of our study, we should note that the question which preoccupied the first Christians, as far as the transmission of the Gospel was concerned, was that this transmission take place faithfully, correctly, legitimately. In other words, the problem of orthodoxy was the primary preoccupation of that time. In comparison with this fundamental problem, all others shrank to insignificance; the Fathers were simply not very interested in the question of the transmission of the Gospel in different cultures, different languages, or in higher or lower social strata. After all, that was trivial; the important thing was that the Gospel be transmitted faithfully. If that were done, all the other questions would fall into place. And this preoccupation of the early church—is it not taken up once again in the Augusburg Confession, when it declares: "The church is the assembly of saints in which the Gospel is taught purely and the Sacraments are administered rightly"?[83]

                                    —*Translated by* Dr. Russell B. Norris

NOTES

1. For information regarding Christian expansion in the first centuries, the basic work remains: A. von Harnack, *The Mission and Expansion of Christianity in the First Three Centuries*, J. Moffatt, trans. and ed., New York, 1908. In this regard, see also the article of E. Molland, "L'antiquité chrétienne a-t-elle eu un programme et des méthodes missionnaires?", in *Opuscula Patristica*, Oslo, 1970, pp. 103-116.
2. Cf. on this subject Oscar Cullmann, "La Tradition," *Cahiers théologiques* 33, Neuchâtel, 1953.
3. On this question it would be worthwhile to consult the article by G. Friedrich on *euaggelizomai* and *euaggelion* in *Theological Dictionary of the New Testament*, Grand Rapids, 1964, Vol. II, pp. 707-737.
4. Once in Matthew 11:5; ten times in Luke, to which must be added another fifteen times in Acts. Outside of Paul, who uses the verb 21 times, we might count two occurrences in Hebrews, three in 1 Peter, and two in Revelation.
5. Cf. Luke 8:1.
6. Luke 3:18.
7. Luke 9:6.
8. Mark avoids the verb, but uses the noun eight times; Matthew employs it four times.
9. There are about 60 occurrences of the substantive in the Pauline literature.
10. 1 Corinthians 15:1-11.
11. Romans 1:1-4.
12. Cf. 2 Corinthians 4:3; 1 Thessalonians 1:5; Romans 1:16-17.
13. Cf. 2 Corinthians 4:3; 1 Thessalonians 1:5; Romans 2:16; 2 Timothy 2:8.
14. Romans 2:16.
15. Cf. A. Benoît, *Saint Irénée—Introduction à l'étude de sa théologie*, Paris, 1960, pp. 106-120.
16. Cf. D. van den Eynde, *Les normes de l'enseignement chrétien dans la littérature patristique des trois premiers siècles*, Paris, 1933, pp. 32 ff. "*Euaggelion* signifies neither a writing, nor a collection of writings, but simply the revelation of Christ. The whole of New Testament literature, of which the latest writings are almost contemporary with Ignatius, understands the word 'gospel' only in terms of good news. . . . Not until the middle of the second century are there certain references to a written gospel" (our translation).
17. "The Letter of the Church of Rome to the Church of Corinth, Commonly called Clement's First Letter," trans. C. Richardson, *Early Christian Fathers*, LCC Vol. I, Paragraph 47:2.
18. The translation given by A. Jaubert ("Clément de Rome, Epitre aux Corinthiens," *Sources chrétiennes*, No. 167, Paris, 1971, p. 177) confirms this interpretation: "Take the letter of the blessed Paul the apostle. What did he write first at the beginning of evangelizing?" (our translation). The verb reappears two times in the Epistle of Clement, in 42:1 and 42:3, and it signifies the activity of the Apostles.
19. "The Letters of Ignatius, Bishop of Antioch," trans. C. Richardson, *Early Christian Fathers*, LCC Vol. I. Philadelphians 5:1 and 5:2. The term gospel is found in a very controversial passage of the same epistle: "If I don't find it in the original documents, I don't believe it in the gospel" (8:2). The gospel here means the same as Christian revelation. Cf. also Philadelphians 9:2; Smyrnaeans 5:1 and 7:2.

20. "The Letter of Polycarp, Bishop of Smyrna, to the Philippians," trans. M. H. Shepherd, Jr., *Early Christian Fathers*, LCC Vol. I, Paragraph 6:3.
21. "The Martyrdom of Polycarp, as Told in the Letter of the Church of Smyrna to the Church of Philomelium," trans. M. H. Shepherd, Jr., *Early Christian Fathers*, LCC Vol. I, Paragraphs 1:1 and 19:1.
22. Cf. P. Prigent, "Epître de Barnabé," *Sources chrétiennes*, No. 172, Paris, 1971, pp. 41 f.
23. "Epistle of Barnabas," *Ante-Nicene Fathers*, Buffalo, 1886, Paragraph 5:9, p. 139.
24. *Ibid.*, Paragraph 8:3, p. 142.
25. Cf. the classification established by G. W. H. Lampe in *A Patristic Greek Lexicon*, Oxford, 1961; the article on *euaggelion*, p. 555.
26. "An Anonymous Sermon, Commonly Called Clement's Second Letter," C. Richardson, trans. and ed., *Early Christian Fathers*, LCC Vol. I, Paragraph 8:5.
27. "The Teaching of the Twelve Apostles, Commonly Called the Didache," trans. C. Richardson, *Early Christian Fathers*, LCC Vol. I, Paragraph 8:2.
28. Matthew 6:9-13.
29. Cf. J.-P. Audet, "La Didachè, Instructions des Apôtres," Études bibliques, Paris, 1958, p. 370: "It is totally contrary to the literary genre of a collection of instructions such as this to suppose that at every moment the author had to depend on a 'text.' The example of the churches, which remained within a common evangelical heritage and even more ancient traditions, was certainly not a less abundant source, nor a source less accessible or less authoritative than the writings, on points such as we are considering. It goes without saying more that Christians did not all await the circulation of Matthew before learning the Lord's Prayer, as if a 'text' had to reveal it to them. . . . Hence it was Matthew who gathered here a tradition and a usage already set around him. Thus it is reasonable to conclude that the quasi-identity of form underlines the proximity of origin in a relatively homogeneous tradition and milieu" (our translation).
30. Didache 11:3.
31. Didache 15:3-4.
32. "The First Apology of Justin Martyr," *Ante-Nicene Fathers*, Buffalo, 1886, Vol. I, Paragraph 66:3, p. 185. In two other passages, Justin uses the term gospel in the singular to designate a written redaction: "Dialogue with Trypho, A Jew," *Ante-Nicene Fathers*, Vol. I, Paragraph 10:2 ("the so-called Gospel") and 100:1 ("in the gospel it is written that he said . . ." followed by a citation of Matthew 11:27).
33. Cf. I Apologia 66:3; 67:3; Dialogos 100:4; 101:3; 102:5; 104:1; 105:1; 105:5; 105:6; 106:3; 106:4; 107:1, for "memoires." Cf. I Apologia 66:3; Dialogos 10:2; 100:1, for written gospel. In addition, it should be pointed out that Justin does not use the term gospel in the general sense of preaching about Christ.
34. *Qui quidem et omnes pariter et singuli eorum habentes Euangelium Dei. Adversus Haereses III, 1:1.*
35. *Ibid.*
36. ". . . handed down to us in the Scriptures. . . . Matthew for his part published also a written Gospel. . . . And Luke too, the attendant of Paul, set down in a book the Gospel preached by him. . . . John . . . again put forth his gospel. . . ." *Adversus Haereses III, 1:1.*
37. Cf. *Adversus Haereses III, 11:8-9.*

38. Apropos—the question of the date of Easter, Irenaeus writes this characteristic phrase: "the disagreement in the fast confirms our agreement in the
faith." Eusebius, *The Ecclesiastical History*, trans. Kirsopp Lake, Cambridge,
Mass., 1965, Paragraph V, 24:13. It would undoubtedly be fair to interpret
Irenaeus by transposing this phrase in reference to the gospels: the difference
in gospels confirms the unity of the Gospel.

39. "Selections from the Work Against Heresies by Irenaeus, Bishop of Lyon,"
trans. E. R. Hardy, *Early Christian Fathers*, LCC Vol. I, Paragraph III, 11:9.

40. *Ibid.*, III, 11:8.

41. Cf. 2 Timothy 2:2.

42. Cf. Ephesians 2:20.

43. Cf. H. von Campenhausen, *Ecclesiastical Authority and Spiritual Power in
the Church of the First Three Centuries*, trans. J. A. Baker, London, 1969,
pp. 12-29.

44. 1 Corinthians 9:1.

45. Luke 1:1-2.

46. 1 John 1:1-3.

47. Cullmann, *La Tradition*. Cf. the chapter entitled: "La tradition apostolique
et le Seigneur élevé à la droite de Dieu."

48. Cf. *Ibid.*, p. 20: "The formula of 1 Corinthians 11:23 leads therefore to the
present Christ, but only inasmuch as he is found behind this transmission
of the tradition. In other words, he is at work in this transmission itself"
(our translation).

49. 2 Timothy 2:1-2.

50. Luke 24:27. Cf. Luke 24:44-48.

51. I Clement 42:1-4.

52. I Clement 44:1-2.

53. Even though the Didache gives a fundamental place to the Apostles, they
play hardly any role at all in the work itself. The Apostles appear there as a
kind of itinerant preacher of whom it is best to be wary. Cf. Didache 11:3-6.

54. Epistle of Barnabas 8:2-3, p. 142.

55. "The Letters of Ignatius," Magnesians 13:1; Trallians 7:1.

56. Cf. Trallians 12:2.

57. Philippians 6:3.

58. Cf. 13:1; 94; 102:2.

59. Cf. Magnesians 16:2; Trallians 2:2; Philadelphians 5:1; Smyrneans 8:1.

60. I Clement 5:3; 47:1; 47:4; Ignatius: Romans 4:3; Polycarp: Philippians 9:1.

61. Cf. the report of the Conference on Faith and Order, Montreal 1963, which
states: "Thus we can say that we exist as Christians by the Tradition of the
Gospel (the *paradosis* of the *kerygma*)" (Section II, §45).

62. Cf. on this subject P. Prigent, *L'épitre de Barnabé et ses sources*, Paris, 1961.

63. Cf. A. Benoît, *Saint Irénée*, the chapter devoted to the demonstration of
apostolic preaching, pp. 234-250.

64. "Irenaeus Against Heresies," *Ante-Nicene Fathers*, Vol. I, Paragraph IV,
26:1, p. 496.

65. The basic work on Marcion is still that of A. von Harnack, *Das Evangelium
vom fremden Gott. Eine monographie zur Geschichte der Grundlegung der
katholischen Kirche, Texte und Untersuchengen 45*, Leipzig, 1921. Cf. also
H. von Campenhausen, "Marcion et les origines du canon néotestamentaire,"
Revue d'Histoire et de Philosophie religieuses, No. 46, 1966, pp. 213-226.

66. It is interesting to note that the reference to the Apostles is affirmed first in
gnostic heresy before ever becoming a claim of orthodoxy. In the letter of

Ptolemaeus to Flora the following passage may be found: "For, if God permits, you will receive later more specific enlightenments . . . when you will have been judged worthy to know the tradition of the Apostles which we ourselves have received by the way of succession." "Ptolémée, Lettre à Flora," G. Quispel, ed., *Sources chrétiennes*, No. 21b, 2nd edition, Paris, 1969, Paragraph 7:9 (our translation).

67. Cf. Clement of Alexandria, "On Spiritual Perfection" (Stromateis VII), *Alexandrian Christianity*, LCC Vol. II, Paragraph VII, 106:4, p. 162.

68. Cf. von Campenhausen, *Spiritual Power*, pp. 158-159.

69. Cf. Origen, *Contra Celsum*, trans. H. Chadwick, Cambridge, 1965, Paragraph V, 62, p. 312.

70. "Irenaeus Against Heresies," Paragraph III, 3:1-4, pp. 415-416.

71. Tertullian, "Prescriptions Against Heretics," *Early Latin Theology*, LCC Vol. V, Paragraph 21:4-5, p. 44.

72. It is surprising to see the number of gospels attributed to an apostle, or to an apostolic personage, or someone in his entourage. It is enough to consult E. Hennecke and W. Schneemelcher, *New Testament Apocrypha*, A. J. B. Higgins, G. Ogg, R. E. Taylor, and R. McL. Wilson, trans., Philadelphia, 1963. Here it is clear that there are a good number of gospels attributed to the "Twelve" collectively (cf. pp. 263-271); there are also several gospels attributed to specific apostles, to Philip, Thomas, Matthias, Judas, James, and Bartholomew (cf. pp. 271-338); there also exist a fair number of gospels attributed to holy women (cf. pp. 338-344) (all references from Vol. I).

73. For information on Acts attributed to apostles, cf. *New Testament Apocrypha*, Vol. II, pp. 167-531.

74. For apocalypses, we might mention those of Peter, Paul, and Thomas. Cf. *New Testament Apocrypha*, Vol. II, pp. 608 ff.

75. Here is what Papias says, according to Eusebius of Caesarea, who quotes him in his *Ecclesiastical History*: "but if ever anyone came who had followed the presbyters, I inquired into the words of the presbyters, what Andrew or Peter or Philip or Thomas or James or John or Matthew, or any other of the Lord's disciples, had said, and what Aristion and the presbyter John, the Lord's disciples, were saying. For I did not suppose that information from books would help me so much as the word of a living and surviving voice." *Ecclesiastical History*, Paragraph III, 39:4, p. 293.

76. *Ibid.*, Paragraph III, 39:8-17, pp. 295-299.

77. "Irenaeus Against Heresies," Paragraph III, 2:1, p. 370.

78. *Ibid.*

79. *Ibid.*, Paragraph III, 3:1-4, pp. 371-373.

80. *Ibid.*, Paragraph III, 4:3, p. 375.

81. *Ibid.*, Paragraph III, 5:1, p. 376. In Latin: *Revertamur ad eam quae est ex Scripturis ostensionem . . .*

82. On this subject see A. Benoît, "l'Apostolicite au second siècle," in *Verbum Caro*, No. 58, 1961, pp. 173-184.

83. Article VII of the Augsburg Confession, in Theodore Tappert (ed.), *The Book of Concord*, Philadelphia, 1959, p. 32. In Latin: *Est autem ecclesia congregatio sanctorum, in qua Evangelium pure docetur et recta administrantur Sacramenta.*

Chapter 6

The Ecumenical
Reconsideration of Tradition

An Evaluation

I.
Basic Consensus and the Core of the Problem

God's salvatory act in Christ was performed once, and yet for all time. The uniqueness and the finality become fused in the eschatological "once and for all" of the event. In this way God's salvatory act in Christ becomes the object of a process of transmission which is continually converting "once" into "for all time" and "there and then" into "here and now." "Handing down," "transference," "transmission," "tradition" therefore signify a fundamental structural element of Christian faith and Christian confession. This is clearly expressed in the command of mission given by the risen Christ (Matthew 28:18ff).

Evidently this command of mission has a two-fold meaning. On the one hand, although the act of transmission is entrusted to men, at the same time it is upheld by the presence of the risen Lord himself: ". . . And lo, I am with you always. . . ." Tradition through men and tradition in the Holy Spirit belong inseparably together and are dependent upon each other. Neither can replace the other or render it superfluous. On the other hand, this act of transmission is indissolubly related to the historical Christ event, to "all that I have commanded you" (Matthew 28:20).

But where can one find a tangible sign of this permanently binding "once" which brings its "and for all" into the present in the act of transmission? Where does this transmission, entrusted to men and

upheld by the Spirit, begin, and where does it find the basis for its
necessary relation to the past?

The concept of "apostolic" or of "apostolicity" gives the fundamental answer to this, as the preceding article has shown. The lasting source and point of reference for transmission are the Apostles
as the Christ-appointed witnesses of his resurrection and the instruments of the proclamation which constitutes the church. Here, in the
Apostles' witness to Christ, lies the point of intersection, so to speak,
of the vertical line of mission between God and Christ and the hori-
zontal line of the act of transmission, by which and in which faith,
proclamation and the church subsist. Tradition of Christ's revelation
must be transmission of the apostolic witness—otherwise it is not a
tradition of Christ's revelation. "Apostolicity" is, therefore, the criterion par excellence for the Christian nature of faith, proclamation,
doctrine and life. The problem of tradition or transmission is thus
to a great extent identical with the question of apostolicity. This is
reflected historically in the fact that towards the end of the second
century the concepts both of tradition and apostolicity receive their
theological formulation simultaneously.[1] To use the concise formula
of Irenaeus: Christian tradition is permanently and essentially "tradition from the Apostles" (ab Apostolis traditio).[2]

On this basic principle all churches were and are in agreement,
despite their divisions. This is precisely why the arguments over true
and false tradition of the gospel, over orthodoxy and heresy, over the
unity or division of the churches were and are concentrated again
and again on the apostolicity issue, i.e., on the question of whether
or not the relation to the apostolic witness basic to the church has
been preserved. For every heresy is at heart characterized and identifiable as heresy by the fact that it lacks this relation. This applies
even if sometimes the concept of heresy seems primarily to be defined ecclesiologically. In other words, the formal earmark of heresy
is that it is a matter of "innovation" as distinct from that which has
been transmitted to us from the Apostles.

The basic accusation of having introduced innovations is made by
both sides in the struggle between "church" and "heretics," and thus
reveals its focal significance. It is raised, for example, in the dispute
with gnosis—by Irenaeus and Tertullian, among others—but appears
also to have been used by the gnostics against their opponents. The
same picture presents itself during the Reformation disputes, when
both sides claim with equal fervour to be the old, true apostolic

church and accuse the other of having introduced innovations, additions, new articles of faith and thus of having become "heretical."

Everything which has so far been said is concerned, as I have already stressed, with convictions which have in reality never been at issue among the churches. The *fact* that transmission forms an essential structural element of Christian proclamation and doctrine, the *fact* that this act of transmission is entrusted to men and yet also upheld by the Holy Spirit, the *fact* that its inexorable source and point of reference must be the apostolic witness and that it must remain faithful to this witness in content and subject to it, all this has not in principle been under discussion, even if interchurch polemics were not always prepared to admit it. But how and where does the problem of tradition come to the fore?

The statement that tradition as a problem is a secondary or derivative issue from the point of view of historical manifestation does not contradict the central prominence it has assumed in the arguments within and between the churches. The great controversies among the churches never began with this problem, although it very soon became the focus of attention. The first bones of contention, as is shown in the dispute with gnosticism and in the Reformation struggle as the two focal points of the debate on tradition in history, were always concrete and factual theological considerations such as, for example, the doctrines of God and of creation, Christology, penance, the doctrine of justification, the conception of the eucharist, etc. These controversies were, however, immediately influenced by the question of whether or not the opinions held by one side or the other were to be regarded as apostolically legitimate, whether or not they "renewed" the apostolic witness or represented "innovations." In short: there has, it is true, never been a church division in which the problem of tradition has failed to become—explicitly or implicitly—a decisive one; on the other hand, however, no division of the churches has ever originated from the problem of tradition as such.[3]

This observation, primarily only a historical or phenomenological one, has its bearing on the right consideration of the whole issue of tradition, and this in two respects. First, it is true that tradition becomes a problem and is crystallized by the contents of tradition, i.e., by that which is in each case transmitted and to be transmitted (*traditum tradendum*). It cannot, however, be fully equated with the question of the transmitted content and of its apostolicity, but rather is in its actual meaning the more comprehensive question of the act or process of transmission (*actus tradendi*). For whether or not transmitted material can be classified as "apostolic" depends in case of controversy ultimately upon the way in which the act of transmission is conceived and executed. It is on this issue of the character and structure of the process of transmission that the divergences which cannot be bridged by the basic consensus sketched at the outset emerged and are emerging. How is the transmission of the revelation fundamentally witnessed by the Apostles carried out? Who are the organs and instruments of this transmission? Where are its fixed points of reference, and what are its norms and criteria?

Second, just as the controversy over the conception of transmission first erupts over the question of the contents of tradition, it can also subside or even cease, depending on the extent to which the dispute over the content of tradition subsides or gives way to increasing agreement. It is therefore quite possible that even radical differences in the conception of the process of transmission might persevere and remain unsolved, but that these divergences might nevertheless fail to become acute because their cause, or their fuel, so to speak, is lacking or is beginning to disappear.

II.
The Convergences in the Catholic and Protestant Conceptions of Tradition

Since the sixteenth century we have become accustomed to viewing the controversies over the character and structure of transmission—under the catchwords "scripture-tradition"—chiefly as controversies between Reformation and Roman Catholic theology. The fact that such a confessionalized view of the issue of tradition is only conditionally accurate from the point of view of theological history can be referred to here only in passing. Nor can I attempt here to trace the path of the ever-changing Catholic/Protestant dispute through all its historical developments. Let us take the present as our starting-point and investigate the present state of the issue.

When one casts one's eye over the last few years one has the impression that the controversy on tradition has subsided altogether. This applies primarily in view of theological literature: by 1967 one could see the oozing away of the broad stream of publications on the subject which had suddenly begun in 1950—again caused by the issue of the content of tradition, in this case the dogma of the assumption of Mary—and which had received a new influx of questions as a result of the anticipation as well as the aftermath of Vatican II and its constitution The Word of God (*Dei Verbum*).[4] Astonishingly, one can also discern an abatement of the problem of tradition when one takes a look at the Catholic/Protestant dialogues triggered by the council: as far as their subject-matter is concerned, one still, it is true, encounters the catchwords "scripture-tradition"; but it seems that the discussions have paused here only briefly.[5] The dialogue between the Lutheran World Federation and the Roman Catholic Church is typical of this. It began deliberately with the question of the tradition of the gospel. However, the problem in its classical form subsided surprisingly quickly during the very first meeting, so that even the report concluding the whole series of discussion deals with the subject in one short paragraph only.[6]

Is all this evidence that this old bone of contention can be numbered among those controversies which have been solved or simply extinguished and whose negotiation can, as Schleiermacher says at one point, be handed over to the history of dogma?

K. E. Skydsgaard, who has contributed to the growing understanding between Catholics and Protestants on this very issue of scripture-tradition as has scarcely any other present-day Protestant theologian, takes this question as the theme of his last publication on the subject —and leaves it open.[7] If one were to attempt a quite general characterization of the present situation, one would be able to describe it precisely in these terms. The controversy on tradition in its old, thoroughly confessionally saturated form is trembling in the balance, so to speak. Whether this is a more or less satsfactory, a more or less reassuring state of affairs remains to be seen. A more important question at present is that of how this seemingly strange situation has come about.

Doubtless one will have to attribute the actual cause to the fact that noticeable rapprochements have taken place in Catholic and Protestant thinking on the issue of scripture-tradition as such. At least one other aspect should, however, be considered before we turn to this main issue.

We have already pointed out that, from a historical point of view, the controversy over the character and structure of the act of transmission does not as a rule develop spontaneously and in isolation. It comes to the fore only when there is conflict over that which is in each case transmitted and to be transmitted, i.e., over important questions of faith, doctrine, piety or church structures. In the absence of such provocation, i.e., without catalytic factors, the issue of tradition is able to rest even if there remain radical differences in interpretation. For divergences in the conception of tradition appear as such not to be among those on which the church may be divided. This very fact seems relevant to a great extent in the current situation. Of course that does not mean to say that there are no longer any church-dividing differences and thus no more cause for serious controversy between Catholics and Protestants where the transmitted content is concerned. But not only is it the general tendency to aim at the overcoming of these theological divergences; it is above all the fact that this rapprochement has already been achieved in essential issues and seems feasible in others as well which is rightly and inevitably forcing the question of the act of transmission into the background and causing it to lose its keenness. Such a development should appear legitimate precisely where Reformation thinking is concerned. For the Reformation *sola scriptura,* the quintessence of the Reformation conception of tradition, was after all not a formal principle maintained for its own sake, but was intended entirely to serve the gospel of justifying grace which was to be transmitted. This explains the sovereignty with which Luther is able to disregard the question of the process of transmission and place Christ or the pure gospel above or, if necessary, even in opposition to Apostles, scripture and church.

Now it would surely be unjustified to regard the current diminution of the Catholic Protestant debate on tradition merely as an indirect result, a kind of by-product, of the growing understanding on the hitherto controversial contents of tradition. Important as this aspect is, it nevertheless explains the present situation only to a certain extent. One is immediately obliged to reverse the relationship and say that it is the growing understanding on the issue of tradition itself which has made a decisive contribution to the rapprochement on the various contents of transmission. In fact both aspects can be regarded as correct. The interplay between them is in accordance with the basic connection between the content of tradition (*traditum tradendum*) and the act of transmission (*actus tradendi*), which we have already pointed out.

Here we find ourselves confronted with the central question: of what does the Catholic Protestant rapprochement on the conception of tradition consist, and how extensive is it?

The first half of our century was a period in which the confessional fronts separated again with particular stringency on the question of tradition. After the partial convergences of the first few decades of the 19th century which had induced a Protestant theologian like F. C. Baur to say that Protestantism and Catholicism had come together in a new, "purified and spiritualized concept of tradition," the paths again diverged radically. This development was marked—on the Catholic side—above all by the dogmatization of immaculate conception (1854), which, for example, caused H. J. Holtzman to mount an attack of unprecedented bitterness against the Catholic conception of tradition and all attempts at Catholic Protestant rapprochement on this issue,[8] and by Vatican I, in which—according to the Protestant verdict—not only had scripture been supplanted by the church's tradition, but church tradition had itself now been engulfed by the papal concept of the church.[9] On the Protestant side it was the conservative theology around the turn of the century, but also and above all dialectical theology, which emphasized scripture as an entity over against the church and as legitimately superior to it, thus dissociating themselves polemically from theological liberalism as well as from Roman Catholic theology.[10] These polemics reached their climax around 1950, the year of the dogmatization of the assumption of Mary.

It might strike one as paradoxical, though, that this very year and the following decade mark a positive turning-point in the history of the Catholic Protestant controversy over scripture and tradition. With regard to Protestant thinking this change has been described by the catchword "rehabilitation" of tradition or of the idea of tradition[11] and—with regard to Catholic theology—as a "turn to Holy Scripture."[12] What is the significance of these two initially vague catchwords?

They are concerned on the one hand with the restoration of a comprehensive, "inclusive" conception of tradition, and on the other with a conception of tradition as an "interpretative" tradition of Scripture". Both concepts, "inclusive tradition" and "interpretative tradition," are key formulas frequently used at present which together—not each one separately—describe the Catholic Protestant rapprochement on the question of tradition.

A. TRADITION AS AN "INCLUSIVE" PROCESS

From the sixteenth century controversies to the present day one has been hearing from the Catholic side that the Reformation advocated an "exclusive"—in the strongest sense of the word—scripture principle and thus reduced the entire process of the transmission of the gospel to self-interpreting scripture. "He [Luther] took the principle of the supremacy of scripture to its extreme by asserting that it alone has any validity," writes Congar, among others.[13] Protestants have for a long time seen virtually no reason to oppose this Catholic interpretation, which to some extent turned the Reformation principle of *sola scriptura* into one of *scriptura solitaria*. On the contrary! They themselves formulated an interpretation of this kind, following the conception of scripture of the early Protestant orthodoxy rather than that of the Reformers. Occasionally they even went as far as to accuse Luther or his followers, wherever they valued and accepted church tradition—e.g., early church dogma, the writings of the church fathers, the decisions of the councils—of vacillation or of abandoning the "purity of the scriptural principle"[14] or of an "unsatisfactory implementation of the Protestant principle"[15] and vestiges of traditionalism.[16]

It was inevitable that in the formulation and application of the Reformation scripture principle its tradition-critical character came to the foreground. It was not, however, a case of denying the whole of church tradition, as would have been the consequence of a truly "exclusive" scripture principle. Some very essential elements of Reformation thinking stood in the way of such an exclusive version of the scripture principle and were responsible for the fact that no break was made *de facto* with church tradition in its entirety. It was probably of particular importance that Luther's interpretation of the scriptures was determined by an understanding of the continuity of the church, which constituted an "integral part of his conception of church and history."[17] This continuity of the church is not conceived by Luther in a biblicist way, i.e. as if it were maintained exclusively and solely by the transmission of scripture. It is rather church fathers, symbols of church faith, early church dogma and councils which play an essential part in this continuity and in the continuing process of the transmission of the gospel. Indicative of this is, for example, the way in which Luther defends himself in his treatise "Against Hanswurst" against the accusation of having introduced heretical "innovations." He defends himself not only by reference to scripture but also and equally by reference to the beliefs of the early church.[18] No less important was the fact that for Luther it is *not* the word of scripture as such which passes on the living gospel and constitutes the "life and substance of the church," but the "word of mouth."[19] E. Schlink says rightly: "The knowledge that the apostolic message is, by its nature, to be handed down primarily not as a book to be read out, but in the act of oral proclamation, prevented Luther from overlooking the living quality of the apostolic tradition in ever-new words and deeds of the church and from despising that which originated from church history."[20]

It is therefore not contrary to, but entirely in accordance with, Reformation principles if Protestants today dissociate themselves more stringently than ever from an exclusive interpretation of the scripture principle[21] and take the view of an "inclusive" conception of tradition which regards scripture as being embedded in a more comprehensive and polymorphic process of transmission.[22] Scripture is not dissociated and separate from the church. It belongs—as is continually stressed—"within the church" and within the comprehensive process of transmission which takes place "in *all* the words and deeds of the church."[23] "The Bible cannot be separated from the church. It belongs in the church with its praise and its confession, with its proclamation, baptism and communion."[24] At the World Conference on Faith and Order in Montreal (1963) this inclusive conception of transmission could be formulated as an ecumenical consensus:

> "Thus we can say that we exist as Christians by the Tradition of the Gospel . . . testified in Scripture, transmitted in and by the Church through the power of the Holy Spirit. Tradition taken in this sense is actualized in the preaching of the Word, in the administration of the Sacraments and worship, in Christian teaching and theology, and in mission and witness to Christ by the lives of the members of the Church."[25]

The fact that the Protestants arrived at a "rehabilitation" of the idea of tradition and at the restoration of a comprehensive and inclusive conception of tradition was not, however, primarily the result of a reconsideration of the genuine structure of the Reformation scripture principle. It can be traced back to a series of motives or causes, some of which had long been exerting their influence and of which three in particular should be accentuated.

Initially there were inducements resulting from historical and critical research of the Bible. An examination of the historically conditioned structure of the biblical canon and its individual writings had profoundly shaken the orthodox Protestant doctrine of scriptural inspiration and thus also its exclusive conception of the Reformation principle of *sola scriptura*. The result was a crisis in the canonical concept which concerned not merely the external delimitation of the scriptural canon but canonicity and the normativity of scripture in general. This canonical crisis has been manifest at the latest since J. S. Semler's *Abhandlung von freier Untersuchung des Kanons* (1771-1775), and provided at least a starting-point for a re-evaluation of the idea of tradition, as is evident from Lessing[26] and F. C. Baur,[27] among others. Above all, however, biblical form criticism and tradition criticism during this century have demonstrated that "scripture" and "tradition" cannot be understood as antitheses, nor as isolated from each other. This research has clarified the manifold process of transmission out of which biblical scripture has grown, and shown that the New Testament authors see themselves as the receivers of tradition and themselves continue the process of transmission by theologically interpreting from their own viewpoint that which has been handed down to them and construing it to suit each audience. The resulting theological multiformity of the New Testament witness rules out the use of scriptures as if it were a homogeneous and unambiguous entity. Only an interpretative transmission of the scriptural witness does justice to the origin and structure of scripture. The biblical scriptures thus stem from a process of transmission, themselves take up this process and lead to its continuation.

Of course this motive for a positive reconsideration of the idea of transmission, originating from exegetical research, must be seen in close connection with that radical change of direction in western thinking which has been characterized as a change from a "metaphysical" to an "historical" way of thinking. Human reality and everything related to this reality are bound up with history as with a moving process in which preservation and change coexist in permanent interplay. Historical continuity does not consist of the timeless and changeless endurance or handing down of something which has once been given. Historical continuity, rather, has the character of a living process of transmission in which that which has come from the past is simultaneously preserved and transformed; indeed, it is only through transformation that it can be brought into the present and there taken over and preserved. Also the gospel and Christian faith exist not outside history, but within it. This means that the handing down of the Gospel and the continuity of Christian faith are not mere matters of maintaining and passing on constant factors but of historical transmission in which preservation and transformation, conservation and modification are not mutually exclusive, but inter-related.[28] From a historical viewpoint the transmission and conti-nuity of the gospel cannot therefore be guaranteed solely and exclu-sively by scripture in its fixed form. What is needed is a living transmission of the original witness to Christ as laid down in the scriptures. This transmission incorporates interpretation and varia-tion of the original witness to Christ in a hermeneutic context pro-vided by the changing historical, cultural and social horizon.

The experiences of the ecumenical movement have, after all, also made their contribution to the fact that the inexorability as well as the legitimacy of tradition were seen more clearly than before. For in ecumenical confrontations it became manifestly clear that even those churches which together advocate the *sola scriptura* principle have developed different "traditions" which are often even felt to be church-dividing—whether in the fields of teaching, of the worship service, of church order, of ethos or piety—and which, according to the convictions of the churches concerned, further the right trans-mission of the gospel and cannot therefore simply be abandoned. Even the *sola scriptura* churches do not live by scripture alone, but at the same time by their particular traditions. The theme "scripture and tradition" therefore rightly and swiftly became a major subject of theological study within the ecumenical movement,[29] and it was clear from the outset that this was not simply a matter of a Protes-tant Catholic controversy, but a problem affecting all churches.

The restoration of a more comprehensive and inclusive concep-tion of transmission may be a task which to a particular degree con-fronts the Protestant churches whose character is based on their heri-tage of a *sola scriptura*, all too often understood in an exclusive, bib-licist sense. But even in the Catholic conception of tradition there are still a past to be brought up to date and constrictions or biases to be eliminated.

Catholic theologians[30] seem to be unanimous in their verdict that there begins a period of disintegration and false priorities after an epoch which had lasted from the time of the early church up to early and high scholasticism and during which the entities responsible for transmission, i.e., scripture, tradition and the church, remained to-gether in a harmonious synthesis. Manifestations of disintegration, often very varied, of the original synthesis were a disproportionate emphasis on the church, particularly in the form of the church or traditions, stress laid on the insufficiency of scriptural content, and papal teaching ministry, the greater prominence of the unwritten traditions, stress laid on the insufficiency of scriptural content, and the predominance given to scriptural authority over the church. They are evident long before the Reformation—approximately since the end of the thirteenth century.

An inclusive understanding of tradition also fails to be re-established during the post-Reformation period. In contradiction to the Reformation scripture principle, the unwritten traditions, and above all the authority of the church's teaching ministry, are given disproportionate emphasis. The rudiments of a re-establishment of the earlier synthesis, provided in the doctrinal statements of the Council of Trent, are not noticed or pursued. The insufficiency of scriptural content continues to be asserted, and more and more stress is put on the third member of the triad, the church, in particular the papal teaching office, to the detriment both of objective historical tradition and of scripture. Not until the nineteenth century is a conception of tradition developed on a relatively broad front which appears to provide once again a right alignment of the three entities scripture, tradition, and church.

It is nevertheless the result of the harsh condemnations of Gallicanism as well as of the Old Catholic position and of modernism that the living teaching ministry of the church once again receives disproportionate emphasis towards the end of the nineteenth (Vatican I) and during the first half of the twentieth centuries and that there was once again dissociation from the great nineteenth-century theologians and their more comprehensive conception of tradition.

At this point the more recent Catholic research into the problem of tradition begins. Its common denominator is the fact that, in opposing an exaggerated emphasis on the church's teaching ministry, it not only brings to bear the function of the entire church in the process of transmission but also affords new prominence to connecting transmission with objective historical tradition and above all with scripture, in order to guarantee once again a right conspectus of scripture-tradition-church.

Some essential parts of the constitution on the Word of God (*Dei Verbum*) of Vatican II are the fruit of this more recent Catholic effort towards a comprehensive conception of tradition. This conception is clearly expressed in the summarizing paragraph at the end of the second chapter ("The Transmission of Divine Revelation") :

"It is clear, therefore, that sacred tradition, sacred Scripture, and the teaching authority of the Church, in accord with God's most wise design, are so linked and joined together that one cannot stand without the others, and that all together and each in its own way under the action of the one Holy Spirit contribute effectively to the salvation of souls."

It is thus evident that developments have taken place on both the Protestant and the Catholic sides which have as their common goal the restoration of an "inclusive" conception of tradition, free of constrictions and false alternatives—a goal which has indeed been reached. If one compares the Montreal text with those of Vatican II, "the convergence is obvious. Both documents take as their starting point a comprehensive concept of tradition."[31] Certainly, one cannot overlook the fact that the individual elements or entities viewed and held together in this conception of tradition with regard to content and character often differ somewhat on the Catholic and on the Protestant side. If one, for instance, takes as a basis the triad scripture-tradition-church, this applies in respect of the second member as well as and above all the third (church teaching ministry). The convergence is nevertheless clear: various entities operate together in the transmission of the gospel—above all scripture, the inherited church tradition and the living proclamation, confession, teaching and action of the church of today.

B. TRADITION AS "INTERPRETATIVE TRADITION OF SCRIPTURE"

A reference to the jointly re-established comprehensive conception of tradition does not, however, fully describe the rapprochement which has been taking place over the last two decades. If that were so, this rapprochement would—especially to the Reformation way of thinking—still seem highly unsatisfactory. For as soon as the false alternatives, biases and claims of absoluteness pertaining to the various entites operating together in the process of gospel transmission have been overcome, one is immediately confronted with the question of the inner structure of this total correlation of scripture-tradition-church, the question of the right differentiation and alignment of the individual entities. This question must be asked, and it can also be asked without once again destroying the comprehensiveness of the process of transmission.

It is true that there is an obvious temptation to be content with the restoration of a comprehensive conception of tradition and to brush aside the question of the inner structure and priority of the elements of tradition, especially if one is guided primarily by the early church's conception of tradition. Such a temptation is certainly particularly strong for the Catholic way of thinking, but it also manifests itself from time to time on the Protestant side.[32]

As I have already mentioned, and as is also made clear at the conclusion of the preceding article by Benoît, the early church had developed during its dispute with gnosis a conception of tradition which had—in the exemplary sense of the word—characteristics of "inclusiveness." There are above all three elements, all essentially in accordance with the triad scripture-tradition-church, which work together in harmonious synthesis and preserve in their cooperation the unadulterated handing on of the apostolic deposit of faith: the christologically interpreted Old Testament and the apostolic writings, the rule of faith (*regula fidei*), initially understood not as a credal formula, but generally as the faith and doctrine of the church, and finally the church's ministry as within the apostolic succession. None of these elements is given an exclusive position in the process of transmission. Thus scripture is incorporated in tradition not simply as a piece of writing, as a text, but always as scripture read and interpreted by the church and in the light of the church's faith. Conversely, church's faith and doctrine are understood essentially as an "interpretation of scripture."[33] The ministerial succession is similarly treated: the process of transmission as the unadulterated handing down of the apostolic witness is assured through the ministerial succession, so that tradition is always *paradosis kata diadochen* (transmission in accordance with the-episcopal-succession).[34] At the same time, however, this ministerial apostolicity remains linked with and keyed to doctrinal apostolicity—and thus to scripture and rule of faith—but not, of course, in such a way that one can separate doctrinal apostolicity from ministerial apostolicity as an independent entity and set it over against the latter as an objective criterion.

All three entities are therefore thought of as "coinherent."[35] Whichever one examines refers to the others, and thus always leads back into the circle which links together all the elements of the process of transmission.

This process of transmission, multidimensional in itself, is encompassed by two major aspects in which the comprehensiveness of tradition is particularly clearly expressed: by the general ecclesiological aspect and the general pneumatological one, with which it is most closely linked. The instrument of transmission in every dimension is the church as a fellowship of all believers, as a "people united with its priest and a fold clinging to its shepherd."[36] It can be the instrument of transmission, however, only because the Holy Spirit is present within it. The whole event of transmission is therefore understood ultimately as a pneumatic event which takes place in the church and through the church.[37]

This description, which is of necessity brief and therefore also a simplification, shows the proximity which exists between the early church's idea of tradition and the comprehensive conception of tradition re-established at present.[38] At the same time, though, an examination of history can make us aware of the whole complex of problems surrounding such an understanding of tradition. It was, after all, not by chance that this complete and harmonious conception, closely encompassed and borne by the general ecclesiological and pneumatological context, became problematic during the waning of the Middle Ages. In any case, one would scarcely do justice to the phenomenon of the subsequent disintegration of the inclusive concept of tradition by seeking its causes outside this conception, in the ideas of individual theologians, for example, or of theological schools, in certain religious movements or even in the political and ecclesiastical circumstances of the time. It was rather the case that the inclusive conception of tradition disclosed its own inner problems and weaknesses. In the last analysis, this is the result of the fact that, wherever apostolic writings, the faith and doctrine of the church and the church's ministry are seen as coinherent and as entirely encompassed by an ecclesiological pneumatology to an extent characteristic of the ideas of the early church, the "difference between the church of that time or the church of the post-apostolic era on the one hand, and the church of the apostles on the other" threatens to dissolve[39] and thus the lasting normative character of the origin is virtually forced to give way, even if one affirms or even stresses it. A clear indication of this is the expansion of the concept *sacra scriptura,* which, in addition to the Old and New Testament scriptures, is now able to comprise the writings of the church fathers, council texts, symbols of faith and papal decrees.[40] Equally characteristic is the fact that one now employs the concepts of divine or Spirit-created "revelation" and "inspiration" to denote post-apostolic

doctrinal utterances, instead of clearly reserving these concepts exclusively for biblical revelation and scriptural inspiration, as advocated by Thomas of Aquinas, for example.[41]

If one is to evaluate the inclusive conception of tradition with its
complex of inner problems and its theological and ecclesiastical consequences it is important to see that religious movements (Walden-
sians, Franciscan movement, Joachimites, Hussites, etc.) often con-
demned as heretical by the church of the time arose one after the
other ever since the twelfth century. In spite of their differing manifestations they reveal one common element: a more or less severely
critical basic attitude toward the church. Congar, who attempts to
see here a type of "heresy" new to the history of the church,[42] says of
these movements supported above all by the people: "With all their
differences they shared in the criticism of the church, of the clergy,
the monks, the bishops and the papacy and claimed that it belonged
more to Constantine than to Peter. They criticized its wealth, its
claim to power. They demanded a Christianity which was closer to
the letter of the gospel, which was less overshadowed by external
modes of action. . . . Certain abuses in clergy circles and among
the bishops and various errors of conduct and discipline were
lamented."[43] As accurate as this characterization may be, it nevertheless risks not quite doing justice to the eminent theological core of
these movements. Certainly criticism of the church is kindled by
those obvious abuses, by a particular "state of affairs" (Congar), and
remains *prima facie* limited to this area. In the last analysis, however, it still indicates the deeper rooted fact that the church of the
times had separated itself from the church of the apostles, and for-
feited its apostolic credibility precisely because it identified itself far
too uncritically with the church of the apostles and failed to take
sufficient heed of the difference between the two, which was, in
effect, a "critical summons." But precisely at this point there lies the
danger of an all too harmoniously conceived inclusive conception of
tradition resting upon an ecclesiological pneumatology: the conception can incorporate the criteriological question only with difficulty,
and tends constantly to shield itself from it.

What, then, is brought to light in the medieval movements aimed
at criticising the church is no less than a crisis of the inclusive understanding of tradition itself—a crisis by no means of external origin,
but stemming precisely from the inner conflict of the conception.

The movements in question adopt this crisis as the focus of their censure. And in this censure reference to scripture plays a—if not the—dominating rôle.[44]

This becomes wholly clear wherever the intentions of this movement, initially only scantily considered from a theological point of view, are more clearly articulated. There is a long list of names one could mention here. To extract the most important of them one ought probably to begin with Henry of Ghent and Gerhard of Bologna and continue via Marsilius of Padua and Occam, the theologians of the Reform councils such as d'Ailly and Gerson, and then Wyclif and Hus, as far as the theologians of the *Devotio Moderna*, like Johann Pupper von Goch, Johann Rucherat von Wesel, and Wessel Gansfort.[45] None of these stops at simply emphasizing the importance and value of scripture, which had in fact always been stressed and never seriously questioned. All continue beyond this to speak, though with varying degrees of intensity and harshness, of the *critical* significance and *critical* function of scripture in relation to the church's faith and doctrine and thus within the process of transmission. The question is the following: does this denote the tearing apart of church and scripture and so the dissolution in principle of an inclusive conception of tradition? There is much that contradicts such an interpretation. It appears that none of the theologians named—not even Wyclif, let alone the others!—can be proved to have advocated a *sola scriptura* principle—understood as isolated, as separated from the church and its tradition and, in an exclusive sense, as the instrument and guarantor of the entire process of transmission. It is rather the case that the theologians named constantly state that for them scripture is not isolated, but is seen and read in the context of other elements which contribute towards the transmission of the gospel: church fathers, symbols of faith, councils, church teachers, the heritage of church tradition. Even where the formula *sola scriptura* occurs—and it occurs frequently in this form or equivalent formulas—it by no means has that strictly exclusive sense which is suspected by some interpreters and desired by others. One could agree with the Catholic theologian P. de Vooght, who has thoroughly investigated this issue: "In reality this 'solum' or 'sola' lacked, among the theologians of the time, even Wyclif, the literal and exclusive sense which is accorded to it today."[46] The *solus*, however, does attribute a particular *rank* to scripture in the process of transmission, together with the function of keeping the principle of *critical apostolicity* alive in the church and of guaranteeing its application.

From this aspect it is impossible to regard the waning Middle Ages simply as an unhappy epoch of false alternatives and of the disintegration of the inclusive conception of tradition hitherto existing. The whole tendency, especially in its basic intention, is one of a justified theological effort to overcome the weaknesses of a harmoniously conceived, comprehensive understanding of tradition— weaknesses which were becoming obvious by their practical consequences—by means of a *modification* of the understanding of tradition. Nevertheless this modification safeguards the "inclusive" character of tradition. It consisted of an attempt to introduce into the prevailing conception of tradition the principle of critical apostolicity in the form of a new emphasis on the normative character of scripture. In other words, the intention was to understand the apostolicity of the church not only as a pneumatic and ecclesial fact, as something given, but also as a challenge, as a "summons"; not only as an indicative accepted in trust, but also as a "reformatory" imperative, if one will.

It is not necessary to demonstrate further how this struggle for the modification of the understanding of tradition engendered a certain amount of shock, that it necessarily provoked counter-relations and that its results were not yet satisfactory. Yet it is equally clear that the subsequent church and theology would never again be released from this struggle. The inclusive conception of tradition in the form characteristic of the church as it was from the time of Irenaeus to that of high scholasticism cannot simply be restored in its pristine form, even if it did continue to provide constructive and critical stimuli for the centuries to come. It rested on a comprehensive trust of the church on the part of the faithful which was as robust as it was naïve and which has been crushed over since the rise of the movements of the Middle Ages that were critical of the church. Ever since, the church has lived with this criticism and with the consequent and never-ending demand for a "reform of head and body." The emergence at that time of a critical consciousness toward the church marks a point in time behind which it is no longer possible to retreat. And therefore even the view that the confessional problem of tradition could be solved by the mere reestablishment of an inclusive conception of tradition such as was characteristic of the early church has something anachronistic about it, not unlike the attempt to re-unite the separated churches in the consensus of the first five centuries.

There is no need to pursue this question further into the Reformation period. What I have said about the Reformation scripture principle has perhaps already made it sufficiently clear that the central issue here is the same as that which lay at the root of the theological struggles of the fourteenth and fifteenth centuries. That is to say that the Reformation emphasis on scripture was concerned with the incorporation, however forcibly demanded and executed, of the principle of critical apostolicity into the alleged frame of a comprehensive conception of tradition and thus with the modification—not with the rejection—of this conception.

One can say that the convergence between Catholic and Protestant thinking is manifest today even on this issue. If Protestants on their side are, as demonstrated in the preceding chapter, complying with a genuinely Catholic concern by integrating scripture more completely than before into the context of a more comprehensive process of transmission and emphasizing that scripture must be read and construed within the church and its tradition, Catholics are also cooperating with the genuinely Reformation concern of viewing and emphasizing more strongly than before the particular and normative position of scripture in the total structure of tradition.[47]

Those who seek a concise and indicative guiding term for these Catholic efforts will find it first of all in the concept "interpretative tradition." Certainly this does not occur in all Catholic authors. There is, however, a consensus on the issue itself: the transmission of the apostolic gospel, taking place in and through the church, is at heart nothing other than a contemporary interpretation, a new and pertinent explanation of the original apostolic witness. And this, with today's widely re-established view of scripture as the sufficient record of this apostolic witness, means that transmission takes place as *traditio interpretativa scripturae sacrae*, as an "interpretative tradition of Holy Scripture." This conception of tradition—according to Catholic opinion—guarantees the retrospective link with the irretrievable apostolic origin and observes the objective and critical primacy of the Word of God over the word of the church. For: "Interpretation necessarily implies obedient subordination to that which is interpreted."[48]

All tradition—even the activity of the church's teaching ministry

—has to take place "in permanent, ceaselessly renewed and necessary reference to that lasting concreteness of origin and beginning which alone is guaranteed 'pure' by God and can be differentiated from the fulfillment of the later church . . . ; this concreteness . . . can be found in scripture and only in scripture."[49] All subsequent doctrine and proclamation therefore have their necessary "counterpart,"[50] "origin, source, standard and norm,"[51] their "normative authority"[52] in scripture as that apostolic tradition[53] which has found expression in the written word as the "objectivation of the beginning."[54]

These results of theological research are also expressed to a marked degree in the constitution on the Word of God (*Dei Verbum*) of Vatican II, particularly in Chapter 6 ("Sacred Scripture in the Life of the Church") : "The Church has always venerated the divine Scriptures just as she venerates the body of the Lord. . . . She has always regarded the Scriptures together with sacred tradition as the supreme rule of faith, and will ever do so. For, inspired by God and committed once and for all to writing, they impart the word of God Himself without change, and make the voice of the Holy Spirit resound in the words of the prophets and apostles. Therefore, like the Christian religion itself, all the preaching of the Church must be nourished and ruled (regatur) by sacred Scripture."[55]

If one now takes a look at the report of the Montreal conference it may strike one at first glance as a sheer reversal of previous confessional positions in this conference, consisting above all of representatives of Protestant churches, refers with positive timidity to the specific and normative position of scripture within the comprehensive process of transmission, if one compares its statements with those of Vatican II. Now this is doubtless a result of the fact that the whole aim of the conference was precisely the restoration of a new and comprehensive view of tradition, the overcoming of an exclusive, biblicist and static scripture principle and the demonstration of scripture's need of interpretation. It would, however, be a fatal misconception to refuse to see what sort of premise determined the background to this. This is also made clear when the report refers to scripture as the "criterion" by which all attempts to determine the original tradition of the gospel have been made.[56] Even the very conscious distinction that "the Tradition of the Gospel . . . [is] *testified* in Scripture, *transmitted* in and by the Church through the power of the Holy Spirit"[57] clearly indicates the particular rank of scripture and thus a corresponding distinction within the total process of transmission. The basic distinction between text and interpretation, whose maintenance was the aim of the Reformation *sola scriptura*, is in any case maintained here in the same way as it is expressed in the Catholic conception of tradition as "interpretative tradition."

We can now begin to sum up the reflections and analyses we have made. The Catholic/Protestant debate on the form and structure of tradition has led to a *double convergence*. *On the one hand* an inclusive conception has jointly been restored, one which no longer defines an individual element as the exclusive instrument of transmission. *On the other hand* it is jointly recognized that there is an order of precedence within the various elements or entities of tradition which fundamentally belong together. This order is determined by the normative primacy of the apostolic writings from which the apostolic summons—which cannot be confused with the factual situation of our churches—reaches us.[58] These two, inclusiveness and order of precedence, do not contradict each other but belong together. To use a quotation from Congar: "Scripture and Tradition are not on the same level. Scripture is absolutely sovereign: it is of God, even in its form. It is the norm for Tradition and for the Church, while neither the Church nor Tradition is the norm for it. . . . However, the sovereign character of Scripture does not prevent it from being *one of the components* of God's works, which include the Church and Tradition; nor does it preclude the existence of a mutual interrelation between these three entities which renders it impossible to isolate them totally, let alone oppose them."[59]

Does this not tally essentially, even literally, with what is said on the Protestant side, e.g., by Skydsgaard: "An approach to the Bible which is separate from living proclamation (and by that Skydsgaard always means proclamation within the church and its tradition), and in this sense an unmediated approach, is an illusion. But *within* the congregation, *within* tradition scripture assumes an absolutely supreme and necessary position?"[60]

This question brings us back to the beginning of our investigation.

III.

The Remaining Differences and the Question of Their Relevance

Is it not possible, after all our analyses and considerations, to say more than just that the discussion on tradition in its confessional form is at present in the balance or temporarily at rest? Has not the problem in fact been solved, so that one should talk frankly and openly of agreements instead of diffidently about "convergences?" Is the present state of the issue not precisely that there is no longer any issue at all?

In spite of everything that has been said one cannot fully agree with this. For it is clear at first glance that the individual entities oı the total process of transmission, scripture-tradition-church, appear different in content and character for Catholics and Protestants. This is true as regards the "tradition" or content of the church's tradition, insofar as there are also "dogmas" involved on the Catholic side which simply do not exist in the Protestant domain, no matter how the structure and authority of confessional statements may manifest themselves *de facto* in the Protestant churches. This applies all the more in respect of the "church," insofar as its magisterium, equipped with a very specific supreme doctrinal authority, is part of the Catholic conception of the church, a factor which again does not exist in the Protestant domain. From this viewpoint alone it would be naïve to overrate the current convergences on tradition by calling them a general and complete consensus, indeed even to expect a flawless consensus, unless one ceases to be "Catholic" or "Protestant."

The remaining differences become concrete above all on the issue of how scripture exercises its—jointly recognized—normative, controlling and critical function as regards tradition and church or ecclesiastical magisterium.

At the same time one must immediately bear in mind that a question arises here which, on the Protestant side, can no longer be answered by a mere reference to scriptural text and a demand for obedient observance of this text. The question has, one could say, become more complex in *substance*, but has lost some of its sting as an *interconfessional* problem. For it is jointly accepted today that scripture can be fully valid only as interpreted scripture and therefore can also exercise its normative and judicial function in the process of transmission only as interpreted scripture. In other words, Catholics and Protestants find themselves together confronted by the hermeneutic circle: scripture has a definitive function where church and tradition are concerned, but it nevertheless exercises this definitive function only as scripture interpreted in and through tradition and church.[61] It remains clear, though, that this hermeneutic circle and its affirmation do not amount to a replacement of the text by its interpretation. The distinction between text and interpretation is preserved. This very conviction is, after all, the essence of the idea of "interpretative tradition," and this is why it was so important that the Catholic/Protestant convergence on the conception of tradition did not stop at an undifferentiated, comprehensive conception, which, as historical investigation had shown, threatens to efface the distinction between text and interpretation.

Although, therefore, deepened insight into the hermeneutic problem relieves to a certain extent the acuteness of the question of how scripture functions as the norm of tradition and at least prevents a relapse into old confessional antagonisms, there remain specific confessional differences on this question which stand in the way of a complete consensus. These reveal themselves above all in two closely related points.

First there is the question: for whom and, as it is always *interpreted* scripture with which one is concerned, in whose hands does scripture become the critical norm of tradition? Protestants would say it is the whole body of the faithful: church leadership and congregation, ministers, theologians and lay people; it remains clear, though, that each believer reads, hears and understands scripture not as an isolated individual, but as a member of the church and within the framework of his church tradition. For the entire church and for every one of its members scripture is therefore the ultimate norm, and it can, therefore, also develop its normative critical power over against the church and its tradition.

According to Catholic understanding, on the other hand, scripture provides the norm in an immediate sense only for the church's teaching ministry, and is the norm for the individual believer only as scripture interpreted by the magisterium. That this is the Catholic conviction is not only shown in the text of the constitution on the Word of God (*Dei Verbum*).[62] It is also stated so clearly and so often even by those Catholic theologians who today put particular emphasis on the normative function of scripture for the church and its tradition that no detailed illustration is required here.[63]

The difference is clear, and one can easily trace its theological roots as far as the differing conceptions of church and of the activity of the Holy Spirit. Even the differing motives emerging from and strengthened by concrete historical experiences, are clear. If Catholics intend to prevent the subjective and arbitrary interpretation and use of scripture, Protestants are concerned with allowing the critical power of scripture to develop more freely and with preventing it from being subjected to the authority of church ministry. It cannot be denied that both motives envisage real dangers.

It would perhaps be as well to point out that there is a growing body of opinion in Catholic theology which to a certain extent attributes a "controlling function" in the process of transmission to individual believers as well, especially to the exegetes.[64] This can only be emphatically welcomed on the Protestant side and seen as a sign of the fact that the Protestant understanding is not entirely alien and unacceptable to Catholic thinking. The question of whether a genuine antithesis exists between Catholic and Protestant conceptions should not, however, be made dependent upon whether or not this view becomes generally accepted.

The question ought rather to be the following: is the difference described above so great that one has to say that the Catholic conception is once again shielding the church with its tradition from the critical summons of scripture, while the Protestant conception exposes it to this summons? In our opinion the difference in question cannot be construed in this way, unless one reverts to the view that scripture always fulfills its normative and critical function as a mere text left fundamentally uninterpreted by church and tradition. But as long as one maintains that scripture—even in the hands of the individual believer—always functions as scripture interpreted within the church and its tradition, it is impossible to construe from this difference an antithesis which would cancel out the convergence achieved. The Catholic/Protestant debate on tradition does not, therefore, necessarily have to be prolonged until even this difference has been ironed out. It can remain in the balance at this point.

Another difference still remaining between the Catholic and Protestant conceptions of tradition seems to be more serious. It is, in fact, related in many respects to the question we have just dealt with, but is fundamentally of an independent nature. It is the question of the status of the church's doctrinal decisions which have been reached in the past.

This question has also to be defined as accurately as possible. It is not simply the problem of the binding authority of decisions on the church's doctrine and dogma, nor is it so much a question of whether or not the magisterium is infallible when it reaches a decision.

It is perfectly true that a confession of a church—or its order—is of binding nature for the faithful even on the Protestant side; nor can it be denied that there is necessarily a claim to truth or authority behind it which, though not described by the term "infallible," nevertheless comes close to this. The complete certainty which Luther, for example, expects of the preacher and which should make the sermon he gives into a "Thus has said the Lord" (*Haec dixit Dominus*) for him and for his audience points very clearly in this direction.[65] In any case the transmission of the gospel in doctrine, confession and proclamation—like faith itself—cannot remain stranded in a "perhaps—but perhaps not," but must rather, according to Luther's well-known saying, have an assertive character if it is to be transmission of the gospel.[66]

This becomes even more obvious when, for example, the member churches of the Lutheran World Federation recognize the Lutheran Confessions, especially the Confessio Augustana and Luther's Small Catechism, as "a pure (in German *unverfälscht*—unadulterated) exposition of the Word of God."[67] It is not very easy to make a clear differentiation between the attributes "infallible" and "unadulterated," particularly if one considers that, for instance, the Catholic German Bishops' Conference, in its criticism of H. Küng's book on infallibility, avoids the word "infallible," replaces it, as Küng does, by "unerring" and thus states that decisions on church doctrine are intended to "retain the Word once spoken and interpret it unerringly."[68]

All these observations are not made with the intention of glossing over the differences between Catholic and Protestant conceptions or of leveling them with glib remarks. The question is that of where the essential difference reveals itself. It will thus perhaps be necessary to go one step further towards specifying where this difference does *not* lie. I have in mind here what one could call the "pneumatological indicative," which occurs continually in the Catholic statements on the ecclesiastical magisterium and its supreme doctrinal authority and which is criticized just as often from the Protestant side. It is characteristic of Catholic statements on the magisterium that they mention less often than Protestant statements do the fact that the church teaching ministry *should* or *must* be in line with scripture. Wherever Catholic theologians or texts intend to be precise, the essential subordination of the magisterium to scripture as the norm is expressed mostly in the *indicative*. It is stated that in its doctrinal decisions the ecclesiastical magisterium *orientates itself* (as a matter of fact and always) in accordance with scripture. And this indicative stems from the certainty that the church, and within it its magisterium, are granted the assistance of the Holy Spirit.

Do the Catholic and Protestant conceptions break apart here? Catholics and Protestants themselves very often picture the situation in this way. G. C. Berkouwer, for example, says: "The controversy as to Scripture and tradition centers increasingly on this *a priori* guarantee (that is, of the Holy Spirit). . . . It is here that we face one of the most profound issues of the controversy, namely the ecclesiological-pneumatological issue."[69]

One can hear similar viewpoints from the Catholic side, for instance from Congar: "In the last analysis, the core of the issue (i.e., of the Catholic/Protestant controversy over scripture and tradition) is ecclesiological"; which for him means—and thus he concludes his monumental work on tradition—that it is a question of "the connection between church and Holy Spirit." "A necessary condition of a more adequate theology of tradition is the elaboration of a more satisfying doctrine of the activity of the Holy Spirit in the church as such."[70]

The "pneumatological indicative" is certainly characteristic of Catholic thinking and once again indicates a clear-cut difference from Protestant thinking. But is it necessary to see a real gulf here which must be bridged without fail if the convergences on tradition are to become valid and effective? Is it not the case that the Catholic "indicative" also contains a very obvious "imperative" note and that —conversely—the Protestant "imperative" is capable of assuming a clearly "indicative" sense?

This, too, can be illustrated here only briefly. One interesting point is the Word of God (Dei Verbum) text of Vatican II (No. 10) : "This teaching office is not above the word of God, but serves it, teaching only what has been handed on as far as (*quatenus* in the Latin text) one is listening to it devoutly, guarding it scrupulously, and explaining it faithfully by divine commission and with the help of the Holy Spirit; it draws from this one deposit of faith everything which it presents for belief as divinely revealed."

Is one not obliged to regard this "as far as" (*quatenus*) as a serious imperative insertion into the indicative statements? It reminds a Lutheran immediately of the confessional documents of his own church and of an old and tough debate which certainly ought not to be resuscitated here. It should nevertheless be pointed out that the binding nature of the statements of the Augsburg Confession is strengthened in the Formula of Concord not—as in the constitution The Word of God (*Dei Verbum*) —by an "as far as," but by a phrase of more strongly indicative overtones: "*because (quia)* it is taken from the Word of God and solidly and well grounded therein."[71]

In short: it undoubtedly could be true, and remain so, that on the Protestant side the *summons* in the word of mission of the risen Christ ("teach . . . all that I have commanded you . . .") is more strongly accentuated, whereas on the Catholic side it is the *promise* ("And be assured, I am with you always . . ." Matthew 28:18 ff.) which predominates. These differing accents no longer need to end in antithesis, but can be held together in the framework of a basic agreement marked by the convergences achieved.

We have thus cleared the way for the question in which the persisting difference between Catholic and Protestant thinking on tradition is, to my mind, most marked and most problematical: the question of the status of the church's doctrinal decisions which have been reached in the past and are binding. Can scripture exercise its critical normativity even where they are concerned? Or are they— once established by the church as "unadulterated" or "unerring" interpretations of scripture—now exempt from scripture's critical voice?

The Protestant conception is unequivocal here, at least in principle: all symbols and confessions of faith are permanently to be subjected to the normative and critical summons of scripture, irrespective of the fact that they are recognized here and now as an unadulterated scriptural interpretation which is therefore binding for the church. This guarantees that interpretation, however adequate it may appear, can never replace the text. As a scriptural interpretation which is in the widest sense conditioned by time and history, the church's confession is open to critical revision and repeated correction through scripture.

What is the situation on the Catholic side? The concept of dogma of Vatican II does not appear to permit such a critical interpretation or even revision. Does the fact that the irreformability of dogma has itself been raised to the level of dogma preclude the possibility of a fresh view of the matter?

It is well known that inner-Catholic discussion has got under way on this point as well, and rudiments and possibilities of an under-

standing of dogma which clearly tends towards the Protestant interpretation are at least beginning to emerge. The view that one should
differentiate between the changeable form and the permanent content of dogma does not yet as such signify an essential breakthrough.
It does, however, lead further, as long as one is conscious of the inseparable integration of form and content. Even the break from a
static concept of dogma towards an "historical," "dynamic," "functional" conception, which makes possible a "critical interpretation
of dogma in the light of scripture,"[72] or the understanding that
dogma "fundamentally and necessarily remains open to possible
further interpretation,"[73] provides important new starting-points for
our efforts towards closer understanding. The same is true of the
increasingly widespread view that the "infallibility" of the church
does not reveal itself primarily in irreformable and infallible dogmatic statements, but that "basically the church remains in the truth
that is unaffected by errors in detail."[74]

The decisive factor, however, will be that the joint conviction
elaborated in the Catholic/Protestant debate on tradition, i.e., the
conviction that scripture assumes normative status in the comprehensive process of transmission, in which it works together with
traditional heritage and the church, including its magisterium—
proves its worth in the conception of dogma as such, and above all
in concrete usage and in the interpretation of already defined dogmas in the church and theology. For "if scripture is really to be regarded as canon, then this also means that each dogma must be
interpreted from the basis of scripture, and that the witness of scripture determines its critical limitations and its positions in the total
witness to faith."[75]

If the Catholic/Protestant dialogue on tradition is to be continued
at all, then it should be continued at this point. Strictly speaking,
though, the aim in dealing with this "sore point"[76] should no longer
be that of prolonging the Catholic/Protestant debate on tradition as
such and obtaining through it new insights and still greater agreements, but rather of making sure that those jointly-held convictions
which have already been reached are put into practice in the task of
transmitting the gospel and thus achieve their full effect.

—*Translated by* BARBARA HALL

NOTES

1. "The idea of tradition in the form of an explicit doctrine first appears in Irenaeus as part of a doctrine of apostolicity." (Y. Congar, *La Tradition et les traditions. Essai historique*, Paris, 1960, p. 42).
2. *Adversus Haereses*, III, 3, 3.
3. One could, it is true, use the example of the formation of the old Catholic Church to contradict this. But even here the actual and central issue was less the understanding of tradition than that of church. This was already the case at the founding of the Church of Utrecht (1723) and remained so after the church had received new members after Vatican I.
4. As far as I can see the only monograph on this subject which has appeared since is G. G. Blum's work: *Offenbarung und Überlieferung—Die dogmatische Konstitution Dei Verbum des II. Vatikanums im Lichte altkirchlicher und moderner Theologie*, Göttingen, 1971. However, even this work reveals, not least by its evaluatory nature, to how great an extent the discussion on scripture tradition has subsided in the interconfessional field.
5. Cf. N. Ehrenström and G. Gassmann, *Confessions in Dialogue—A Survey of Bilateral Conversations among World Confessional Families 1962-1971*, Geneva, 1972, pp. 94 f., esp. pp. 96-107.
6. Report of the Lutheran-Roman Catholic Study Commission "The Gospel and the Church," No. 17 (referred to hereafter as "Malta Report"), published in *Lutheran World*, 1972-1973, pp. 259 ff., among others.
7. "Ecriture et Tradition, un problème résolu?", in *Ecriture et Tradition—Journées oecuméniques de Chevetogne*, Paris, 1970, pp. 9 ff.
8. *Kanon und Tradition—Ein Beitrag zur neueren Dogmengeschichte und Symbolik*, Ludwigsburg, 1859.
9. Thus F. Loofs in his verdict which is constantly being repeated by Protestants: *Symbolik oder christliche Konfessionskunde*, Tübingen, 1902, p. 109.
10. K. Barth's argument against the Catholic conception of tradition, which is as detailed as it is radically critical, is plainly characteristic of this; *Church Dogmatics*, Edinburgh, 1956, Vol. I, pp. 544 ff.
11. E.g., K. E. Skydsgaard, "Schrift und Tradition—Bemerkungen zur Traditionsproblematik in der neueren Theologie," in *Kerygma und Dogma*, 1955, p. 170; J. R. Geiselmann, *Die Heilige Schrift und die Tradition*, Freiburg, 1962, p. 89; G. C. Berkouwer, *Das Konzil und die neue katholische Theologie*, Munich, 1968, p. 116.
12. Geiselmann, *op. cit.*, p. 90.
13. *Op. cit.*, p. 185; similarly in Vol. 2 (*La Tradition et les Traditions II—Essai Théologique*, Paris, 1963, p. 178) and in Tavard: "In the person of Martin Luther the cleavage between Scripture and tradition became irreconcilable." *Holy Writ or Holy Church*, New York, 1959, p. 80.
14. H. Preuss, *Die Entwicklung des Schriftprinzips bei Luther bis zur Leipziger Disputation*, Leipzig, 1901, p. 47; cf. p. 44.
15. F. C. Baur, *Der Gegensatz des Katholizismus und Protestantismus nach den Prinzipien und Hauptdogmen der beiden Lehrbegriffe*, Tübingen, 1834, p. 352.
16. Cf. e.g., A. Harnack, *Lehrbuch der Dogmengeschichte*, 4th edition, Tübingen, 1910, Vol. III, pp. 863 ff.
17. W. Höhne, *Luthers Anschauungen über die Kontinuität der Kirche*, Berlin, 1963, p. 123.
18. *Luther's Works*, Philadelphia, 1966, Vol. 41, pp. 194-199 (WA 51, esp. pp. 477-487).

19. Our translation of WA 7, p. 721.
20. "Zum Problem der Tradition," in *Der kommende Christus und die kirchlichen Traditionen*, Göttingen, 1961, p. 102. Similarly H. Rückert: "Luther understands the Word of God always as the *viva vox evangelii*, the living word proclaimed in a church, so that the history of this church is thus included as the element in which proclamation and tradition take place" (*Schrift, Tradition und Kirche*, Lüneburg, 1951, p. 23).
21. Even in his bitter dispute with the Catholic conception of tradition, which had in his opinion received fatal confirmation in the dogma of the assumption of Mary, Rückert was nevertheless able to say: "The manner in which the *sola scriptura* is generally understood among us and applied as a so-called 'formal principle of the Reformation' turns it into an unjustifiably one-sided concept. Catholicism is simply in the right when it tells us that there is a false alternative in the dilemma of 'scripture' or 'scripture and tradition'" (*op. cit.*, p. 22).
22. W. Trillhaas, for example, speaks thus of the "stream of tradition of Christian proclamation," which includes the Bible as the "first stretch of Christian tradition . . . but also as the most highly qualifying stretch." "Even liturgy, even hymns, customs and usages, the law, art and symbol valid to the congregation, all these are included in the great complex of historical tradition," through which the Word of God reaches us (*Dogmatik*, Berlin, 1962, p. 69).
23. Schlink, *op. cit.*, p. 196.
24. Skydsgaard, "Tradition und Wort Gottes," in *Schrift und Tradition*, K. E. Skydsgaard and L. Vischer, eds., Zürich, 1963, p. 146.
25. Section II report, No. 45.
26. In his "Axiomata" (1778), directed against the orthodox Lutheran Pastor Goeze. Esp. Chapters V-VIII.
27. For F. C. Baur also, "criticism of the canon" such as he demands from an introduction to the New Testament (*Theologische Jahrbücher*, 1850, p. 474) and positive re-evaluation of tradition (*Der Gegensatz des Katholizismus und Protestantismus nach den Prinzipien und Hauptdogmen der beiden Lehrbegriffe*, Tübingen, 1934, esp. pp. 341-342, 361 and 431-436) go hand in hand.
28. Also see on this G. Ebeling, *Die Geschichtlichkeit der Kirche und ihrer Verkündigung als theologisches Problem*, Tübingen, 1954, pp. 31-38.
29. The importance of this issue was already emphasized at the 2nd World Conference on Faith and Order (Edinburgh, 1937). The next World Conference (Lund, 1952) decided on the formation of a study commission on "Tradition and Traditions." In Montreal (1963) the entire work of Section II was devoted to the theme "Scripture, Tradition and Traditions."
30. Here I have in mind chiefly the strongly historically orientated presentations of Congar, Tavard and Geiselmann, which I have already mentioned, and also: H. Holstein, *La Tradition dans l'Eglise*, Paris, 1960.
31. L. Vischer, "After the Fourth Session of the Second Vatican Council," in *The Ecumenical Review*, 1966, p. 156. Esp. J. L. Leuba ("La Tradition à Montréal et à Vatican II—Convergences et questions," in La Révélation Divine, t. II, *Unam Sanctam* 70b, Paris, 1968, pp. 475 ff.) and recently G. G. Blum again (*op. cit.*, pp. 70-75) have stated this clearly.
32. Here lies the weakness in the above mentioned work by Blum.
33. Irenaeus, quoted from Congar, *op. cit.*, p. 51.
34. Irenaeus, *Adversus Haereses*, III, 3, 1 and 2.
35. Tavard, *op. cit.*, p. 244.

36. Tertullian, Epist. 66, 8, 3; quoted from Congar, *op. cit.*, p. 55.
37. "Ministerial succession, unanimity and tradition are spiritual and supernatural realities which in the last analysis originate only from the Holy Spirit as the 'Vicar' of Christ (Tertullian) and soul of the church" (*op. cit.*, p. 52).
38. Cf. esp. Blum's work (*op. cit.*).
39. Congar, *op. cit.*, p. 128.
40. Cf. Congar, *op. cit.*, p. 127 and pp. 170 f., Notes 24 and 25; Tavard, *op. cit.*, pp. 15 ff.
41. Cf. Congar, *op. cit.*, pp. 127 f. and 151 ff. In the continuation of this the idea of post-apostolic revelations, clearly rejected in the dispute with Joachimism, finds greater acceptance (cf. Tavard, *op. cit.*, pp. 27, 53, and 55).
42. In *Mysterium Salutis. Grundriss heilsgeschichtlicher Dogmatik*, J. Feiner and M. Löhrer, eds., Einsiedeln, 1972, Vol. 4/1, pp. 449 f.
43. In *Lutheran World*, 4, 1967, p. 352.
44. F. Kropatschek's work (*Das Schriftprinzip der lutherischen Kirche. Die Vorgeschichte. Das Erbe des Mittelalters*, Leipzig, 1904, Vol. I), for example, shows this clearly.
45. Cf. esp. P. de Vooght's presentation (*Les sources de la doctrine chrétienne d'après les théologiens du XIVe siècle et du début du XVe . . .*, Bruges, 1954), but also Tavard and Kropatschek, *op. cit.*
46. De Vooght, *op. cit.*, p. 254.
47. The Malta Report (No. 17) confirms this double rapproachement. "The Scripture can no longer be exclusively contrasted with tradition. . . . Yet as the witness to the fundamental tradition, Scripture has a normative role for the entire later tradition of the church."
48. P. Lengsfeld, *Uberlieferung—Tradition und Schrift in der evangelischen und katholischen Theologie der Gegenwart*, Paderborn, 1960, p. 195; similarly Holstein: "Interpretation and discernment: the primacy therefore remains with scripture, since tradition is subservient to it" (*op. cit.*, p. 267); Tavard, "Explicatio—or tradition . . . is subservient to scripture insofar as it is born of the existential reading of the Bible by the Church" (*op. cit.*, p. 21).
49. K. Rahner, *Lexikon für Theologie und Kirche*, 2nd edition, Freiburg, 1958, Vol. II, column 450.
50. Lengsfeld, *op. cit.*, p. 111.
51. *Ibid.*, p. 191; cf. Geiselmann, *op. cit.*, p. 272.
52. K.-H. Ohlig, *Woher nimmt die Bibel ihre Autorität*, Düsseldorf, 1970, p. 202.
53. Geiselmann, *op. cit.*, p. 21.
54. K. Rahner, *Uber die Schriftinspiration*, Freiburg, 1958, p. 82.
55. No. 21.
56. No. 51.
57. No. 45.
58. It is very difficult to understand why this extremely strong emphasis on scripture and its normativity for the entire process of tradition is given so little serious consideration, indeed intentionally devalued, in such detailed Protestant presentations of the Catholic conception of tradition as those of R. Daunis ("Schrift und Tradition in Trient und in der modernen römisch-katholischen Theologie," in *Kerygma und Dogma*, 1967, pp. 132-158 and 184-200) and R. Boeckler (*Der moderne römisch-katholische Traditionsbegriff*, Göttingen, 1967). G. G. Blum (*op. cit.*), despite the entirely different tenor of his work, sees things similarly. He tends to see the positive side of the development—where both Catholics and Protestants are concerned—far

too one-sidedly as the attainment of an "inclusive," "dynamic," and "pneumatological" conception of tradition and for this reason deliberately brushes aside the normative rank of scripture together with the whole question of the criterion of tradition, as this would again endanger tradition's comprehensive character.

59. *La Tradition et les traditions II—Essai théologique*, Paris, 1963, pp. 177 ff.

60. Thus in the above mentioned article in *Kerygma und Dogma*, 1955, p. 177.

61. This had already clearly been seen in Montreal. The report reads thus: "Throughout the history of the Church the criterion has been sought in the Holy Scriptures rightly interpreted. But what is 'right interpretation'?" (No. 51). And this question had then led to the hermeneutical problem (No. 52) and the abundance of hermeneutical options (No. 53), so that the necessity arose for "further thinking about the hermeneutical problem" (No. 55).

62. No. 8; cf. No. 12.

63. Simply for the sake of clarification I am including two fairly recent statements by such theologians. W. Kasper, for example, says in view of the decision of Vatican I that scripture should be interpreted according to the norm of dogma (Denzinger, 1507): "This (decision) does not mean that the church wishes to set itself above scripture. In the construction of the canon the church has set itself clearly under scripture, and it is taking nothing back from this. It is not a question of the superior rank of the church over the Word of God, but of the superiority of the church's understanding over the subjective judgment of the individual" *(Glaube und Geschichte*, Mainz, 1970, p. 192). K.-H. Ohlig states even more briefly: "Scripture is the judge here (i.e., vis-à-vis church and tradition), but not in the hands of the individual *(op. cit.,* pp. 202-203).

64. W. Kasper, for example, says: ". . . Exegesis has a critical function within the church. Exegetes have controlling responsibility in the church, which means the task of making sure that the faith and proclamation of the church do not become separated from their origin" *(op. cit.,* p. 184). K. Rahner states it even more sharply in his commentary on the dogmatic constitution of the Church (Lumen Gentium) (No. 22): "Even if there is no juridical instance which can . . . challenge the validity of the Papal decision, there can still be in the church the 'charismatic and prophetic' opposition to the face" (Galatians 2:11) *(Lexikon für Theologie und Kirche*, Freiburg, 1966, Das Zweite Vatikanische Konzil Vol. I, p. 227). The Malta Report also indicates this state of affairs, however reservedly. In the context of the question of the "criteria" of tradition the Catholic participants make the following formulation: "In the Catholic view, the Lord authenticates his word through the *reciprocal interaction of official and unofficial charisma*, both of which remain under scripture" *(op. cit.,* No. 20). Here one should, of course, refer particularly to H. Küng, who not only contends the possibility of a scripture-based criticism of the church and its doctrinal tradition in almost all his major works, but also often puts this into practice.

65. It is not by chance that K. Barth objected here that the pastor is thus putting himself in the place of the church and the church in the place of the Word of God. P. Schempp, for example, was certainly right in countering this protest with the argument that the Word of God is to be heard in this very interpretation of the scriptures, in the "viva vox," and that the preacher is "referred back to scripture" *(Luthers Stellung zur Heiligen Schrift*, Munich, 1929, p. 44). But this would be said quite similarly on the Catholic side.

66. *Luther's Works,* Philadelphia, 1972, Vol. 33, p. 20. Luther defines the concept of "assertio" here as follows: "And by assertion. . . . I mean a constant adhering, affirming, confessing, maintaining, and an invincible persevering."
67. Lutheran World Federation Constitution, Article II.
68. *Una Sancta* 1971, Vol. 1/2, p. 24.
69. *Op. cit.,* p. 110. Similarly Skydsgaard in: *Challenge . . . and Response. A Protestant Perspective of the Vatican Council,* W. Quanbeck, ed., Minneapolis, 1966, p. 57.
70. *La Tradition et les traditions, op. cit.,* Vol. II, pp. 232 and 243.
71. *The Book of Concord,* Philadelphia, 1959, p. 504.
72. Thus, e.g., W. Kasper, *op. cit.,* pp. 203-206 and 183; see also the complete article "Evangelium und Dogma," pp. 197 ff.
73. K. Rahner, "Kritik an Hans Küng," in *Stimmen der Zeit,* 1970, 12, p. 373.
74. H. Küng, *Infallible?,* London, 1971, p. 149; similarly in the Malta Report: "The church's abiding in the truth should not be understood in a static way but as a dynamic event which takes place with the aid of the Holy Spirit in ceaseless battle against error and sin in the church as well as in the world" (*op. cit.,* No. 23).
75. W. Kasper, *op. cit.,* p. 206.
76. *Ibid.,* p. 182.

Chapter 7

Dogmatic Statements and the Identity of the Christian Community

I.
Preliminary Considerations

A. THE HORIZON WHICH GOVERNS OUR
CONSIDERATION OF DOGMATIC STATEMENTS

This study and everything asserted in it is governed by the horizon of understanding within which we locate dogmatic statements. What follows in this essay is governed by a view of the church as a dynamic community which concretizes its identity as it moves through time and space. In its career through history and nature, the church does indeed, like all other worldly phenomena, function as a part of the world in which it lives, and it coexists as such with all the other parts of that world.[1] It shares the processes by which all communities are shaped and by which they make their impact upon their environment. As all other communities, the church exists as a distinctive group in its world, with a distinctive identity among the plurality of distinctive groups with which it coexists. The life of the Christian community, then, can be said to share in two moments—that in which it shares common elements with its world, actually ingests, culturally and physically, its environment and that in which it takes distinctive shape and makes a distinctive impact upon its world. Dogmatic statements take their place as part of the activity by which the church reflects upon its distinctive identity and actualizes that identity. If the church is a life-phenomenon which is always assuming a distinctive identity in its world, dogmatic statements are a dimension of that thrust toward identity-formation.

This horizon of understanding sets two tasks for us. The first is to clarify that the very term "dogmatic statements" is a complex one, which in fact refers to a cluster of elements, among which we must make distinctions while at the same time holding all the elements together in a whole. The second task suggests that a conceptuality of the identity-forming process within a community is useful for throwing light on what dogmatic statements are, how they function, and how problems concerning dogmatic statements are to be resolved. The elaboration of these two tasks and an attempt to deal with the issues inherent within them comprise the substance of this essay.

B. THE CLUSTER OF ELEMENTS TO WHICH THE TERM
   "DOGMATIC STATEMENT" REFERS

Actualizing identity and reflecting upon it within the Christian community is a process which moves with the life of the community itself and which is sensitive to the terrain over which the church moves in history, of which it sometimes becomes a part. Identity-formation, in other words, is a thrust, not an established, once-for-all accomplishment. Identity-formation (which includes both actualization and reflection upon identity) brings to focus a number of different activities and gifts within the community. Because identity-formation is a process which encompasses several activities, we must acknowledge that what we call "dogmatic statements" actually refers to a cluster of elements.

The identity-formation process includes more than dogmatic statements and the efforts that go into those statements. It includes liturgy, ministry, church organization, ethical action, and private prayer and adoration—to name a few. But the term "dogmatic statements" refers to the cluster of activities that have to do with *beholding* the central truth of revelation which is associated with the church's identity, *reflecting* upon that truth, and intelligently *articulating* it. Everything that pertains to this beholding, reflecting upon, and articulating the central truth of revelation which animates the church is in some way related to dogmatic statements. In a broad sense, this would, quite rightly, include every aspect of the church's life, but we shall here narrow our discussion so as to include only the elements most relevant to our subject.

These insights, which emerge directly from the horizon which illuminates our perspective, help us to understand the difficulties that surround any attempt to define the term "dogmatic statements." In English, the term can refer both to statements that qualify as "dogma" and also to those that qualify as "dogmatics." In German, the same linguistic phenomenon is not so clear. However, there is confusion in both languages. When Roman Catholics use the term, they recognize that their church's understanding of dogma is to be reckoned with as an important element of the discussion, although they do tend to move into a discussion of dogmatics, defined as the theological reflection of individual theologians. Karl Rahner, for example, in the introductory section of his essay, "What is a dogmatic statement?" speaks both of the statements of dogma issued from the magisterium of the church and also of "that aspect of dogma which includes theological statements."[2] When Wolfhart Pannenberg and Edmund Schlink write, the former in an essay entitled exactly as Rahner's, it is clear that although they wish to speak of a faith-statement that includes more than the activity of individual theologians, they are basically speaking of the discipline of dogmatics as it is carried out by professors of theology.[3]

1. Dogma

In an important sense, the definition of the term "dogmatic statement" must be set by the Roman Catholic understanding of dogma. At the very least, it must include the Catholic term "dogma." This term is itself not unambiguous, but the starting-point is the understanding set forth by Georg Söll:

> The current definitions of "dogma," particularly as they appear in dogmatics textbooks, ordinarily lift up two components: (1) the identity of the contents of dogmas with the truths of revelation, and (2) the formal establishing of this identity by the ecclesiastical magisterium. Designating these two elements—the theological and the juridical—expresses what is most important in dogma, but nevertheless not its entirety. Five essential characteristics of dogma are set forth clearly, both in the formulation of Vatican I and in the whole history of the concept of dogma up until the present time. Dogma is (1) in its content, a truth of revelation; (2) in its form, a doctrinal proposition; (3) in its objective validity, an infallible utterance of faith; (4) in its subjective claim to efficacy, a guideline that is obligatory in the conscience of every believer; (5) in its development, a certainty upon which the church in the course of history has resolved.[4]

As several writers have shown, the term "dogma" has a history of its own. The present understanding has grown up in relatively recent times. In the New Testament (Acts 16:4) the term referred to publicly affirmed teachings pronounced by the leading authorities in the early church. For most of the church's history, and as recently as the late nineteenth century, dogma referred to what Roger Haight terms the "stable teaching of the revealed truth of Christianity."[5] What has been added to the Roman understanding as a consequence of the defensiveness of attitude associated with Vatican I and the Modernist crisis of 1907-1910 is the emphasis that dogma is doctrine that has been publicly defined by the magisterium in its infallible character and that is binding upon believers.[6] As Avery Dulles points out, it is possible not only to point to a long period of developing opinions prior to the Roman concept of dogma that crystallized in the late nineteenth century, it is also clear that that concept has been superseded by Vatican II in a number of respects, particularly as that is manifested in the understanding of revelation embodied in *Dei Verbum*.[7]

If it is true that allowing the Roman Catholic concept of dogma to set the ground rules for the discussion of dogmatic statements makes things more difficult for us, it also follows that the discussion will be more substantial and that it will be more productive for a dialogue both with the Roman Catholics and also with the tradition of the ecumenical church. On the one hand, it would seem less useful to include the concept of "dogma," because presumably that leaves the Protestant theologian with little to talk about, since he recognizes a minimum of dogma and does not have to relate his work to dogma with any great frequency. On the other hand, two things must be said: (1) It is useful for the Protestant to deal with the question of dogma, because he can then both help the Catholic theologian and also talk more realistically with him; (2) As George Lindbeck and G. C. Berkouwer have pointed out, every ecclesial community does have its *de facto* dogmas, which do indeed function with the characteristics which Söll has described, recognizing that *mutatis mutandis* every ecclesial community defines dogma in terms of its own understanding of magisterium, revelation, etc.

There is a sound instinct, however, in the discussions that define "dogmatic statements" more broadly, so as to include dogmatics. The ground of this instinct is the awareness that what now qualifies in Roman Catholicism as dogma is described by a concept that is itself relative to a given time, dating roughly from the 1860's to the 1960's. This awareness recognizes that it is more in harmony with the mainline Christian tradition and more adequate theologically to define dogma as more nearly synonymous to "doctrine."[8] The lack of unanimity today in the discussions of what qualifies as a "dogmatic statement" is in part a confusion caused by the recent narrow-

ing of the term "dogma" and in part an attempt to alter that
narrowing.

Our intention in this essay, however, corresponding to the horizon
that guides our work is to broaden the context within which dogma
occurs. We share the intention of others to alter directly the understanding of dogma, but our efforts will serve that purpose indirectly.
Our image of the church as a community that actualizes its identity
while moving through time and space, moving over the terrain of
its world, existing both as a part of that world and yet over against
the world in its distinctive identity, recognizes dogma, *however it is
specifically conceived*, as the apex of the cone that is formed by the
total complex of beholding-reflecting-articulating activities that we
call "dogmatic statements." Our image recognizes that dogma is
central, but that it coexists with and depends upon a support system
of elements. And while we do permit the Roman Catholic understanding of dogma, as enunciated by Söll, to be our reference point,
we will insist that the only ecumenically viable concept of dogma
that is binding on the total church is one that has received the
acknowledgment of the entire Christian community. Dogma thus
stands as the vortex of an exceedingly complex process within the
life of the church. On the one hand, it rests solidly upon the prior
beholding and reception of God's revelation, with the faith, humility, and discipline which goes along with the beholding. Even though
our considerations here are directed toward the phenomenology of
the church's process of dogmatizing and the function of dogmatic
statements within the church, we are presupposing at every point
that dogmatic statements are *responses* to the prevenient grace of
God and his revelation. Dogma, therefore, although a fully human
phenomenon in the church is more than a human product, inasmuch
as its content is the revelation of God himself. Being a fully human
phenomenon implies, on the other hand, that dogma includes the
formulation of that which the church has beheld, which involves the
complex process by which the church reflects upon its vision of
revelation and articulates it in a manner that is received by the
church. This reception by the church has been symbolized in different ways—by the action of a council, by the pope as the head of the
church. The point remains, however, that in the long run the acknowledgment and reception of the dogma must be that of the
parish clergy and the laity, otherwise the very meaning and authority
of dogma is lost since dogma's claim rests on its being an articulation

of revelation which can guide and edify the whole body of Christ. Acknowledgment and reception are thus "from above," in that the church-political leaders of the church and the leading theologians have worked out and approved the dogma, and also "from below," since the conscious and unconscious affirmation of the people, in their regular parish worship and study as well as in their daily lives, demonstrates the correctness and edifying power of the dogma.

The function of dogma is correlated to the characteristics we have just enumerated. It functions to clarify revelation, as a hermeneutical key for interpreting revelation, as a criterion by which to judge false interpretations, and as an image which enables a correct internalization of Christian truth. It follows from the horizon within which we are approaching this question that dogma is a gift of God's Spirit to the church as it seeks to actualize its identity in its pilgrimage through this world. Dogma serves as part of the church's guidance system, an instrument of the *kubernetikos* which keeps the community on course, checking and redirecting it in its ongoing attempt to live faithful to its original inputs of identity-bestowing revelation as it moves over unknown terrain through an uncharted history.[9]

What we have said thus far about dogma is in agreement with much of what Lutheran and Roman Catholic theology hold concerning dogma. Our discussion is also tendentious, however, with respect to Roman Catholics at the point where we speak about the reception and acknowledgment of dogma by the entire church. It is tendentious vis-à-vis some Lutherans in its assertions that dogma is a formulation of revelation that serves to guide the church. These questions will be discussed in detail later, but here we may simply say that acknowledgment by the church cuts against the Roman grain, since it ties the understanding of dogma to an ecclesiology which broadens the concept of acknowledgment so much that no pronouncements dating after the break between the Eastern and Western churches can be recognized as dogmas, since there was no acknowledgment by the "whole" church. The close relationship we have drawn between dogma and revelation offends the sensibilities of many Lutherans, since they are intent either in so exalting Scripture as the vessel of revelation that dogma must be denigrated or they are so persuaded of the historicity of the church's tradition that they cannot take dogma seriously as a permanent expression of revelation.

The understanding of dogma that I am representing here implies, for all practical purposes, that there are only two formulations that qualify as ecumenical dogmas: the Holy Trinity and the Two Natures of Christ. No other formulations can meet the definition that I have set forth—formulation by the church and full acknowledgment "from above" and also "from below." Theoretically, this definition differs from the Roman Catholic view which uses dogma to refer to certain teachings enunciated by their magisterium. Practically, it also differs from the Lutherans and other Protestants, who give only their own peculiar basic teachings the operative force of dogma, as for example, *sola gratia* and *simul justus et peccator.* Roman Catholics and Protestants alike prefer to give the status of dogma to pronouncements that are not fully ecumenically received and acknowledged, but which obtain only within their own ecclesial communities.[10]

2. Dogmatics and Confession

Dogma is the pivotal manifestation of what we mean by "dogmatic statements." This pivotal location is clearly observed when we note dogma's relation to confession and dogmatics. Confession is a response to the Gospel which has grasped an individual or a community under circumstances which demand that one's commitment be professed in clearest possible terms. Confession expresses not only the shape of the Gospel that has grasped a community but also the specific implications of that Gospel in the face of the community's foes. It is therefore a distinguishing factor which sets the community apart from others. This confession grows out of a central vision of God's grace that has become determinative for human existence, and it requires dogma to formulate that central vision in clear, balanced, and reflective manner so that the spirit of the confession is not distorted or lost. The most universally significant dogmas (the ones on which ecumenical consensus can be obtained) are contained within the Niceno-Constantinopolitan creed, although the christological dogma of the Two Natures was not properly enunciated until Chalcedon. For a Protestant, therefore, dogma is always closely associated with the confession which he raises up in the liturgy and in which he acknowledges his God and commits himself to that God. Despite this close association, he distinguishes between the dogma and confession, and he reflects upon the dogma in its own right and permits it to illumine his mind and spirit and deepen his understanding of God's revelation. Confession raises the necessity for dogma for its preservation and clarity.[11]

If dogma is demanded by confession to give it focus and preserve it, dogma in its turn demands dogmatics, since dogma requires theological reflection and can be properly understood only in the context of such reflection. Theological reflection is required, on the one hand, because the movement from confession to dogma is not a direct one, and on the other hand, because once a dogma has been defined, it gives rise to new reflection. The space of time it required to convince the church that the homoousion was indeed faithful to revelation concerning Jesus' relation to God the Father and even required by that revelation demonstrates how complicated and difficult the pathway is from confession to dogma. The decades between Nicea (A.D. 325) and Constantinople (A.D. 381) saw the most energetic theological reflection at work attempting to give solid intellectual form to the undeniably authentic confession of Jesus' oneness with the Father. The decades from Constantinople to Châlcedon (A.D. 451) can also be interpreted as an indication of how the incipient form of the Trinitarian dogma expressed in the late fourth century gave rise in its turn to intense reflection upon how this Jesus Christ could in fact be both man and yet of one substance with the Creator.

Although the developments from Nicea to Chalcedon are not as direct and unambiguous as this sketch would suggest, history nevertheless bears out the fact that dogma exists in a support system of dogmatics. Dogmatics is understood here to be both corporate theological reflection (doctrine) and individual theological thinking. Dogmatics prepares the way for dogma as the preservation of the central vision which animates confession, and it also follows after dogma, picking up the questions that dogma raises and pursuing the provocative implications that inhere in dogma. The revelation of God grasps man and evokes his confession which both acknowledges the revelation and signifies man's commitment to it. The confession demands dogma for its continued life, but that dogma depends on theological reflection and doctrine for its formulation and spawns further reflection after its pronouncement.

We are approaching dogmatic statements within the context of the church as a living organism living within its world. This implies that the lines which separate and distinguish one aspect of the church's life from the others are not clear-cut, but rather that they shade off into one another, and that each aspect is related in a living way to the coexisting elements within the ecological system which is the church in its world. Therefore, it is not surprising that we are forced to admit that "dogmatic statements" refers to a cluster of functions within the church. The processes by which this cluster does its work will be our theme in later sections, but the thrust is clear: The revelation which evokes confession is the substance of the community's Christian identity; the confession makes that identity more concrete in setting it apart from others; dogma crystallizes that identity in cogent statements; dogmatic reflection fashions dogma and follows up its implications. *"Dogmatic statements," then, refers to dogma and the support system of doctrinal and theological reflection in whose ambience dogma comes into being and makes its impact.* Revelation (Gospel), confession and doctrine are the nearest antecedents of dogmatic statements. Since identity is at stake, dogma must be understood to be pivotal in the process, but it cannot stand alone. This definition places the peculiar "dogmas" of Roman Catholicism and Protestant communities in a position that is somewhat less authoritative than dogma in its proper sense and more authoritative than theology as done by theologians. These "dogmas" belong in the cluster we have described.

Other elements of the church's life are also linked to dogmatic statements, even though they receive little attention here. The relationship is illuminated by the horizon of identity that we assume. Thus, preaching and teaching stand in reciprocity with dogmatic statements, since their proclamation and edifying work influence dogmatic statements by virtue of their being more concrete manifestations of the identity which dogmatic statements concern themselves with. At the same time, preaching and teaching are corrected and shaped by the formulation of identity which dogmatic statements aim at.

II.

Five Areas of Controversy Concerning Dogmatic Statements

There are at least five problem areas to which we must attend today if we are to contribute to a better understanding of the dogmatic statements and their role in the church.

A. THE AUTONOMY OF DOGMA

Both Lutherans and Roman Catholics struggle with the question whether dogma possesses autonomy when it makes its truth claims.

They face this question when they confront each other, as well as when they carry out their theological efforts within their own traditions. The question of dogma's autonomy is basically a question of the *relationship of dogma to the rest of the church's life.* This question arises naturally for Lutherans, since the Reformation pressed them to find a basis for calling into question the dogmatic statements which they considered objectionable. Their invoking of the authority of the Word of God gave them the lever they needed. The authority of the Word did not necessarily denigrate dogma nor eliminate obedience to it, but it did undercut radically the autonomous authority of dogma and all dogmatic statements. For Roman Catholics, the question arises today especially because the church is receiving the brunt of the consequences of the rediscovery of Scripture as a primary norm for faith and life, as well as the unavoidable impact of relativizing forces that attend the consciousness that all human history and institutions that live in history share in historicity. Both of these factors—the greater stress on Scripture and the concern for historicity—raise the question of dogma's relationship to and even its dependence upon other aspects of the church's life. The kinds of questions that are raised for both traditions are these: Is there an appeal from dogma or an authority alongside dogma, on the basis of which dogma can be judged? This question comes to the fore in all examinations of dogma, but particularly with respect to dogmatic formulations subsequent to the seventh ecumenical council, that is to say, with respect to formulations whose authority is rendered controversial by the separation of the churches. Can dogmas be evaluated and ranked according to their significance? What is the relationship between dogma and scripture, revelation, faith, and the Gospel? Can dogma be reformed or repealed?

On the Lutheran side, Edmund Schlink has given thorough, if not exhaustive, attention to the relationship of dogmatic statements to the rest of the church's life.[12] Roman Catholic theology in this century has produced a monumental amount of reflection on this question, some of which is reflected in Vatican II.[13] Hans Küng, Walter Kasper, Karl Rahner, E. Schillebeeckx, and Bernard Lonergan are especially important.[14] Although there are differences among these men, we can summarize their reflection thus: they have insisted that dogma is a vehicle of God's revelation and therefore subordinate to that revelation; they have broadened the concept of dogma so as to place it within the total framework of church's process for appre-

hending revelation and articulating its apprehension; they have at
the same time rooted dogma both in divine revelation and in human
experience and knowing; they have differentiated between the intention of the dogmatizing process and the propositional forms
which that process assumes, so as to relativize the latter and place
them firmly in a network of processes of expressing faith, over which
dogma can in no sense be supremely autonomous.

B. THE NEED FOR DOGMA

The question whether dogma is needed is also a *question of the
relationship of dogma to the rest of the church's life,* since it is the
question whether dogma is necessary as protection for the Gospel.
The discussion centers on whether the Gospel carries within it the
irresistible thrust toward dogmatic reflection and dogma. This question is also a *question of the role of dogma in human experience,*
however, since there are arguments for the view that the human
spirit cannot live without fulfilling its thrust toward dogmatic
statements.

For Roman Catholics, the conviction that the Gospel itself moves
faith toward the formation of dogma has been a basic assumption.[15]
Hans Küng has to a certain extent called this into question in his
book, *Infallible? An Inquiry,* in his demand that a dogma justify
itself to the individual theologian, and this deviation from the
Roman custom of theology has been challenged severely.[16] For
Lutherans, even though Catholic teaching was affirmed in the Augsburg Confession,[17] the necessity of dogma has not been felt in the
same way. The perennial Lutheran concern for *pura doctrina evangelii,* first voiced in Augustana VII, does reveal, however, that a high
premium is placed on dogmatic statements, even if they are not
acknowledged as dogma. The *articulus stantis et cadentis ecclesiae*
certainly functions as a normative dogmatic formulation that is demanded by the Gospel itself. For Lutherans, the necessity for dogma
as such is perceived in the light of two important assumptions: The
first is that *doctrina* is closely identified with preaching, both lin-
guistically in that the Latin word can be translated as preaching and
also in the fact that the *articulus stantis et cadentis* is the *sola gratia*
which from Luther onward has been placed in the very center of
the church's concrete ministry of Word and Sacrament.[18] Second,
the Lutheran understanding of adiaphora recognizes that doctrinal
and dogmatic forms themselves are not of the essence of the faith,

although they are necessary and worthy of great attention. The Lutheran adiaphoron doctrine would approximate, in its implications, the current Roman Catholic view that dogmatic forms are not of the essence, but the Gospel-content or intention is. Neither of these considerations would necessarily lead Lutherans to deny the need for dogma, but they would certainly determine the manner in which that need is asserted and the way in which that necessity is understood. Even though Roman theologians emphasize the difference between the form of dogmatic statements and the "deposit itself of faith,"[19] they certainly face different tasks than do Lutherans in dealing with this distinction and interpret differently just what the distinction implies.

Roman Catholic theologians have greatly broadened the question of whether there is a need for dogma in their suggestion that dogma is rooted intrinsically in the processes of human psychic and intellectual life. Although this analysis dates from the medieval tradition of theology, it has assumed particular force today, especially in the thought of Rahner, Lonergan, and Schillebeeckx.[20] Lutheran theology, shunning as it traditionally has, the philosophical task, has not approached the sophistication of the Roman theologians at this point. The judgment by Melanchthon is deeply rooted in the Lutheran *Geist*: "Hoc est Christum cognoscere, beneficia eius cognoscere non quod isti (scholastici) docent, eius naturas, modos incarnationis contueri."[21] This is not to say that the foundations of dogma in the basic structure of the human spirit have been left totally unexamined. Edmund Schlink and Wolfhart Pannenberg, for example, have given attention to this issue,[22] but it is still necessary to say that Lutherans have yet to give proper study to it. The Roman theologians have opened up this avenue of discussion as a means of coming to terms with relativism and historicity, but their highly refined epistemological and metaphysical discussions of the need for dogma as rooted in the human spirit itself are of enormous significance for interconfessional discussions, as well. In a later section we shall take up the great relativizing impact of the work of Albrecht Ritschl and Adolf von Harnack upon our understanding of dogma. Here, however, we simply point out that their epoch-making studies, which spoke of dogma as a peculiarly time-bound phenomenon, tied to the Hellenistic phase of Christianity, are countered head-on by the assertion that the formation of dogma is a perennial dimension of the human being. Although the Roman theologians are more in-

clined to relate their assertions to the twentieth-century offspring of
the Ritschl-Harnackian thesis, namely, the demythologizing proposal
of Rudolf Bultmann, the debate with the nineteenth century theologians must be taken into account, inasmuch as they devoted such
exhaustive attention to tracing the history of dogmatic statements
and demonstrating on the basis of their research that dogma is demanded neither by the Gospel nor by the structures of the human
spirit.[23]

C. DOGMA AS CRITICAL AND CONSTITUTIVE

How do dogmas function? Do they actually assert something constitutive or are they rather critical in their function, drawing lines
of demarcation *against* assertions that threaten the faith? Does dogma function so as to make a substantive truth-statement or does it
rather draw the circumference outside of which reflection and teaching and preaching cannot go? Or is it possible to say that dogma
functions in both ways. This also is a *question of the relationship of
dogma to the rest of the church's life*. It is also a response to the
problems of historicity and ecumenical conflict, inasmuch as it affects the *way* in which dogma is taken seriously.

To say that dogma is constitutive, that is, that it sets forth a substantive vision of truth, demands that we take dogma seriously for its
positive content. If we hold to this view, we must attend carefully to
the psychic and intellectual processes which inform the dogma-
forming process, as well as to the historical context of the dogmatic
statement, so as to be able to ascertain precisely what the dogma intends to assert. Such careful attention is rendered necessary, because
the dogma's vision of the truth is a vision out of which we live as
Christians, which is a fountain of nourishment for the faith and life
of the church and its theology. No less careful attention will be
given to dogma if we hold that it functions primarily in a negative,
critical manner, but the motivation for this attending to dogma and
its consequences are quite different. If we hold to the latter view,
we do not expect that we shall find nourishment from the dogma as
such,[24] but rather look for methodological clarity. This position
frequently criticizes sharply the Nicene and Chalcedonian formulations, for example, for their ambiguity, philosophical naivete, and
failure to assert any substantive truth. George Lindbeck has recently
presented a forceful variation of this position in his assertion that
the dogmatic definitions at Nicea and Chalcedon function "as rules

for correct Christian linguistic usage."[25] This has been a not uncommon Protestant device for minimizing the value of dogma, although Lindbeck does not seem to propose his variation of the argument to this end. He, rather, proposes it as a way of coming to terms with problems which historicity pose for the validity of dogma. This argument, in whatever form, seems to run directly counter to the thought of Schlink, Rahner, Schillebeeckx, Kasper and Lonergan, which would root dogma in the basic human drive toward grasping and articulating the truth. It would seem also to contradict the evidences of history which reveal how positively stimulating and productive of further reflection the dogmatic formulations have been. The argument that dogma functions critically *does*, however, lift up in an important way the conciliar processes by means of which dogmatic definitions are hammered out, namely, in discussion and consideration of varying positions. As a consequence, every dogma must be interpreted in light of what it rejects. The role of the *relatio* in relation to each *schema* at Vatican II bears this out. It is because dogma does play this critical function that the hermeneutics of dogmatic interpretation are so complicated, necessitating an investigation of the background documents that are pertinent to any given dogmatic definition under consideration. It is doubtful, however, whether the constitutive function of dogma can be set aside so easily, since dogma *does* grow out of an encounter with God and Christ.[26]

D. THE UNITY AND UNIFORMITY OF DOGMA

Must there be unity and/or uniformity of dogma across the lines of differing ecclesial communities? This is the *question of the ecumenical function of dogma*. A number of considerations enter at this point, so as to render the question rather complicated, even though the basic issue is clear: to what extent are the dogmatic statements of one ecclesial community valid for another community, and can there be unity between communities that do not recognize the binding validity of each other's dogmatic statements? The complexity of the question arises, in the first place because dogmas have multiplied, particularly within Roman Catholicism, since the division of the church, first in the eleventh century and later at the Reformation. The very existence of the Roman Catholic church, therefore, places a dogmatic burden upon the other ecclesial communities that come into contact with her. Both the Eastern churches and the Reformation churches share a body of dogma with the Roman church, a deposit of faith that binds them with her, since it grew in the period prior to the ruptures. At the same time the issue is very clear that in one sense they hold to different faiths from her and from each other, because they do not share her dogmas, nor do they acknowledge their binding claim. Since the existence of a forceful magisterium which proclaims dogma has not existed in the eastern churches, the role of dogmas as such is not an issue in their relations with Rome as it is with Protestants, who have proclaimed doctrines which serve as *de facto* dogmas. Although the locus and authority of the magisterium is a very ambiguous thing among Lutherans, for example, dogmatic reflection has been at work in their tradition so as to promulgate dogmatic statements that do function as dogma in ecumenical relations. Therefore, it is not only a question of Lutherans not accepting as binding the dogmas proclaimed by the Roman church since 1530. Lutherans have in fact established a set of their own distinctive dogmatic statements which distinguish them, toward which the Roman church must also take a position. These dogmatic statements include, for example, the definition of justification, the dogmatic reflection upon the presence of Christ in the Eucharist, the distinction between the Gospel and adiaphora, the concept of the church, church-order, and ministry. Because the Lutheran tradition is itself predisposed to sophisticated theological reflection, it, too, places a dogmatic burden upon the ecclesial communities that seek conversation with Lutheran communities.

The question of how dogmatic statements function ecumenically is, as these observations indicated, a question of *how the distinctive identities of different ecclesial communities interact*, since dogmatic statements are one intense form of that identity. George Lindbeck has stated this in an argument that proceeds from the interpretation of dogma as "rules for correct Christian linguistic usage."[27] Catholics and Protestants are likely to continue to differ in their understanding of what qualifies as dogma and what the status of dogma is,

for though they share a common Christian language, they speak different dialects of it. What is appropriate or essential in one dialect is not in the other. To be sure, there are ways of carrying on arguments and dialogues across linguistic boundaries even when these mark chasms between different ways of living the Christian life; but these are rather like discussions between the English and the Americans as to which of their two versions of the same language is superior, with the English including post-seventeenth-century English usage and the Americans post-seventeenth-century American usage in their respective normative traditions, while both agree that Shakespearian and pre-Shakespearian literature is canonical.[28]

Another way to put this ecumenical question is to say that dogma confronts us with working out a viable conceptuality for understanding the necessity and viability of dogmatic pluralism. Protestants have perhaps made greater progress toward fashioning such an understanding, largely because of their decades of experience together in the World Council of Churches. This progress should not be overestimated, however, since it has not really come to terms with serious claims of dogma as binding for the adherents of the various churches, nor has the progress that has been made between theologians on this issue been translated into practice by church leaders. The various churches have discussed the question of dogmatic pluralism within their own communities, but not across lines to other churches. The recent work of Lonergan is a case in point here. In his 1971 lecture, "Doctrinal Pluralism," it is clear that he is dealing exclusively with pluralism within the Catholic church and not across confessional boundaries.[29] Lutherans are perhaps even farther from adequate resolution of this question. Lindbeck is correct when he states concerning the Protestant that no proposition need possess for him permanence, that neither the Trinity nor the Christological formulations, nor even the justification *sola fide* is really the *articulus stantis et cadentis ecclesiae*.[30] But this is correct only in theory for Lutherans. In practice, not only is the justification *sola fide* central, but even the doctrinal form in which that affirmation was enshrined in the sixteenth century resists relativizing. Although some biblical scholars may recognize that the center of Scripture cannot be identified with Luther's understanding of justification, no Lutheran church to date has formulated a theological conceptuality which allows for the *sola fide* to stand alongside a plurality of other centers of truth. In practice it is *the* center and functions as dogma does within Roman Catholicism. This centrality lies behind the perennial effort of Lutherans to locate a "canon within the canon" as they interpret the New Testament. This ecumenical question concerning dogma poses the task for each church to deal with the issue of pluralism within its own midst and also as a cross-ecclesial problem. It challenges all ecclesial groups to define what infallibility of dogma means for them. Dulles and Kasper have spoken of dogmatic pluralism, and they have pointed to the model of the Council of Florence in its formula for allowing unity between East and West, despite basic disagreement over the *Filioque*.[31]

E. THE WORLDLINESS OF DOGMA

When we consider the worldliness of dogma, we are raising the *question of the extent to which dogma participates in the world in which it lives*. This question is really a cluster of four questions: (1) To what extent does the world influence the forms and language of dogma? (the question of cultural conditionedness), (2) To what extent does dogma participate in the movement and change of the process of history? (the question of historicity and doctrinal development), (3) To what extent is dogma the expression of "interests" that are political, social, cultural, economic, and psychological, rather than more purely the interests of faith and revelation? (the question of the sociology of knowledge), (4) To what extent can dogma be influenced by the forms, language, historical process, and non-theological "interests" of the world and still be faithful to the truth of the Gospel (also a question of the sociology of knowledge)?

These questions have been felt as problems for centuries, but it is only in modern times that historical consciousness has raised them to sophisticated expression and rendered them unavoidable. Although they did not originate the statement of these problems, F. C. Baur (1792-1860), Albrecht Ritschl (1822-1889) and Adolf von Harnack (1851-1930) raised these issues in a normative manner for Protestants, and their work has had a great impact, at least negatively, upon Roman Catholic theologians as well.[32] Because the questions of cultural conditionedness and doctrinal development arose for Catholics most sharply in the sixteenth century Reformation and in the later Modernist controversy, they have been obliged to react to the very raising of these questions even more defensively than Lutherans, and for that reason have only in the post-World War II period been able to reflect more soundly on them. There is a sense in which both Lutherans and Catholics have only recently been liberated to reflect honestly on their nineteenth-century experience of historical consciousness—Lutherans by the passing of neo-orthodox theology and Catholics by Vatican II.

Baur, building upon a Hegelian base, was able to speak powerfully of dogma's movement through history, participating fully in the world, and yet bringing to embodiment the Absolute Spirit of

God under all circumstances. His was a positive appreciation of dogma under all circumstances, and therefore his was a spirit that Catholics should also share, at least in principle, even if his specific judgments—which saw Lutheran dogmatic statements as the apotheosis of the Spirit's unfolding—were objectionable to them.[33] Ritschl combined careful historical analysis and an awareness of change and cultural conditionedness with a concept of the "fall of the church," so as to suggest that dogma was not universal in time or space, but rather bound to a particular time and place and serving a particular purpose. Ritschl likened dogma to "Keimblättchen," that is, vestigial leaves that protect a seed that is in the early stages of its germination, but which fall aside when the plant can support itself.[34] It was Adolf von Harnack, however, who built upon both Baur and Ritschl so as to give powerful form to the argument that dogma is indeed worldly. The *substance* of his argument, in his *History of Dogma*, is that Gospel is not identical to dogma, but rather prior to it and distinct from it; dogma belongs to a particular culture and period, namely, to the Greek soil of the Hellenistic age, since it is the offspring of the Gospel's mating with the Greek mind. The intention of his hellenization theory was neither depreciation of nor disregard for dogma. On the contrary, Harnack recognized that dogma served very specific purposes in behalf of the Gospel, not the least of which is that it opened up the gifts of the Greek mind for the expression of the Gospel. If the Gospel had not become hellenized, there would have been no Christian penetration into the hellenistic world. Harnack had a definite bias which compelled him to subordinate dogma to first-century Gospel and to pinpoint every distortion which dogma perpetrated, and in the process he forged a scientific-historical basis upon which dogma could be criticized and at times dispensed with in his day. But we should be clear that the intention of Harnack's theory was not the denigration of dogma, but rather its drastic *relativization*. This relativization was not simply an identification of dogma with its rootage in a particular time and place, but also with a particular cultural context, a particular type of human spirit.[35] Dogma is the product of the Gospel's particular interaction with a certain culture, certain forms of human thinking at a specific time.

Harnack's thesis has often been criticized, but not to this day superseded. We know now the places where he erred; we do not, as yet, have a fullblown alternative interpretation of the history of

Christianity that matches his for brilliance and suggestive power. We know now that dogmatic forms are closer both in time and in space to the Gospel of Jesus than Harnack allowed,[36] just as we know that he was not wholly accurate in his description of the Greek spirit.[37] But two implications of his work have remained as irreplaceable components of our understanding: that dogma and Gospel are not to be equated and that the very form of dogmatic formulation itself has temporal-spatial-cultural roots. In other words, dogmatic form cannot escape the sociology of knowledge. Where Lutherans have learned to live with Harnack, it is because they have generally believed that they could do so without binding dogma anyway.[38] Where they have felt obliged to oppose Harnack, they have done so by insisting that his historical judgments are in error or by underlining the continuities between Gospel and dogma which transcend historical accident and relativity. Neither of these strategies is an adequate response to Harnack.

Roman Catholic theologians have devoted an enormous amount of effort to dealing with the impact of relativity and historicity upon dogma. Rahner, Lonergan, Schillebeeckx, Schoonenberg, and Kasper have all dealt at length very persuasively with this theme.[39] Although they do not often refer to Harnack, they meet his argument on the two points which have proven to be of lasting significance: they attack the problem of the continuity between Gospel and dogma, and they attempt to deal with the sociology of knowledge. They grant that Gospel and dogma cannot be equated, but they insist that Gospel requires dogma.[40] As we mentioned above, they insist that Gospel is normative over and determinative for dogma, but they argue that the career of the church through history demands that Gospel be explicated in dogmatic formulations. They accept Harnack's insight that penetration into the real world of the centuries subsequent to the first would be impossible without dogma.

With regard to the second of Harnack's crucial conclusions, relating to the sociology of knowledge, the Roman theologians respond very provocatively and persuasively, even though they do not choose to meet him head-on, a factor which renders their thinking less persuasive than it might otherwise be. On the one hand, they acknowledge the historicity of the forms of dogmatic formulation by distinguishing between the *depositum fidei* and the formulations that embody the *depositum*,[41] between the meaning of the dogma and the context of its formulation (Lonergan),[42] between intentionality which is preconceptual and formulation of that intentionality (Rahner and Schillebeeckx).[43] These arguments ultimately go back to Thomas.[44] On the other hand, these theologians reject the main brunt of the sociology of knowledge perspective by insisting that dogma is related to recurrent operations of the intelligence and processes of the human psyche that are permanent, not simply the manifestation of the human mind in one cultural setting. Lonergan speaks on this point:

> Now later we shall find that doctrines named dogmas are permanent, but our conclusion will not rest on classicist assumptions. Again, we are not relativists, and so we acknowledge something substantial and common to human nature and human activity; but that we place not in externally valid propositions but in the quite open structure of the human spirit—in the ever immanent and operative though unexpressed transcendental precepts: Be attentive, Be intelligent, Be reasonable, Be responsible.[45]

This sort of argument does not ignore sociology of knowledge and Harnack, since it acknowledges that forms of dogmatic formulation are subject to historicity. But in its assertion that the dogmatizing thrust is intrinsic to and permanently a characteristic of the human mind, this position is a blunt and strong contradiction of the basic Harnackian position and its subsequent Protestant progeny (as in Rudolf Bultmann). It in fact rejects the relativization that Harnack asserted; it does not argue out its disagreement fully enough. It sets up an agenda for discussion that demands vigorous prosecution.

Sociology of knowledge also includes the question of "interest" (Habermas).[46] This concern grows out of nineteenth-century analyses, including those of Marx, Feuerbach, and Freud, and it has received special attention from Mannheim and the Frankfurter Schule of sociology. Harnack himself showed some awareness of this sort of consideration when he wrote that after the sixth century, there is little history of dogma as such, since what purported to be dogmatic discussion in the church was really subordinated to ecclesiastical policy and national politics.[47] This aspect of the question of dogma's worldliness is of enormous significance, and it has scarcely been touched by the theologians. From one perspective, the phenomenological approach of the current generation of Roman Catholic theologians might be inclined to bypass this consideration altogether, in its assertions that dogma is rooted in an invariable structure of the human mind and that it proceeds from revelation itself and is accepted by God. This may indeed happen. On the other hand, since "interest" is also an invariable factor in human knowing, this approach might well be able to deal with it.[48] "Interest" must also include the psychological dimension which is expressed unconsciously in every work of the human mind. This aspect of dogma and dogmatic statements is also virtually unexplored territory.

Dulles has touched lightly, but insightfully, upon this question of "interest" in his comments on the interpretation of dogmatic statements.

> We too often forget that popes and councils sought to speak in ways common *for high officials of their time*, and that they were aiming not simply to communicate a content but to do so in a manner that would evoke a suitable emotional and practical response on the part of the faithful. Ecclesiastical pronouncements from the Middle Ages until the First Vatican Council (inclusively) commonly were phrased in a majestic, even triumphalistic, style that would not be considered appropriate today. . . . I doubt whether any well-informed theologian, if he were speaking for the first time on the subject, would think of saying, as did Vatican I, that Christ made Peter "prince of all the apostles and visible head of the entire Church militant," and gave him "primacy of true and proper jurisdiction." *The phraseology, at least, is bound up with the political experience of Western Europe in a certain historical era.* If the question were coming up for new decision today, we would doubtless look for other ways of talking about the Petrine office in conformity with current New Testament scholarship *and contemporary political forms.*[49] (Italics added.)

Both Dulles and Harnack intend something more detailed and more subtle than simply asserting, as many do today, that the "interest" of dogmatic Christianity is governed by the so-called "Constantianian Era." Rather, their hints demand further investigation, as to how "interest"—political, economic, church-political, and psychological— influences dogmatic statements. Dulles is correct in suggesting that the tools of form-criticism (and let us add traditions-criticism and redaction-criticism) must be applied at least as carefully to dogmatic statements as they are to biblical texts. Of course, such tools have been applied with great skill. But we must remember that such critical tools dig up not only theological "interests," but also the sociological and psychological dimensions that we have referred to above. We agree with Lonergan: "One cannot infer what a church document must mean from one's knowledge of theology."[50]

III.
A Philosophical-Theological Model
for Understanding the Function of Dogmatic Statements

We said at the outset that the horizon which governs our understanding of dogmatic statements is the church as a living community, existing within a larger ecosystem, actualizing its identity as it moves through history and nature. Now we turn to the description of a model of the church's functioning which is grounded in that horizon and which we set forth as a framework within which dogmatic statements and their role in the church's life can be located and understood. Specifically, we focus on the identity-formation process within the Christian community, remembering that this is a life-process itself in which the church, along with all other communities, participates. This identity-forming process is one within which the community and its individual adherents find their identity and participate in the maintaining and strengthening of that identity. Since it is a living process within a living community, it cannot be approached as if it were static, hence our larger assertion that identity formation takes place as the community moves through time and space within its ecosystem.

A. THE IDENTITY-FORMING PROCESS:
PHILOSOPHICAL AND PSYCHOLOGICAL PERSPECTIVES

Identity refers to what Erik Erikson describes as the sense "which provides the ability to experience one's self as something that has continuity and sameness, and to act accordingly."[51] Although the specific reference by Erikson here is to individuals, the same applies to groups and institutions, although the processes of forming identity differ in groups from individual processes. Continuity and sameness imply participation in meaning, which enables action which maintains that participation and extends that meaning. For the church, then, *the identity-forming process is the way in which the church experiences an ongoing participation in the central meaning of the Christian faith, a meaning which in spite of changes in time and space possesses a continuity and sameness, and then acts in ways that are commensurate with this meaning.*

The process of forming identity has to do, therefore, with meaning—both the meaning that gives intelligibility and the meaning that that makes life possible. This latter, "the meaning that makes life possible," points to the under-lying *meaningfulness* which is necessary for life and which serves as a basis for the functions of life. What is at stake in the identity-formation process is life itself, because without clear and comprehensive identity, a community and its individual adherents cannot function in a way that is consonant with the intention of the community, nor can the community as a whole be faithful and effective in embodying what the community stands for.

In the identity-forming process, meaning must function in several different ways: (1) it must form *an overarching universe of meaning* which makes all reality—including the community, its world and other communities—understandable; (2) it must *focus* the center of distinctive meaning that informs the community itself; (3) it must *clarify the community's relationship* to other communities, in terms both of commonalities and differences; (4) it must be *the source of life-style and action*, both individual and corporate, of the community. In order to actualize these thrusts adequately, as the community moves through history within its world, the community permits an executive function to develop which can preside over the stimuli that the community encounters from its world, coordinate the components of the community and make the appropriate judgments that differentiate clearly the community from its world and its co-existents and also proclaim for the community the meaning that undergirds its life-style. This executive and presiding agency may be formally designated or it may emerge informally and be acknowledged informally. Its functioning may be conscious or unconscious, but in any case it is real and effective, if the community is vital—which is another way of saying that where there is clear identity within a community, this agency will be at work, in whatever way that may be.

1. Meaning and Symbolization

In order for the process of identity formation to succeed, so that meaning as we have just described it is achieved, one major task must be carried out: *the ordinary experiencing of the community and its adherents must be brought into conjunction with symbols.* This bringing-into-conjunction is the process in which meaning appears and takes hold, and therefore it is necessary for the enabling of life. Having once been brought into existence, meaning must be centered and given sharpest possible focus on the one hand and broadened so as to give the most comprehensive wholeness, on the other. All the while, however, there must be unrelenting honesty so that the lived experiencing of the community is not falsified by joining it heteronomously to a given symbol or set of symbols. If it is falsified, then the meaning achieved is not authentic, it becomes oppressive rather than life-enabling. In Tillich's terminology, such meaning would be heteronomous rather than theonomous.

The elements of this major task deserve some further clarification. The basic formula, *experiencing plus symbol equals meaning* is one that is generally acknowledged, but we draw specifically upon the work of Paul Ricoeur and especially Eugene Gendlin.[52] Because "experience," is already a concept and loaded with philosophical connotation, we follow Gendlin in using the term "experiencing." It denotes "*concrete* experience . . . the *raw*, present, ongoing *functioning* (in us) of what is usually called experience."[53] "Meaning is formed in the interaction of experiencing and something that functions as a symbol."[54] This experiencing is the ongoing flow of feeling which is prelogical and preconceptual. It is not limited to data received by the five senses, but is also what Whitehead called organismic knowledge and what Heidegger speaks of as moods. It makes up all but a small portion of human thinking, it is the broad substratum to which all verbalizations and conceptualizations refer, the nine-tenths of the iceberg, so to speak, which lies below the surface of verbalization and conceptualization. These latter comprise the one-tenth that is publicly manifested.[55] This experiencing is the concrete response of individuals and their communities to what is happening in their world. It is the interior life of fantastic variability which is the correlate of the external world of nature and history. We cannot begin to understand properly what identity-formation is and how meaning functions within this formation unless we have a clear recognition that the encounter of the external world with human beings and their response to that world takes place first of all and most comprehensively *within this dimension of experiencing*. There is no attempt here to discredit or reject concepts, logical precision, and thinking, but rather only a desire to indicate that experiencing is involved in them and that without experiencing, they have no meaning. If it is true that experiencing without these more refined meanings is blind, they on the other hand are empty apart from experiencing.

The second component in the equation we mentioned above is *symbol*. The sense which we (and Gendlin) give to "symbol" in this

discussion is anything that gives meaning when brought into conjunction with raw experiencing. This means that symbols are infinite in their diversity and combination; they vary tremendously
both in form and in significance, in simplicity and complexity. A
symbol, therefore, can be a thing, a person, an event, a behavior, a
color, a concept, an image, to mention only a few possibilities. The
symbol can be elemental or extremely complex, limited or comprehensive, trivial or profound. Experiencing can be symbolized (moving on a continuum from elemental to complex) in the following
ways, for example: "I have a strong feeling"; "I feel pressured"; "I
am experiencing tensions and difficulty"; "I am struggling because
I am participating in the final stage of the dialectic of material history, in which we as proletarians are establishing the socialist society
that eliminates the bourgeois exploitation of persons, and I must
work to defeat the bourgeois foes that threaten our cause." Each of
these statements is a symbolization of what might conceivably be
the same experiencing; each provides meaning when it is brought
into conjunction with felt experiencing; each statement employs
different symbols in ascending degrees of complexity. There is a
movement from simple recognition of the experiencing to description, naming, and finally comprehensive location and interpretation
of the experiencing. This example suggests that the same experiencing can be symbolized and given meaning in different ways, in
successively deeper and more profound ways. The examples given
here are of course oversimplified and not explained. Gendlin, for
example, shows in meticulous detail at least seven different models
which can explain how symbols relate to experiencing so as to provide meaning.[56]

The symbols which allow meaning to emerge must, finally, be
organized. This organizing takes a number of forms. The *formation
of myth* is one way of organizing symbols, in a narrative system,
which may reach deeply into history and into the psychical structures of humankind and give profound meaning by putting things
together within this narrative. *Conceptuality and theory* are still
other ways of organizing, in that they attempt to represent the experiencing and at the same time clarify the interrelations of the
various symbols that give meaning to experiencing, clarifying both
their relationship to experiencing itself and to other symbols. They
perform this latter function by judging the relative significance of

each symbol and by integrating them into a totality, a *system* of meaning.

2. Symbolization and Identity

The formation of identity rests very squarely upon this rather complicated process of meaning-coming-into-being through the interaction of experiencing and symbols. To advert to our earlier definition of the identity-forming process, the task that confronts identity-formation and maintenance is *to fashion* the felt and thought-out "continuity and sameness of meaning" that can persist throughout the infinite variety and stages of experiencing. Identity-formation and maintenance, then, is an important part of the process of *organizing* the symbols that give meaning to the experiencing of the church and its members.

B. THE IDENTITY-FORMING PROCESS APPLIED TO THE CHURCH

1. The Overarching Framework: Divine Providence

In a relatively undifferentiated manner, the Christian community has chosen to accept a presupposition which is in fact a set of symbols that give meaning to its experiencing in that they provide a background for its existence. In response to its world, it has operated with the understanding that this world is under the dominion and providential guidance of God, and thus it interprets its own experiencing, in interaction with its world, to be part of God's own historical presence and intention for his world. Thus, the experiencing and the symbols which give meaning to that experiencing are all understood as taking place within a matrix of divine presence and revelation. The Christian community has not considered its experiencing nor its symbolic meanings to be accidental nor to be the autonomous fabrications of its own imaginative efforts. In sum, the Christian community considers that its own experiencing, the symbols that give it meaning, and the external events to which it responds are under the dominion of God. This is a very comprehensive symbol, itself made up of lesser symbols, but it nevertheless is not properly understood, unless we recognize that it rests fundamentally *not* on a *principle* of divine sovereignty from which experiencing is deduced, but rather it emerges as a conviction that gives meaning to experiencing when that experiencing is listened to and interpreted honestly. The persuasiveness of this overarching symbolic is continually tested, as each experiencing of pain, perplexity, and bewilderment compels the individual and the community to reassess the honesty of the interaction between experiencing and the symbols of divine presence and providence.

2. The Identity-Bestowing Symbol: Jesus as Christ

If divine providence is the *overarching framework-symbol*, which according to the Christian community's own testimony, encompasses its experiencing vis-à-vis its world, the community's central *identity-bestowing symbol* is Jesus the Christ. It is noteworthy that the experiencing of the community interacted and continues to interact with the Christ symbol. It underscores for us that the community has accepted as a central meaning-giving symbol *the life of a man*. This central symbol is comprised of the life, death, and subsequent presence of Jesus of Nazareth among his followers. The experiencing of the community interacted with this man—as that man and his actions and words were interpreted by means of symbols, it is true—and out of the interaction there emerged meaning. This meaning was brought about in the process by which the church allowed the life, death, and later presence of Jesus to function as a symbol. This symbol has interacted so powerfully with the experiencing of the community and its individuals that it has become central, hence our designating it the identity-bestowing symbol of the community. The power of this interaction throws light on the dynamics of the process by which Christians affirmed Jesus as the Christ, Son of God. It is this symbol, in its diverse interaction with the community's experience, that forms the substance and basis of the continuity and sameness of meaning that constitutes the identity of the church and both demands and enables it to act in harmony with that meaning.

The emergence of this symbol and its interaction with the community's experience so as to bestow normative meaning is itself a fascinating phenomenon. The community did not imagine or fabricate the man Jesus of Nazareth or his life, death, and subsequent presence in resurrection. But the community was active in the process of interaction with him, out of which meaning and therefore also identity emerged. It was active in the complex process by which the life of this man and the events in that life assumed the form and status of the symbol which bestowed decisive meaning. The community was active also in *affirming* this symbol as central and identity-forming. It is difficult to speak of this process. That the church was active in it does not mean to imply that the community manipulated the process, controlled the process, or otherwise assured its outcome. The community could well have disintegrated, forming no identity or meaning out of its interaction with Jesus, or it could have found its meaning and formed its identity in other ways.

The various types of historical-critical analysis help us to describe this interaction between the experience of the community and Jesus. They enable us to understand the diversity and confusion of that experiencing and how the community had to wrestle through to meaning and identity. The community had to wrestle with the various titles ascribed to Jesus, for example, at some points accepting some titles, rejecting others, reaccepting some of those that had been rejected.[57] It had to come to terms with Jesus' crucifixion, inasmuch as the death of Jesus was itself a meaning-disrupting event.[58] The resurrection had to be set within a framework that was not immediately clear and upon which there was no unanimity. Historical-critical studies remind us forcefully that this was a *life process*, a living enterprise of a community of human beings existing in a certain world, seeking to gain clarity about their experiencing, to remain honest and faithful to that experiencing, and to discover its meaning, so that their own identity as a community could be forged. The process was not under their control, and it was not as self-conscious as our discussion indicates. It was largely unself-conscious, groping, full of coincidence and fraught with uncertainty.

3. The System-Forming Symbol: The Trinity

The Christian community, although it began its career in the conviction that its experiencing and discovery of meaning took place under God's providence, moved toward greater clarity and fullness in the shaping of a larger symbolic structure into which the identity-giving symbol could fit. This larger structure speaks of God in terms of his relationship to the origins of the world and of man, to the life of Jesus of Nazareth, and to the ongoing process of the world—natural and historical—and its consummation. This trinitarian symbol *is the system-forming symbol* of the community. The complexities of this larger symbolic structure can hardly be touched upon here. We can, however, simply sketch the meaning afforded by the various components of this larger symbolic structure. We can see that certain kinds of experiencing lie behind the symbols which speak of God as creator and as *mysterium tremendum et fascinosum*, and we can understand how these symbols provided meaning for that experiencing. Similarly, we can imagine for ourselves how the experiencing that grew out of the encounter with Jesus moved to questions of his relationship to the Creator God, the question of how the symbol of identity is related to the symbol of origins and power. Finally, we recognize the experiencing that underlies the question of what is the status of this present life-process in which man exists and what its relationship is to the man who shapes our identity (even after his removal from the earthly scene) and to the creator God. A very complex meaning-forging process led finally to a total system of symbols which suggested that one and the same power is correlated to all three of these types of experiencing. The *clearest* of these symbols is the identity-symbol of Jesus the Christ, whereas *the most powerful* is the symbol of the Holy Spirit. The symbol of the Holy Spirit asserts that the power of God is present in the ongoing life of the community; it enabled the original interaction with Jesus that engendered the formation of the central symbol with the consequent fashioning of meaning and identity; and it enables the representation and continuation of that interaction today.

Again, we must say that although the community was active in the process in which the trinitarian symbol emerged, it was not autonomous in that process, nor did it fabricate the symbol or control the process. Rather, the symbols and meaning were born out of the process of experiencing, which was the subjective correlate of the prelogical, preconceptual, premeaning encounter with the world in which God was active.

This larger, trinitarian system-forming symbol incorporates innumerable symbols, encompassing the diversity of both the Old and the New Testaments. It embraces several levels of significance, and it gathers up within itself the experiencing of many generations of Christians in several cultural settings. Furthermore, it is related again and again in an infinity of ways to the experiencing of the subsequent generations of Christians.

4. Identity Within the Full Symbol System

When the identity-bestowing symbol, Jesus the Christ, is placed in its proper framework of the system-forming symbol, the trinitarian God, it becomes clear how the Christian community finds its identity and maintains it. This complex symbol—identity-symbol placed within the system-forming symbol—provides the meaning in which the Christian community participates, namely, the life, death, and resurrection of Jesus Christ. It provides the possibility of sameness and continuity in that meaning through the assertion that the creator God (the High God) continues to be present in this ongoing life-process after Jesus' departure, enabling the community in later generations to relive the interaction with Jesus: this is expressed in the symbol of Holy Spirit. Finally, it elaborates how action, within this continuity of meaning and consonant with it, is demanded and enabled—this too, under the Holy Spirit as the symbol of God's ongoing presence, a presence that is the power which sustains the community and drives it forward. If, as we noted above, based on the work of Erikson, identity in its fullness includes *meaning, continuity and sameness within that meaning* despite movement in nature and history, and *action* that is commensurate with meaning—then, the total symbolic system we have described constitutes the Christian community's manner of forging that identity, in an interrelation of Christology and Trinity. Furthermore, if our comments above, based on the work of Ricoeur and Gendlin, speak adequately of the meaning with which identity has to do as the consequence of the interaction of experiencing with symbol—then, we must recognize that in a complex manner, these symbols of Christology and Trinity are not imposed upon Christian experiencing, but rather are brought authentically into conjunction with the honestly felt experiencing of the community and its adherents so as to give the meaning that is the cornerstone of identity. The dangers are clear: the admirable symbolic system apart from experiencing is empty. The experiencing of the community apart from the symbol system is blind. Apart from the utmost honesty in perceiving the actual experiencing of the community and the flexibility to allow the symbols to be dynamic and plastic, the symbols become heteronomous tyrants which stifle experiencing and thus preclude authentic meaning and encourage false identity. These dangers are counterbalanced by the possibility of the genuinely theonomous meaning which enables life.

C. DOGMATIC STATEMENTS AND THE IDENTITY-FORMING PROCESS

Dogmatic statements (remembering that we earlier defined this term to refer to the cluster constituted by dogma and its support system of doctrine and theological reflection which precede it by way of preparation and flow from it to follow up its implications)

are essential components of this life-process in which the Christian
community responds to the creative and renewing power and presence of God in its world. Within the framework that we have just
delineated, dogmatic statements are construed in their relationship
to the experiencing of the community and to the emergence of
meaning and identity-giving symbols. We believe that the structure
of meaning- and identity-formation which we have set forth provides
a basis for affirming essentially what George Lindbeck elaborates on
the grounds of linguistic analysis, and it clarifies further the grounds
for the validity of his proposal. He speaks of primary statements and
"second-order statements." Primary statements grow out of the practice of the religious faith. Second-order statements reflect upon the
primary uses of language.[59] Lindbeck states the matter vividly:

> Christians not only worship and preach, they also reflect on these
> primary uses of their language. They do theology in formal and in-
> formal ways. They become not only speakers of the Christian tongue,
> they also become grammarians and linguists who try to distinguish
> reflectively between the essential and accidental, the infallible and
> fallible parts of their discourse.[60]

Primary statements emerged from the doing of faith, from what the
Pragmatic philosophers termed "knowledge of" in contradistinction
from "knowledge about." Second-order statements are more nearly
related to the latter, "knowledge about."

What we have called "experiencing" is prior yet to primary statements and to the practice of the faith, although it takes place in the
context of and simultaneous with the practice of faith in worship,
preaching, comforting, acting, and meditation. This experiencing is
the most immediate response to the presence of God in his world.
The symbols (defined in Gendlin's sense) which emerge from this
most immediate response go into the constitution of the primary
uses of language. These primary uses often represent a level of reflection, conceptualization, and coordination that has advanced beyond the first symbols of meaning that emerge from experiencing,
although in prayer, testimony, and meditation it may well be that
there is an identity of these most immediate symbols of meaning
and the first order of language related to the practice of faith. The
point is that symbols of various sorts and levels of significance, some
of them more immediate and private than those Lindbeck refers to
as the primary order of language, have emerged in the life of the

Christian community to give meaning to the experiencing of that community, and these are more or less *directly* related to that experiencing. These symbols follow the contours of that experiencing. For example, if we follow closely the dynamics of the formation of the Synoptic gospel traditions we can see that the symbols used to name Jesus and his activity did follow the shifts and turns of the community's experiencing of him and their attempt to find the meaning of that experiencing within the framework of the symbols that were available to them. Some of this is visible, for example, in the changing attitudes toward the symbol "Messiah"—apparently some connotations of that term were commensurate with the community's experience, whereas others (particularly the political overtones) were not. Another level of this process, probably more primitive, we see reflected in a pericope like the one concerning the "doubting" Thomas, where the search for adequate symbolization of the experiencing of interaction with Jesus takes the form, not of searching for a name, but of deciding whether to believe that the risen man was Jesus, whether to acknowledge the wounds as his, whether to avoid his presence or to bow down to him.

Dogmatic statements are a "higher level" of symbol, in the sense that they are more abstract, some steps farther removed from the experiencing and its immediate symbolization. They are more comprehensive than the immediate symbolizations, they follow only indirectly the contours of experiencing, and they function to clarify the immediate symbolization (or "primary uses" of language) by organizing them. Dogmatic statements are thus a kind of "macro-symbol" or "hypersymbol," or perhaps it is more helpful to call them "secondary" (and in some cases, as Lindbeck says of the dogma of Infallibility, "tertiary") orders of language.

Here we would take possible exception to Lindbeck's analysis, although this may represent a difference of intention rather than a real difference of outlook. He seems, as we indicated above, to want to restrict dogma to a critical, negative function of clarifying the rules of usage for the language of the Christian community, and he uses this as his chief characterization of "second order" statements. Our interpretation of dogmatic statements includes the function he outlines, but it also intends to say that dogmatic statements give constitutive meaning simultaneous with their negative, critical delineation of how Christian language is to be used. The organization of more immediate symbols *does* constitute a positive, constitutive affirmation of meaning that is significant for the experiencing of the community and its immediate symbolization of that experiencing to form primary meaning. Although it is true that artistic organization of the Christian meaning, in poetry, painting, and music, may be more powerful, initially more impelling visions of Christian meaning, we should not wish to deny that dogmatic statements also intend to envision that meaning, that they, too, are products of the human yearning for meaning in a positive, constitutive form. Even such abstruse and on the surface aesthetically displeasing testimonies such as the Tome of Leo and the Lutheran dogmatizing concerning the *communicato idiomatum* organize the more immediate symbolizations so as to provide a vision of who and what the experiencing of the man Jesus in the Christian community *means*.

The consequence of our analysis is the enumeration of three levels in the meaning-forming process which comprises the identity-establishing of the Christian community:

LEVEL III—Dogmatic statements (dogmas and the support system of doctrine and theological reflection that prepares for dogma and flows from it).

LEVEL   II—The more immediate Christian symbols that provide meaning for Christian experiencing (worship, teaching, preaching, action, confession, etc.).

LEVEL   I—The immediate experiencing of the Christian community.

In clarification of this scheme, we can say that the heart of the identity-giving symbols occur on Level II; it is the primary locus of what we call "revelation" and "gospel." The system-forming symbols occur on Level III. This level shares the process of revelation, but not in so direct a manner. The three levels are all part of one dynamic living process, and they ought not to be separated except for analysis.

The distinctions that are suggested by our analysis and the scheme of the three levels must be understood within the horizon we mentioned at the outset, namely, the Christian community as living, dynamic community which concretizes its identity as it moves through history and nature within a world. The substratum of the experiencing and immediate symbolization of that experiencing in word, deed, and other symbols is the broadest and most significant portion of this phenomenon. Level III symbols can do no more "than express a very small part of the truth to which the intellect assents in the act of faith. Unless they are embedded in the living matrix of Christian language in its primary uses, they are quite literally unintelligible."[61] But they do play a role that is indispensable, even though it is limited. Without them, identity-formation and therefore the reception of revelation would be incomplete. Dogmas, as such, are the apex of Level III in the sense that they are received so broadly by the community in a public and overt manner. They are not the only intense symbols of identity, nor the only ones that function in an organizing manner. Rather, they are symbols that have emerged out of conflict and special threat to the community. Since threat generally strikes the community at times and places that seem to be dangerous to its very existence, they speak of the most central themes of identity, however. Theological reflection, the other component of dogmatic statements is an ongoing activity which is always necessary, since the community is always a *thinking, reflecting* community, and it is fortunate that this is the case, because it provides a ready base upon which dogmas can be constructed when it is necessary and possible.

We further elaborate the three levels in the following theses:

The entire life-process which is clarified by the three levels we have described is rooted in God and his powerful revelatory and creative-redemptive work.

Everything in the life and belief of the Christian community is persuasive—and thus evaluated—in virtue of its proximity to the central symbols of meaning and identity, that is, to those symbols on Level II that pertain to the life-death-resurrection of Jesus.[62] This we take to be the basis, in our analysis, for the concept of "hierarchy of truths" as set forth in the Decree on Ecumenism.[63]

All of the symbols located on Levels II and III emerge within the ambience of the world in which the community and its adherents live. That is where the experiencing took place; that is where Jesus lived, died, and manifested his subsequent presence; that is where the symbols took shape.

The entire process of the community's life and all of the symbols are caught up in the historicity of the world.

All of the symbols, whether at Levels II or III, share in both relativity and absoluteness. They are relative with reference to time, place, and cultural influences upon the forms of their being perceived and expressed, and with reference to the God to whom they respond. They are absolute (Lindbeck terms this "infallibility"[64]) in that they contribute more or less to the community's identity. The farther they are from the center of identity, the less they share in absoluteness. This kind of absoluteness, as we have said, is not distinctive to Roman Catholicism, but is typical of Protestant groups as well. Since these symbols are essential for the meaning of the community and its identity, they are symbols by which Christians live and upon which they act and thus they become functional absolutes as the community and its adherents live out their lives in Christian identity.[65] When we consider dogmatic statements and the more primary symbols from this perspective, it is clear that it is a contradiction of the very life of the community to deny this absoluteness, since such a denial would in effect be a loss of identity. When such denial does take place, it indicates febrility of identity, which may presage creative change or demoralizing identity crisis. Dogmatic statements are no more absolute or infallible than the symbols occurring on Level II, but to the extent that they are publicly received in a formal manner, they may be more authoritative. This applies particularly to dogma.

The *interrelationships* of the levels may be clarified in the following theses:

Of the two levels on which *meaning* occurs, Level II is the most dynamic and the broadest. The symbols on this level range from the trivial to the profound. Symbols which are mere "signs" occur on this level, as well as myths. Myths may serve to organize primary symbols, just as dogmatic statements do (for example, the myth of Creation or of the Fall), but they are closer to the contours of experiencing than the intellectually reasoned out dogmatic statements, and they do not qualify as second-order statements. Furthermore, they differ from Level III dogmatic statements in that the latter are not cast in narrative form, but rather in the form of reasoning, even if that reasoning form is misleading, as Ian Ramsey points out, because it "is likely to bristle with improprieties" and "logical oddities."[66]

Level III is less dynamic than the other two levels and it does not interact with experiencing in the immediate manner that Level II does, although such interaction is not impossible.

Level II generally mediates between Levels I and III. It is necessary to avoid confusing Levels II and III. The two levels function differently. Level II symbolizes experiencing and brings that symbolizing directly to bear upon efforts to deal with experiencing through worship, preaching, comforting, etc. Dogmatic statements reflect and organize the symbolizations of Level II, both critically, setting forth rules for the usage of symbols at Level II, and positively as the steersman (*kubernetikos*) or gyroscope that keeps Level II on even keel and also as a constitutive vision which opens up mysteries of God for illumination.

The three levels affect one another: I sets the contours for II. II mediates the demands for meaning that emerge from I to III. II reverberates back upon I and in turn shapes it. III deepens and clarifies II and thus also I. III is never autonomous from II and I, nor can it manipulate them. The organizing symbol-systems make their impact upon that which they organize, but they cannot obliterate its integrity nor exercise autocracy over it.

Level III is necessary, inasmuch as human beings and human communities demand clarification and organization of the meaning that emerges from their experience.

Whereas II follows the contours of I, III has other principles for shaping it, such as logic, intellectual structures, etc.

All three levels are susceptible to the influence of the world.

IV.
The Areas of Controversy in Light of the Philosophical-Theological Model

The test of the value of the model we have suggested, which relates dogmatic statements to the identity-formation process within the Christian community and which approaches the issues within the horizon of the church as a living community that concretizes its identity as it moves through history and nature, lies in its ability to throw light on the five areas of controversy that we enumerated earlier. We now turn to this task, rather briefly.

A. THE AUTONOMY OF DOGMA

Protestants have from their beginning sought for levers by which they could exert some independence of judgment vis-à-vis dogmatic statements, and they insisted that they found those levers in Scripture and in their own experiences of grace. Roman Catholic theologians, at least since the early years of the twentieth century, have also, in their own ways sought for such levers, and they claim to have found them in their analysis of the character of the dogmatizing process itself, which has also led them to Scripture and contemporary experience.[67] The model outlined in the preceding pages clarifies why dogmatic statements, particularly dogmas, may lay claim to autonomous authority and also why this autonomy is unjustified and how it is that levers have been discovered by which to criticize dogmatic statements and range them in terms of their importance.

As the model suggests, the decisive factor in the life of the community is the meaning which bestows its identity—meaning and identity which the community believes are gifts of God. Therefore, dogma and theological reflection can in no way be independent within the community, nor self-initiated and self-sustaining. The substance of dogma's claim to autonomy, and also that of theological reflection, is its function of organizing the symbols of identity, including as that does an inevitable executive function in the identity-formation process. What we have called the "gyroscope" function of the dogmatic statements may engender this claim to autonomy. The model also clarifies why this claim to autonomy can never be honored, even though the organizing and executive function is affirmed. Dogmatic statements exist in symbiosis with a total living community, and within that community identity is not created by the dogmatic statements which organize the symbols of identity. Rather, that identity and its symbols emerge at a much more primal level. Even if they are not so articulate nor so facile as dogmatic statements, just because they are so primal and because they are concerned with the wellsprings of identity, symbols at that level carry an intrinsic power, directly related to the integrity and survival of the community essence. This power simply cannot be denied, and for this reason it has always been simply a matter of time until the meaning that emerges directly from this primal realm challenges dogmatic statements in their inadequacies and presses for flexibility and even revisions where they are demanded by the power of the community's life itself. In terms of the levels, we must say that Level III can never hold out against the pressures exerted from Levels I and II—not simply because Level III is dependent upon them, but also because they are so dynamic and intrinsically compelling.

The Protestant and Roman Catholic strategies for putting dogmatic statements into proper perspective and thus mitigating their claims to autonomy are clarified by the model. These strategies invoked the historicity and febrility of the process of identity-formation itself, and this could not be ignored for long. Furthermore, these strategies invoked Gospel and revelation as being primary over dogmatic statements. This claim, too, has to be recognized, since Gospel and revelation are what the church's identity is all about. They are the most precious elements of Level II, following the contours of Level I, and therefore they had to prevail.

In other words, the horizon we have adopted for interpretation insists that dogmatic statements be put into relationship with the rest of the church's life, and that means at the same time that the central identity-bestowing symbols of the community be given their due, both as source for dogmatic statements and also as check over against those statements. This helps us to understand the force of Edmund Schlink's celebrated essay, "The Structure of Dogmatic Statements as an Ecumenical Problem," as well as Wolfhart Pannenberg's "What is a Dogmatic Statement?"[68] Both essays, particularly Schlink's insist on elaborating the fuller range of the community's life and indicate, thus, how dogmatic statements are subject to revelation and how they emerge from confession of faith and teaching of faith.[69] The Roman Catholic analyses by Rahner, Schillebeeckx, Lonergan, and the Pannenberg essay rely more on relating dogma to the dogmatizing process itself—the Catholic insisting that the intentionality of that process be given its due over against its own formulation and including the historicity of that process, whereas Pannenberg insists that the eschatological dimensions of that process (correlated to the eschatological character of the Kingdom of God itself) makes dogmatic statements provisional and proleptic. Pannenberg and the Küng-Kasper position also emphasize starkly the primacy of Gospel over dogmatic statements—the internal logic of which our model readily substantiates.

Our model makes it clear that dogmatic statements, as organizing symbol systems, stand in the service of the life of the church. This recognition is the greatest safeguard against their becoming unjustifiably autonomous. The model clarifies how the harmony as well as the tension between dogmatic statements and the rest of the church's life is correlated to the nearness or distance in which those statements stand from the central symbols of the church's identity.

B. THE NEED FOR DOGMA

The model of the identity-forming process within the Christian community shows immediately why dogmatic statements are needed: There can be no identity without the centeredness of meaning which dogma and theological reflection intend. In saying this, it is clear why dogmatic statements are demanded both by the Gospel and by the human spirit itself. They are demanded by the Gospel, because the Gospel is God's Word, which does not return empty, but which takes root and transforms human lives. This transformation includes identity-formation around the power of God that is manifest in Jesus, and identity-formation demands the stability of expression which dogmatic statements afford. They are demanded by the human spirit because to be human is to live out of identity. To be without that identity, which is centered by dogmatic statements or their equivalents, is in a profound sense to be non-human.

From this perspective, it is clear why Lindbeck and Berkouwer are correct in saying that all Christians have their dogma and every ecclesial community has its own way of asserting the infallibility of its dogmatic statements.

C. DOGMAS AS CRITICAL AND CONSTITUTIVE

Within the perspective we have set forth, the critical function of dogma, in which it sets forth the boundaries within which certain kinds of statements can be made, clarifying the rules for usage of Christian language, is undeniably large. The very notion of *kubernetikos* that we have used is one that describes this function. Dogma as organizing agent and check against imbalance is certainly a description of dogmatic statements as critical principles. At the same time, this perspective indicates why dogmatic statements, dogma included, are also constitutive. They are constitutive in their vision because they are intimately concerned with safeguarding and intensifying identity. In order to do this, the dogmatizing process must be grasped powerfully by the identity symbols that occur on Level II, and when the process is so powerfully grasped, it can never divorce its critical function from a positive vision of Christian identity. So, for example, the Trinitarian dogma could hardly lay down the rules for language, hardly negate the tendencies which endangered identity in the fourth, fifth, and later centuries, without at the same time affirming strongly that God is real as creator, redeemer in Jesus, and present power of life. In the process, furthermore, it was also affirming that the experiencing of the community that received meaning by the symbols which comprise this larger symbol system was indeed a response to that God. Without this constitutive vision, the critical function would be impossible. This two-fold functioning of dogma stands in analogy to generally human processes, in which it is impossible for individuals or groups to defend their identity or rule out elements which threaten that identity unless they have some strong, if not clear, sense for what their identity really is.

D. UNITY AND UNIFORMITY OF DOGMA

The problem of unity and uniformity, as we suggested earlier, is the problem of how pluralism of dogmatic statement can be tolerated and even celebrated within Christendom. Our model suggests that this is a question of how a plurality of life-manifestations of a single identity can coexist and be celebrated within one over-arching community. The life-process horizon which governs our interpretation suggests on the one hand that since dogmatic statements can never hope to express more than a small part of the deep springs of identity that move the Christian community as it symbolizes its experiencing in its pilgrimage through history, it would be counter to clear thinking itself to suppose that a plurality of dogmatic statements could ever be avoided. This is suggested by our image that dogmatic statements are the one-tenth of the iceberg that lies above the surface of life. On the other hand, this horizon demands that we cherish the dynamic and variety of life itself which has been centered and illumined by the identity that flows from God's gift in Jesus Christ. It seems by no means an overwhelming task for dogmatic statements to preserve the vision of Christian identity within each branch of that life-process which bears the identity and defend it against errors and yet at the same time to witness to (and thus celebrate) their humility and incompetence to order adequately the total life-phenomenon called the Christian community. It should also be possible for dogmatic statements, while they call attention to their own limitations, to point to the real sources of Christian unity within the life-process that Christ has transfigured.

E. THE WORLDLINESS OF DOGMA

The problems we posed earlier with respect to the worldliness of dogma were: the question of cultural conditionedness, doctrinal development, relativization, the sociology of knowledge, and non-theological "interest." The horizon which directs our inquiry presupposes from the very beginning that the Christian community coexists with other worldly groups within an ecosystem that moves through time and space in complex interrelationship with that ecosystem and its constituents. This perspective assumes that the community actually ingests its world in various ways, even as it exerts an independent influence upon that world. Finally, our view affirms that the entire process transpires in the hand of God, under his guidance, responsive to the power of his presence. The identity-formation process is, indeed, the quest for clarity about the community's oneness with its world and its distinctiveness which must be asserted in balance and in tension with that world. This quest is a continual struggle to maintain identity against the tendency to be absorbed by the ecosystem, against deterioration and loss of the sense of the continuity of that distinctive identity.

As a consequence of the horizon we have chosen to govern our study, it is unthinkable for us to deny that cultural conditionedness, doctrinal development, relativization, sociology of knowledge, and non-theological interest are operative in every aspect of the church's life. But our perspective understands that this is true simply because, as a living community, the church shares the conditions that all living organisms exist under. Thus, it is not a question of whether the operative force of these five factors indicate unfaithfulness or error in the church's life. Rather, these factors are the inescapable conditions under which all communities live, and the task is to understand how God works under these conditions, which he himself has created, and what the imperatives for the church are.[70] Our discussion to this point has emphasized that the imperative for the community is to be faithful to the central symbols of its identity, the Christ-oriented symbols which symbolize its experiencing. We believe that God works through his presence in the world today as Holy Spirit to quicken the identity-formation process and sustain the community in that quest for identity.[71] Conditionedness in this framework is simply participation in the ecological situation in which the church is placed at any given time. Development and historicity are participation in the process of living advance through time and space which all life shares in as long as it remains alive. Any living community is caught in relativity, in the sense that its identity and the knowledge inherent in that identity is relative to time, place, and to the ways God has manifested himself in any given ecological situation. Similarly, sociology of knowledge and interest are simply ways of saying that all facets of the ecological situation intersect in every life-expression that emerges in that situation.

We must underline that faithfulness and perseverance in the quest for identity is the imperative. Dogmatic statements are never unambiguous, but they represent the critical, organizing thrust of the community to check itself within its total immersion in its ecosystem so that this immersion does not become in fact a drowning of identity. Conditionedness is always there, development and relativization are also present. A non-theological "interest" will always be represented, even in the most precious utterances of faith. The question is whether the conditionedness and the "interest" are proper to the church, or whether they are distorting its identity in ways that present the church in a false light. Since even Jesus could not prevent his contemporaries from misunderstanding him, sometimes as a political insurrectionist, sometimes as a gnostic hero, we must reckon with the fact that dogmatic statements will also prove less than fully effective in their effort to articulate the purest identity of the Christian community. Such ambiguity, however, is a constant factor we must live with, and it does not weaken the imperative to concretize our identity faithfully. Rather, the ambiguity demands that the community exercise vigilant, ongoing self-criticism upon itself, to discern the actual shape of its conditionedness and "interests."

The horizon of our reflections upon dogmatic statements impresses strongly upon us the recognition that the chief imperative for the church (which is at the same time the indicative which animates the church) is to be faithful to its identity. This identity is centered in Christ, initiated by the Creator God, and is preserved efficaciously by the present power of God the Holy Spirit. The church remembers its identity and projects it forward in every moment as a living organism within its world of nature and history, and not as a static entity that exists above time and space. This recognition tells us a great deal both about the revelation that vivifies the church and the processes by which the church appropriates that revelation. Dogmatic statements take their meaning from this horizon of life, and they receive their characteristics from their role in the beholding, reflecting upon, and articulating publicly the central truth from which identity emerges in the community in which these statements themselves live.

NOTES

1. See P. Hefner, "Ecological Perspectives on Communicating the Gospel," *Lutheran World*, 19 (Oct., 1969), pp. 322-338.

2. K. Rahner, "What is a Dogmatic Statement?", *Theological Investigations*, V, Baltimore, 1964, pp. 42-66. The same can be said of E. Schillebeeckx, "The Concept of Truth," *Revelation and Theology*, II, New York, 1968. And of B. Lonergan, *Doctrinal Pluralism*, Milwaukee, 1971.

3. E. Schlink, "The Structure of Dogmatic Statements as an Ecumenical Problem," *The Coming Christ and the Coming Church*, Philadelphia, 1967, pp. 16-86. W. Pannenberg, "What is a Dogmatic Statement?", *Basic Questions in Theology*, I, Philadelphia, 1970, pp. 182-211.

4. G. Söll, *Handbuch der Dogmengenschichte*, I, Fascicle 5, "Dogma und Dogmenentwicklung," M. Schmaus, A. Grillmeier, L. Scheffczyk, eds., Freiburg, 1971, p. 20.

5. R. Haight, "An Understanding of Dogma: A Study of the Notion of Dogma in French Modernism," unpublished Ph.D. diss. University of Chicago Divinity School, 1973, p. 52.

6. A. Dulles, *The Survival of Dogma*, Garden City, 1971, pp. 154-155. W. Kasper, *Dogma unter dem Wort Gottes*, Mainz, 1965, pp. 28-38.

7. A. Dulles, *ibid.*, p. 155.

8. R. Haight, *ibid.*, p. 52.

9. St. Augustine, *de trinitate*, I.

10. A. Dulles, *op. cit.*, p. 167. G. C. Berkouwer, *Gehorsam und Aufbruch. Zur Situation der katholischen Kirche und Theologie*, Munich, 1968. G. Lindbeck in *The Infallibility Debate*, J. J. Kirvan, ed., New York, 1971, p. 117.

11. E. Schlink, *op. cit.*

12. *Ibid.*

13. Vatican II, Unitatis Redintergratio.

14. Works cited above by Kasper, Schillebeeckx, and Lonergan. Also H. Küng, *Infallibility*. B. Lonergan, *Method in Theology*, New York, 1972.

15. See, for example, V. Schurr, "Kerygma and Dogma," *Concilium*, Vol. 3, pp. 150-152.

16. H. McSorley, in Kirvan, *op. cit.*, pp. 89-90.

17. Confessio Augustana, Articles on Abuses. *The Book of Concord*, p. 48.

18. CA, IV, V.

19. Vatican II, Unitatis Redintegratio 6. Also A. Dulles, *op. cit.*, p. 163.

20. See Note 14.

21. *Corpus Reformatorum* XXI, 85.

22. See Note 3.

23. A. Ritschl, *Die Entstehung der altkatholischen Kirche*, Bonn, 1850, 1857. A. von Harnack, *History of Dogma*, 7 vols., New York, 1900.

24. See Note 15. McSorley quotes the Jesuit theologian J. McKenzie, who expresses this negative attitude, as saying he has no problem confessing the dogmas of the Assumption and the Immaculate Conception because he has "not the slightest idea of what either dogma means," p. 90.

25. G. Lindbeck, in Kirvan, *op. cit.*, p. 136. We would have to take issue, however, with Lindbeck's suggestion that Lonergan supports him in this opinion.

26. G. Söll, *op. cit.*, p. 22, n. 93. Note the disagreement between W. Kasper and P. Schoonenberg on this point.

27. See Note 25.

28. G. Lindbeck, *op. cit.*, p. 136.

29. B. Lonergan, Doctrinal Pluralism, pp. 48-52.
30. G. Lindbeck, *op. cit.*, p. 131.
31. A. Dulles, *op. cit.*, pp. 163-170; W. Kasper, "Geschichtlichkeit der Dogmen?", *Stimmen der Zeit*, 1967, pp. 410-411.
32. The Modernists did react directly to Harnack, particularly A. Loisy.
33. F. C. Baur, *Das Christenthum und die christliche Kirche der drei ersten Jahrhunderte*, Stuttgart, 1966.
34. A. Ritschl, *op. cit.*, and also "Prolegomena" to *The History of Pietism*, in *Three Essays*, Philadelphia, 1972, pp. 134-135.
35. A. von Harnack, *op. cit.*, Vol. I.
36. J. Danielou, *Théologie du Judéo-Christianisme*, Paris, 1958, Vol. I.
37. P. Tillich, *Systematic Theology*, Chicago, 1951, Vol. I, p. 157.
38. See Note 30.
39. See Note 14.
40. V. Schurr, *op. cit.*, H. Schlier, "Kerygma und Sophia: Zur neutestamentlichen Grundlegung des Dogmas," *Die Zeit der Kirche*, Freiburg, 1958, pp. 206-232.
41. J. R. Geiselmann, "Dogma," *Handbuch Theologischer Grundbegriffe*, Munich, 1962, Vol. I, pp. 225-241. See also T. Livernois, "The Recovery of Dogma: A Contribution to the Critical Understanding of Dogma," unpublished dissertation, Lutheran School of Theology at Chicago, 1974.
42. B. Lonergan, *Doctrinal Pluralism*, p. 54 and *Method in Theology*, p. 325.
43. See Note 14.
44. S. T., II-II, q. 1, a. 6, and 1. See J.-M. Parent, *La Notion de dogme au XIIIe siècle*, Premiere Serie, Ottawa, 1932. See also discussion in T. Livernois, *op. cit.*
45. B. Lonergan, *Method in Theology*, p. 302.
46. J. Habermas, *Erkenntnis und Interesse*, Frankfurt, 1968.
47. A. von Harnack, *op. cit.*, Vol. II, pp. 304 and 432-444.
48. See for example, B. Lonergan, *Method in Theology*, pp. 312, 316-317, and 320.
49. A. Dulles, *op. cit.*, p. 180.
50. B. Lonergan, *Method in Theology*, p. 312.
51. E. Erikson, *Childhood and Society*, New York, 1963, p. 42. See also P. Berger and T. Luckmann. *The Social Construction of Reality*, Garden City, 1966.
52. P. Ricouer, *The Symbolism of Evil*, Boston, 1967. E. T. Gendlin, *Experiencing and the Creation of Meaning*, Glencoe, 1962.
53. E. Gendlin, *ibid.*, p. 11.
54. *Ibid.*, p. 8.
55. Note the similarity to G. Lindbeck's argument, *op. cit.*
56. E. Gendlin, *op. cit.*, Chapter III.
57. F. Hahn, *Christologische Hoheitstitel*, Göttingen, 1963.
58. E. Lohse, *History of the Suffering and Death of Jesus Christ*, Philadelphia, 1967 and T. Weeden, *Mark-Traditions in Conflict*, Philadelphia, 1971.
59. G. Lindbeck, *op. cit.*, pp. 121, 127.
60. *Ibid.*, p. 127.
61. *Ibid.*, p. 127.
62. E. Schlink, *op. cit.*, W. Pannenberg, *op. cit.*
63. Unitatis Redintegratio, 11.
64. G. Lindbeck, *op. cit.*, pp. 117-118.

65. L. Gilkey, *Religion and the Scientific Future*, New York, 1970, Chapter II. Also K. Rahner, *Sacramentum Mundi*, p. 910.
66. I. T. Ramsey, *Religious Language*, New York, 1957, p. 191. Also A. Dulles, *op. cit.*, p. 157.
67. R. Haight, *op. cit.*, Chapter V.
68. See Note 62.
69. E. Schlink, *op. cit.*
70. P. Hefner, *op. cit.*
71. See P. Tillich, *Systematic Theology*, Vol. III, Part IV.

Contributors

André Benoît is Professor of Patristics at the University of Strasbourg, France.

Philip Hefner is Professor of Systematic Theology at the Lutheran School of Theology, Chicago, Illinois.

Harding Meyer is Research Professor at the Institute for Ecumenical Research, Strasbourg, France.

Regin Prenter is a former Professor of Systematic Theology at the University of Aarhus, Denmark.

John Reumann is Professor of New Testament at the Lutheran Theological Seminary, Philadelphia, Pennsylvania.

Jürgen Roloff is Professor of New Testament at the University of Erlangen, Germany.

Vilmos Vajta is Research Professor at the Institute for Ecumenical Research, Strasbourg, France.

Gustaf Wingren is Professor of Systematic Theology at the University of Lund, Sweden.